James Campbell was born in Glasgow
and now lives in London. Between 1978
and 1982 he was editor of the *New
Edinburgh Review*. Among his previous
books is a biography of James Baldwin,
Talking at the Gates. His play *The
Midnight Hour* was performed in
Philadelphia in 1993 and 1995.

PARIS INTERZONE

Richard Wright, Lolita, Boris Vian
and others on the Left Bank, 1946–60

JAMES CAMPBELL

Minerva

A Minerva Paperback
PARIS INTERZONE

First published in Great Britain 1994
by Martin Secker & Warburg Ltd
This Minerva edition published 1995
by Mandarin Paperbacks
an imprint of Reed Books Ltd
Michelin House, 81 Fulham Road, London SW3 6RB
and Auckland, Melbourne, Singapore and Toronto

Copyright © 1994 by James Campbell
The author has asserted his moral rights

A CIP catalogue record for this title
is available from the British Library
ISBN 0 7493 9869 8

Printed and bound in Great Britain
by Cox & Wyman Ltd, Reading, Berks.

to Vera

Contents

List of Illustrations

Acknowledgements

I am grateful in particular to Vera Chalidze, for consistent help and advice, and to Patrick J. Kearney, whose bibliography *The Paris Olympia Press* proved an essential tool of research. Many other people have assisted in the writing of this book, including Maureen Allen, Pip Benveniste, Mary Briault (aka Muffie Wainhouse), Jane Lougee Bryant, Ed Clark, William Rossa Cole, John Coleman, J. P. Donleavy, Michel Fabre, Otto Friedrich, Richard Gibson, Lee Goerner, Dominique Goy-Blanquet, Michael Greenberg, Danny Halperin, Lucien Happersberger, Ollie Harrington, Antony Harwood, Jim Haynes, Lesley Himes, Rohan Jayasakeera, Eric Kahane, Juliette Kahane, James Knowlson, Jim Lesar, Christopher Logue, Gerald Mangan, Geoffrey Mulligan, Maurice Nadeau, Rachel Peddie, George Plimpton, Roger Rosen, Richard Seaver, Leslie Schenk, George Solomos (aka Themistocles Hoetis), John Stephenson, John de St Jorre, Diana Vowles, George Whitman, Alain Woisson, Barbara Wright. Anthony Bernardo of the Beinecke Rare Book and Manuscript Library at Yale was helpful in locating buried documents, and I would also like to express thanks to Kevin Ray of the Washington University Library, St Louis, and Diana Latchatanere of the Schomburg Center for Research in Black Culture, New York Public Library. Finally, I remain mindful of my debt to James Baldwin and to Alexander Trocchi, each of whom spoke to me on matters relevant to this work, though both died before it was begun.

Author's Note

La Zone is the old-fashioned word for *la banlieue*, the suburbs; according to *Petit Robert*, *la Zone* comprised 'les faubourgs misérables'. The people described here lived, mostly, in the heart of Paris, but, being on the margins of French society, they were confined, in a way, to *la Zone*.

'Zone' is also the title of a lyrical vision of Paris by Apollinaire (translated into English by Samuel Beckett). 'Interzone' was the original title of William Burroughs's *Naked Lunch*, first published by the Olympia Press. These things, among others, suggested the title of this book.

Many people have shared their views and reminiscences with me. In the text, the statements of an interviewee are usually signified by the use of the present tense, or by the introductory phrase 'According to . . .', but seldom otherwise. Thus, 'John Brown says', etc., or 'According to John Brown', indicates that the remarks were made in an interview with me; but 'John Brown said' (recalled, complained, etc.) means that the statement is taken from a written source which the reader will find referred in the Notes.

As regards the word 'Negro', now disliked by some, I have simply followed the usage of the time. A certain amount of overlap with my biography of James Baldwin, *Talking at the Gates*, is unavoidable, but I have sought to keep it to the minimum.

ONE

Un Enfant du Pays

I

> . . . and so naturally it is I an American who was
> and is thinking in writing in America and lives in
> Paris. This has been and probably will be the his-
> tory of the world.
>
> Gertrude Stein, *transition*, Fall 1928

In early May 1946, Gertrude Stein received an American visitor at her apartment on rue de Fleurus, just off the Boulevard
Raspail, on the Left Bank of the Seine. As the city's most
famous American resident, a leader and leading survivor of
the modernist revolution in art which broke out in Paris during the first two decades of the century, Stein was accustomed
to admitting strangers to the spacious rooms which she shared
with Alice B. Toklas, where the walls were hung three and
four deep with paintings by Cézanne, Bonnard, Picasso,
Matisse. Sometimes, letting go of politeness, she would
remind a caller who had been welcomed in the past and had
returned with friends, to see 'the pictures', that her house was
not a museum.

Her present visitor was there by consent. Indeed, he had
sailed to Paris from New York on the raft of an official invitation from the French Government, initiated by Stein. Without

1

her intervention, his application for a passport to leave the United States, rejected when it was made the first time, would probably have been turned down again. This happened, and would happen increasingly, to Americans of dubious allegiance in the post-war years, when the actual fight, on the ground and in the air, against fascism had ended and the ideological battle against Communism was just beginning. One of its most famous victims was Paul Robeson, who had been welcomed in the Soviet Union, and who, when refused a passport to fulfil a singing engagement in Canada, set up loudspeakers on the American side of the border and broadcast a concert to Canadians listening on the other.

Like Robeson, the man who was visiting Gertrude Stein had been a Communist. Like Robeson, he was black – a Negro, as Gertrude Stein, and he himself, would have said. He was also a writer, and this, taken together with his race, made him seem to Gertrude Stein something new. Not new in the sense of being a novelty, for amusement; but new in the sense of being *modern*.

Stein was not unacquainted with black people. She was rare among white American writers in creating a novel-length work of fiction with an all-black cast: 'Melanctha', which she published in 1909 in her book *Three Lives*. The story is chiefly notable as an early example of Stein's innovatory techniques: repetitious, insistent, circular sentences, which urged words to perform in the way of an artist's line, sometimes without regard for realistic meaning – as Matisse would disregard 'reality' to create a true form. But 'Melanctha' also exhibits the racial attitudes of its time (shared by blacks themselves), for example in equating a light-brown or 'yellow' skin with gentility and a very dark one with coarseness, in manner and spirit.

The man standing before Gertrude Stein was dark, but if Stein retained any of her subliminal prejudice, he, by his presence alone, demolished it. He was the author of two recent books – a novel, *Native Son*, and a memoir of his Mississippi childhood, *Black Boy* – which had impressed her deeply. So much so that she regarded Richard Wright as 'the most important writer in the States since herself'.

This compliment – greatly welcomed by Wright, in spite of its self-regard – was delivered in a note sent by one of Stein's friends in April 1945. Wright, as it happened, was already an admirer of hers, and a correspondence began which ranged over many topics, including the daily humiliations, large and small, endured by the American black – for example, Wright had trouble finding a barber in Greenwich Village who would cut his hair – the jazz craze now sweeping Paris, and the black GIs Stein saw in the city streets. She perceived in their expressions and gestures, and heard in their speech, the American anthem played in a different key. Wright sent her books, including his own collection of stories, *Uncle Tom's Children*, and a pamphlet called 'Handbook of Harlem Jive'.

> You, of course, have heard of the words *jive*, *hot*, *cat*; you have no doubt heard the phrases, 'laying it in the groove', 'beating it up', 'blowing your top', etc., etc. All of these are called jive words.

Jive, he told her, meant 'hiding things with words', and generally enhancing the tempo of life 'through talk'. America had made Negroes into a strange people, Wright went on. By 'strange' he meant twisted, and it was this twistedness he had set himself the task of unwrenching. It is a terrible thing to live with, he told Stein in one letter, 'but for writing it is great'.

Wright had wanted to visit France some years before, but had been prevented from doing so by the War and the Nazi occupation. The friendly contact with Stein reawakened his desire. Even before receiving the initial note from her friend Joseph Barry he had thought about Stein and her situation: 'Melanctha' had captured, as no other work had, the 'deep Negro dialect' of his ancestors; Stein had given a form so distinct to something that Wright had been hearing all his life, that it was for him, 'as if I were listening to my grandmother for the first time, so fresh was the feeling it gave me'. Not only had she drawn the rhythms of Negro speech on the page with

3

an exactness which enchanted and surprised him, she had done so while living in Paris. Could there be a connection between her exile and this clarity of imagination?

'I'd say', Wright told his journal one night in January 1945, as he broke off from reading Stein's *Narration*, reminding himself once again that this woman 'who is distrusted by everyone' had made him hear the speech of his grandmother;

> I'd say that one could live and write like that only if one lived in Paris or in some out of the way spot where one could claim one's own soul.

It took a year, but the idea was born. He had to find out if there was another country, a place where life was lived differently.

*

> 'Gee, I'd like to go to France.'
> 'Me too.'
> 'Me too.'
> 'Me too.'

Richard Wright, *Lawd Today!*, 1936

But: on applying to Washington at the beginning of the New Year, 1946, for a passport to enable him to travel, Wright was told by the State Department that he would not be granted one. A friend of his, a magazine editor, Dorothy Norman, wrote a letter to the Department, saying that she wished to appoint Wright to go abroad to represent her journal, *Twice a Year*, so that he could 'report on cultural, social and political events in France' (culture being one of the best ways to get round the State Department's reluctance to allow 'meddlesome' Americans to leave their own shores at the end of the War). 'We were generally warned', Norman reported later in an article written for the *New York Post*,

> that it would be difficult for Richard Wright to get a passport because he was a Negro. We were warned that the Government would not like to have Wright, in particular, go abroad, because

4

of the way in which he had always spoken out against injustice at home, and against racial discrimination in particular.

I was asked why Wright, who was 'after all' a 'Negro', would want to go 'abroad' anyway. Wasn't it his 'place' to stay 'here'? What 'interest' could he possibly have in Europe?

The refusal stuck. 'Our State Department is really a tough nut to crack,' Wright unassumingly told Stein, but he appealed to her for help, if she could provide it. At her instigation, with support from Marc Chagall and Jean-Paul Sartre, an official invitation was issued to Wright to visit France with his wife and infant daughter, as guests of the Cultural Relations Section of the French Foreign Ministry. Their passage across the Atlantic would be paid, and living expenses in Paris met for one month. Wright could then stay on for as long as he wished.

Following some confusion (when the offer was made, by telephone, an elated Wright exclaimed, 'It's not possible!', whereupon the Frenchman at the other end of the line assumed the gesture had been declined, and replaced the receiver), the invitation was confirmed; this by itself was enough to sway the State Department. Richard Wright, ex-Communist, present left-leaning liberal, Negro radical but, in his own words, 'a human being before being a Negro', author of a book (*Black Boy*) described by a Mississippi congressman as 'the dirtiest, filthiest, lousiest, most obscene piece of writing that I have ever seen', set sail on April 30 aboard the SS *Brazil* with his wife and daughter for a visit to the City of Light and the city of Stein that was to last nine months.

They docked on May 8. The left-wing daily *Combat*, co-edited by Albert Camus, sent a journalist and photographer to meet the boat-train at Gare St-Lazare. It reported Wright's arrival on the front page. The journalist, Maurice Nadeau, asked Wright if the black problem in the United States was nearing a solution. 'There is not a black problem in the United States,' Wright told him, 'but a white problem. The blacks know what they want.... The whites don't.' A chauffeur-driven car, sent by the American Embassy, pulled up alongside the kerb. Nadeau noted that the white chauffeur doffed his cap. 'Richard Wright, holding his daughter, got in, not before giving me a slap on the back, accompanied by a peal of laughter.'

In Paris, the trees were blossoming and the flowers were out in the gardens. Under an open sky, the effect of space and stone to one who had never laid eyes on it before was ravishing. 'How beautiful!' the cultural attaché Douglas Schneider heard Wright exclaim under his breath as he instructed the driver to take them on a brief tour through the early-morning, traffic-free streets, down the Champs-Elysées, past the Tuileries on to the rue de Rivoli, then along the quais to the Trianon-Palace Hotel on the Left Bank, where a room had been reserved. 'How absolutely beautiful.' He could never have imagined that a city could contain 'in so little space so many treasures, so many flowers, so many grey stones, all so very beautiful'.

And now, finally, he was sitting down to tea with the woman who was at once an admirer, an idol, a supporter, even a sponsor. There was no hint of condescension in the relationship – Stein respected nothing more than talent in an artist, and sincerity in the person, and Richard Wright, at thirty-eight still young enough to appear boyish to the septuagenarian modernist, was happily in possession of both attributes. More than those qualities, though, Stein looked for the new. What stimulated her most was to witness the twentieth century breaking out, in painting, in writing, in dress, even in war. The nineteenth century had come to an end in 1943, Stein wrote in her recent book *Wars I Have Seen*; the Second World War had finished it off, but she herself had played a part, 'killing it dead, quite like a gangster with . . . a tommy gun'. In his every aspect, Richard Wright struck Gertrude Stein as new. In an article which he wrote about her for *PM*, a magazine he contributed to in New York, he declared that his main impression of her

is this: perhaps more than any other mind of our time, she has realized acutely the difference between Yesterday and Today.

6

The piece was datelined 'July 13, 1946'; less than two weeks later, Gertrude Stein was dead. Following a ceremony at the Hôtel de Ville, Richard Wright was made an honorary citizen of Paris.

*

> I like Sartre's face. Some say it is ugly. It cannot be ugly: his intelligence irradiates his features. Hidden ugliness is the most repulsive; Sartre's face has the candour of an erupting volcano. When he enters the Dôme or La Coupole, he is like a suppressed bull. ... Some faces are stingy, denying one even the flicker of eyelids. They appear starched. I love his lower lip like a white negro's, his squint, his wandering eye, his shipwrecked eye, a slip-stream of light when he enters our troubled waters.

> Violette Leduc, *La Folie en tête*, 1970

'It is precisely in her stomach that Paris has recovered least,' wrote the *New Yorker* correspondent Janet Flanner, another survivor from the era of Stein and Montparnasse. It seemed as if the gunpowder used to scatter the Nazis had been made by grinding down every available ounce of meat, fruit and sugar, every shred of writing paper and toilet paper, by liquidizing every drop of milk and ink. There were shortages of all imaginable kinds. Parisians could lunch off a legal menu in a modest restaurant for a few francs, Flanner wrote in May 1946, 'if they can afford it. The white-collar and working classes cannot.'

The de Gaulle government (from which de Gaulle had temporarily resigned) was trying to take steps towards a recovery, aided by two unlikely allies, each unacceptable in its own way, the American government and the French Communist Party (PCF). Unusual attempts were made to sway the allegiance of the people. One spring day a large consignment of underwear landed unexpectedly in shops all over the city, to the relief of

7

the general public. Each garment was stamped with the phrase 'Renaissance Française', the slogan of the PCF, which had manufactured the clothes and organized their supply. They were quickly snapped up, nevertheless, by a grateful public. 'New underdrawers are vital to a civilized reconstruction of Europe,' quipped Flanner.

The occupation of Paris had happened more or less silently, but it had ended with a bang, and the explosion caused fits of creative agitation, in theatres, publishing houses, magazine offices, night clubs and cafés. The strait-jacket had been turned inside-out, and an entire populace was free again, flexing muscles made slack by lack of use, and taking steps unhindered towards the resumption of normal life. The chief representative of this new energy in artistic circles was a writer, Jean-Paul Sartre, and his headquarters were in a café. Many of the eminent pre-war figures were still active: Gide, Cocteau, Colette, Breton; the world's attention was no longer on their grand salons, however, but on the downstairs room at the Café de Flore, on the corner of the Boulevard St-Germain and rue St-Benoit, where Sartre held court, a philosopher-king who was not above lifting dog-ends off the floor to stuff his pipe with tobacco when he ran out, who gave freely of his conversation to whoever stopped at his table, so long as he or she was eager to discuss things – the peace, Marxism, American fiction – with seriousness and commitment. 'It is certain', he wrote in *L'Etre et le néant* (*Being and Nothingness*), 'that the café by itself, with its patrons, its tables, its books, its mirrors, its light, its smoky atmosphere, and the sounds of voices, rattling saucers, and the footsteps which fill it – the café is a fullness of being.' Next to the Flore, forming a corner with the ancient Place St-Germain, was another café, the Deux Magots. Between them, these two constituted the base-camp of the post-war Parisian avant-garde.

Among Sartre's inner circle, apart from his intimate companion Simone de Beauvoir, were Camus, Jean Genet, Raymond Aron, the singer and actor Mouloudji, Boris Vian, and Maurice Merleau-Ponty, editor-in-chief of *Les Temps Modernes*, the journal founded by Sartre in October 1945 with the express purpose of giving 'an account of the present, as complete and faithful as possible'. Talent existed in such abundance and variety in this group, and the idea of an intellectual king and queen with courtiers in the heart of Paris was so appealing, that the *Temps Modernes* circle became a tourist attraction in itself, admired as much for its glamour as for its products. To talk of existentialism was very much *dans le vent*, or as the Americans were starting to say, 'with it'.

The freedoms of the individual which Sartre wrote about in *Being and Nothingness*, in over 500 pages of dense philosophical argument – the limits of knowledge, the nature of the emotions, the transphenomenalism of being, the distinction between *en-soi* and *pour-soi*, the intuition of nothingness and the alternatives of choice – also had their accessible side, in concepts such as the authenticity of the individual and 'mauvaise foi' (bad faith). Phrases such as 'The individual creates his own values', and 'There is no human nature because there is no God to have a conception of it', and 'Man simply is', became the common currency of the young people who had come of age under the Nazi occupation, and who were now in the bloom of liberty. Sartre by himself stood for the new freedoms, and many people had taken to hanging around the Flore in the hope of catching a glimpse of him, at his table in the corner, writing in his notebook. *Being and Nothingness* had, after all, been written in a café. Anyone who had ever drunk *un petit express* could recognize the waiter in the portrait drawn by Sartre to illustrate the concept of *mauvaise foi*:

> His movement is quick and forward, a little too precise, a little too rapid. He comes towards the patrons with a step a little too quick. He bends forward a little too eagerly; his voice, his eyes express an interest a little too solicitous for the order of the customer. Finally, he returns, trying to imitate the inflexible stiffness of some kind of automaton, while carrying his tray with the recklessness of a tightrope-walker by putting it in a perpetually bro-

ken equilibrium which he perpetually reestablishes by a light movement of the arm and hand. All his behaviour seems to us a game. . . . He is playing, he is amusing himself. But what is he playing at? We need not watch long before we can explain it: he is playing at being a waiter in a café.

It became *dans le vent* to call everything that was traditional 'bourgeois', to renounce the institution of marriage, to dress in black and to profess a liking for modern jazz.

'New York is buzzing over existentialism,' Richard Wright had written to Gertrude Stein a month before his departure from New York, 'trying to understand it. It frightens most folks here. Too gloomy.' For Wright, who had a tenacious and enquiring, if not a fine mind, it required first-hand contact with the matter behind an idea before he arrived at a full understanding of the idea itself. He had, so to speak, to touch and feel the existentialists before he could see what the doctrine everyone was talking about was really about. When he had done that, he discovered that existentialism was all about him.

*

The Wrights hardly suffered from the austerity. Their needs were well catered for. The franc was cheap, and, as they were guests of the government during the first month of their stay, most things were paid for anyway. Wright found himself at the centre of a host of official gatherings in his honour. Throughout his sojourn he was treated, for the first time in his life, as a great man of letters.

He responded with typical curiosity and enthusiasm, taking a strong interest in Parisian literary life and seeking contact with the leading writers. He was introduced to Gide, Cocteau and Camus (who told him that the French writers' affection for him was 'fort'). He corresponded with German and Italian publishers over the translations of his books, got his passport amended to enable him to visit England, and generally felt like a citizen of a different world from the one he had left behind. To his editor at Harper and Brothers, he wrote: 'There is such an absence of race hatred, that it seems a little unreal.'

Unlike the tourists who peeped round the classically proportioned pillars of the Café de Flore, Wright read his Sartre – but slowly, and piecemeal. *L'Etre et le néant* was not yet translated into English, and in any case its great philosophical universe was difficult to encompass for someone not trained in its conceptual vocabulary. The long essay 'Anti-Semite and Jew' was published in *Partisan Review* in 1946; he read that, and the lecture 'Existentialism and Humanism', a summary of the themes of *Being and Nothingness*, which came out in English the following year. One of Sartre's themes was that alienation, self-mutilation, the inauthenticity of the individual, grew out of the individual's acceptance of the social labels used to define him: Jew or Aryan, even ugly or handsome. In 'Existentialism and Humanism', Sartre declared that 'Man is nothing else but what he makes of himself. . . . Man is condemned to be free in his choice of action. He is doomed to bear the burden of responsibility.'

Those words made sense to Richard Wright. But, he argued with Sartre when they met, from where he stood the attempt to choose to be something other than what society had determined for you, might be fatal. What use was 'choice' if it led to a lynching? In America, the Negro who 'chose' freedom was fundamentally no more free than the Negro who chose to dwell in the forms of obsequious submission to which society had directed him. The latter was trapped by a social tyranny; the former was trapped by the knowledge that his choice might bring persecution or death.

This was the problem Wright had tackled in his novel *Native Son*, the story of a black youth in Chicago who takes a job as chauffeur to a rich liberal family. On his first night, after carrying home the drunken daughter who has been flirting with him, he smothers her with a pillow, in order to avoid being discovered in her bedroom. Wright had not read any Sartre at the time of writing his novel, but his purpose was 'Sartrean' enough, to explore which ways to freedom were open to his hero:

11

> Having been thrown by an accidental murder into a position where he had sensed a possible order and meaning in his relations with the people about him; having accepted the moral guilt and responsibility for that murder because it had made him feel free for the first time in his life . . . he chose not to struggle any more.

This is Wright in the act of formulating an 'existentialism' – without at the time having the word in his vocabulary – of the black American mind. Where Sartre's decision to choose freedom led to freedom itself, for Bigger Thomas it led to the electric chair.

Contemplation of the example of Richard Wright would eventually contribute to a change in direction in Sartre's thinking, as he began to focus more on the colonial, rather than the proletarian, as the victim of capitalist oppression. He devoted several pages to the American author in the essays he was currently writing for *Les Temps Modernes*, which would later be published as *Qu'est-ce que c'est la littérature?* (*What is Literature?*). And Wright drew on the rich fund of Sartre's ideas, which in Paris were in the air, part of the atmosphere of every café and salon, for the novel he started work on soon after his arrival.

As he dwelt on Sartre's ideas, there occurred a shift in the way Wright actually began to experience himself. When he went to Paris he made a discovery, which was that *Angst* did not begin and end with the fact of being a Negro. The condition of the outsider had dimensions he had never previously had cause, or even opportunity, to explore. *Angst* was not spelled b-l-a-c-k. Until now, colour itself had stood between him and this discovery. The realization made him feel like a man and not a 'black man'. Paris and Sartre revealed this to Richard Wright; as a revelation, it meant a great deal more than witnessing at first hand the famous sites of the Lost Generation. This was why he came to Paris – not to walk gaily up the rue Cardinal Lemoine sniffing the footprints of Hemingway. Paris seemed to endow all its visitors with the ease of gesture that refreshed the whole person, a freedom of expression that surprised and renewed the speaker – whether an artist of the last century or a tourist stepping off the boat in 1946. But the freedom it gave Richard Wright was distinct, and he would describe it in poetic rather than philosophical terms: all his life he had felt as if he was carrying a corpse around with him; when he came to Paris, he felt the corpse slipping off his back.

*

When he boarded ship to take him back to New York at the end of January 1947, Wright did not imagine that he would be returning to France in a little more than half a year. In the interviews he gave to French magazines, he spoke out forthrightly against the racial situation in America, particularly in the South (his remarks were carefully noted by the FBI), contrasted American materialism with the rich cultural outlook of the French, complimented his hosts in the government for having had the 'courage' to invite a black writer as an official guest (though it's doubtful they felt that any particular courage was required), remarked on the esteem in which France held her own writers . . . . And yet, he said, 'My home is over there', tilting his head in the direction of the ocean he was about to cross. My anger, meant, my struggle, my inspiration as an artist — 'for writing it is great' — are over there.

So he spoke while in Paris. The moment he stepped off the boat, however, the corpse climbed on to his back again. He had dreamed of packing his new-found ease in his luggage and bringing it home with him. Instead, he found that when he left his apartment with his white wife, Ellen, he was waiting — and he realized he would always be waiting — for someone to come up and shout 'Nigger lover!' in her face.

America was his subject; but to have to live in America in order to be able to witness what he called the 'thousand little dramas' of black life as it related to white life, now seemed too punishing an ordeal to endure. He had had hopes of a new brotherhood between black and white in the 1930s; but the leftist liberalism of those times had been thrown out of joint

13

by the War.

Wright was no longer connected with the Communist Party. The admiration he had had for Stalin before the War – 'the most politically sensitive volume' was his description of the dictator's *Marxism and the National Question* – had evaporated as his understanding of the reality of the Soviet experiment matured. In his own country, the party which had once regarded him as a potential spokesman on intellectual affairs had turned on him at the first sign of scepticism. 'Intellectuals don't fit well into the Party,' Wright was told one night by a visiting comrade, who warned him that he should make his writing serve the revolutionary cause, or risk being disciplined by the Central Committee.

In a long article published in the *Atlantic Monthly* in 1944, 'I Tried to Be a Communist', he had made public his disillusionment. But, in the elephantine memory of the FBI, there was no mechanism for forgetting, and Wright still ran the risk of being called before one of the growing number of committees formed by the Senate to investigate the activities of Communists and former Communists – just about anybody who'd ever known a Communist, in fact. At the same time as Wright was trying to settle back into American life, the newly formed House UnAmerican Activities Committee (HUAC) was setting in motion its investigation of the film industry – 'the loathsome, filthy, insinuating, unAmerican undercurrents . . . running through various pictures', in the words of the Democratic congressman who proposed the investigations. This was the beginning of the prosecution of the Hollywood Ten, all members or past members of the Communist Party, all sent to prison.

Many other people in the entertainment or literary worlds were called to answer questions by McCarthy's committees. Had he remained in the US, Wright would have been among them. At this time, when he felt fortified by his prestige, it is unlikely that he would have compromised either himself or his present and former friends, in which case his problems would have multiplied. At the very least, he would have found it difficult to leave the country.

And so he decided, shortly after his return to New York, to take the family back to France, this time to stay. The word was spreading. 'All the young people I meet are longing to go to France,' he wrote to Sylvia Beach at the end of May; writers and painters who had heard that Paris was where the interesting work was being done, that you could live cheaply in hotels there and write in cafés; ex-soldiers who had sampled the pleasures of the city during the Liberation, and who wanted more, and soon, with the implementation of the GI Bill, would be able to get it; jazz musicians who had heard that Europe – especially Paris – was in the grip of a 'hot music' craze . . . all were 'longing to go to France'.

Wright's letter to Sylvia Beach was concerned with helping her find an agent and publisher in New York for her memoir about running the bookshop Shakespeare and Company, and publishing *Ulysses*, during the 1920s. This kind favour frames the process of Wright's migration neatly. Two years earlier, a pillar of the old expatriate establishment, Gertrude Stein, had been instrumental in assisting him on his way to Europe. Now, on the eve of a self-exile which would last the rest of his life, he found himself in a position to offer a helping hand to another central figure of the generation that had gone before, symbolically displacing it. 'If I could not have April or May in Paris, I shall have August or September,' Wright told Sylvia Beach; 'but in any case I shall have Paris.'

*

I insist, call me 'racist' if you like, that white people will never be able to equal blacks when it comes to jazz; I'm sorry to repeat it so often . . .

Boris Vian, *Jazz Hot*, 1948

15

The American Negro was already familiar to inhabitants of Paris in two forms: the GI and the jazz musician. Stein had questioned Wright about the black soldiers she saw swinging through the streets after the Liberation – What were they like? What were they thinking? – and received in reply a disquisition on 'jitterbugs'. Had she seen any jitterbugs in Paris yet? Wright had a suggestion to make: the next time she saw 'some of the Negro boys' she should go up to them and ask them about this new music that seemed to have got into everybody's system. 'Just say, hello, boys. I don't dig this jive. What's it all about? Who is this Armstrong and what makes him so hot? They will tell you.'

They would, would they? It's not easy to picture: Gertrude Stein meets the jitterbugs. Wright was well-informed in one sense, though: Paris, or at least St-Germain-des-Prés, was going through a jazz craze. It was not Armstrong they were listening to – it was Dizzy Gillespie, king of *le be-bop*. 'Gillespie's sixteen black musicians will play for the first time in France, at Salle Pleyel, tomorrow night,' Boris Vian told readers of *Combat* on February 19, 1948. 'Just about every young American jazz musician now plays bebop . . . one more inexorable step in the evolution of jazz, which was born centuries ago when the first slaves arrived from Africa in the southern United States.'

The indefatigable Vian – he wrote novels, plays, songs and just about everything else, as well as playing the trumpet himself – reviewed the latest sounds from across the ocean in a number of newspapers and magazines, all at the same time, including one he founded himself, *Jazz News*. For him, as for others of the St-Germain élite, this taste in music was inseparable from an interest in the social conditions in which blacks lived, particularly in the American South. Vian wrote in his jazz column in *Combat* about the introduction of anti-lynch laws in Southern states which previously did not have them, and about the censoring in Memphis of the film *New Orleans*, because of the appearance in it of Louis Armstrong. ('It's an astonishing decision when you see to what point the poor Mr

16

Armstrong is exploited in this movie.') He also ridiculed the racist remarks which had been directed against Gillespie by a few hooligans in the Salle Pleyel.

For most of the *rats-de-cave* of St-Germain, whether committed café-thinkers or not, jazz was the modern thing. Even Sartre liked it, especially when his friend Vian was leading on trumpet at Club du Tabou, on rue Dauphine. Jazz was the doh-ray-me of the newly fashionable philosophy. It spoke of the new liberalism and permissiveness. It was blue. It spoke of defiance and protest. It was rude and erotic. It was supremely of the moment. 'Man simply is' – and what could be more simply 'is' than the black man playing his way out of a past that had enslaved him? The black jazz musician was man-simply-is *par excellence*, improvising his freedom nightly, clearing a playground of sensual delight in the existential gloom. His notations, a new aesthetics of *Angst*, delivered the message which the young *rats-de-cave* were prepared to hear: jazz, the black man's mastercrime of cultural defiance, was the ultimate anti-bourgeois art. In its very first cry of origin, from the auction blocks of the Deep South, as Vian reminded the serious readers of *Combat*, it was freedom music.

*

The Wrights arrived back in Paris at the end of the first week of August 1947. They stayed at first with friends near the river, and eventually bought a house on rue Monsieur le Prince, a broad street in the Latin Quarter, running from the Carrefour de l'Odéon to the Jardin du Luxembourg. 'I shall have Paris' – but the novelty had faded, and he saw France through eyes a little less dewy now. French plumbing exasperated him. He had to drive halfway across Paris just to pick up half a dozen packets of cigarettes, or to buy his coal on the black market. He had brought his large American car with him, an Oldsmobile, and people stopped on the pavements to look at it, and at him, when he was driving through the streets. 'I don't know whether to feel proud or ashamed. I'm ashamed most of the time.'

But his love-affair with the intellectuals continued. On ship, he had read Sartre and de Beauvoir and Camus. 'How those French boys and girls think and write,' he told his journal. 'How keenly they feel the human plight.' Nothing like their movement existed anywhere else in the world. They were serializing the French translation of *Black Boy* in *Les Temps Modernes*. When Wright went into a restaurant for lunch one day, a group from the magazine, eating at another table, sent over a bottle of red wine, with their compliments. He and his wife often dined with Sartre and de Beauvoir; Wright found them generous and sympathetic; de Beauvoir called him her favourite American. Ellen Wright became de Beauvoir's literary agent. Sartre asked Wright to read over the film-script of his play *La Putain respectueuse* (*The Respectful Prostitute*), which told the story of a prostitute in the American South who found herself in the absurd position of sheltering a Negro being hunted by a white mob for the supposed crime of raping her on a train. Wright also wrote an introduction to the English translation of the play.

By the end of the year, three of Wright's own books had been translated into French: *Les Enfants de l'Oncle Tom*, *Un Enfant du pays*, and *Black Boy*, which kept its original title. *Black Boy* had particular success. Black boys were *dans le vent*. Indeed, the most talked-about novel of the year in Paris in 1947 was the work of an American black writer, but he was not Richard Wright. The book was published in French as *J'irai cracher sur vos tombes*, by Vernon Sullivan. The English title would be 'I Will Spit on Your Graves', but, as was explained in a preface by the book's translator – Boris Vian, again – Sullivan had no hope of seeing his work published in his native country. For one thing, it was obscene, containing many descriptions of sexual acts. For another, it was extremely violent, and the violence was that of a black against whites. *J'irai cracher sur vos tombes* charts the erotic adventures of a light-skinned Negro, Lee Anderson, after he takes up a job managing a bookshop in the small Southern town of Buckton. Like

Joe Christmas in Faulkner's novel *Light in August*, Lee is light enough to pass for white. He becomes fixated on two sisters, but his desire to dominate them sexually is morbidly, fatally, connected to a need to obtain vengeance on behalf of his darker-skinned brother, a victim of white violence in the past. Seducing a series of white girls with pathologically inspired energy, Lee revels in a private revenge (they do not realize he is a Negro); but it is not sufficient to satisfy him, and in the end he murders both sisters, before being killed himself by a police bullet.

According to the translator, Sullivan's light skin would have enabled him to live, like his protagonist, among whites, but he preferred 'les Noirs'. While *J'irai cracher sur vos tombes* became highly successful, Sullivan remained an enigma. In fact, this Afro-American novel was a hoax. The book had been written in French, and 'Sullivan' was a ghost. His real name was Boris Vian.

The book earned Vian a good deal of money, but he was correct in pointing out the dangers of publication in his spurious preface, for *J'irai cracher* was prosecuted for obscenity: the first such trial of a French novel since that of *Madame Bovary* in 1857. Did Vian read *Native Son*? *J'irai cracher* was written in August 1946 (in two weeks) while Wright was in Paris. *Native Son* would not be published in its French translation until several months after the appearance of the pseudo-American novel, but Vian read English, was up to date in things American – especially Afro-American – and it seems unlikely that he would have ignored the major work of the black American everyone was talking about. In fact, he translated a fifty-page story by Wright for the French-African journal *Présence-Africaine*, 'Bright and Morning Star', which came out in the same month as *J'irai cracher*. In the preface to *J'irai cracher*, Vian mentions as influences on 'Sullivan' the works of Henry Miller and James M. Cain, both of whom were enjoying a vogue in French translation, but the theme of the 'black' novel is almost identical to that of *Native Son*, in

19

which a young Negro kills a white girl, half accidentally, but also with feelings of triumphant revenge – 'it made him feel free for the first time in his life' – for the slow death he has suffered throughout his entire life.

Wright and Vian were acquainted through Sartre, but not intimately. Neither man recorded any comment on the other. Vian, tall and handsome and up to the minute in everything, might even have regarded Wright as a bit of a *vieux jeu*, a 'square': he didn't know about be-bop, he didn't know how to dance, and the sight of French boys throwing French girls into the air to the sound of ersatz New Orleans rhythms at the Club du Tabou made him feel depressed. 'I hated that place,' he confided to his journal. He wanted France to be France, not a paler version of America.

But, writing to Gertrude Stein shortly before his first departure for Europe, he had noted that 'Negro hot music' was a crossroads at which white and black could meet. As a child in the South, he would never have thought it possible, but when he came North, white boys 'would corner me and tell me the deep meanings buried in a solo trumpet'. It was among the many surprises Paris held in store that there was a white boy there who would do that too.

II

. . . the ritual of opening the morning mail, invariably rich with amusements and doubly so when a mail boat had arrived from New York the previous day. There were the unbelievably bad manuscripts from Americans who interpreted modernism as an unsystematic garbling of words and from Englishmen who apparently thought emancipation meant the spilling of the nastiest thoughts left over from puberty. There were threatening unpoetic letters demanding whether *transition* were going to publish that poem sent a year ago – *yes or no*!! There were those precious

20

newspaper clippings which, with few exceptions, ran true to form – preliminary sneers at the Joyce-Stein contributions (the names, for some reason were always linked together), the inevitable wisecrack about the small 't' in *transition* and the naive speculations about the magazine being composed on the terraces of Montparnasse cafés. And then, in magnificent contrast, the occasional appearance of an excellent manuscript from some person completely unknown.

Eugene Jolas, letter to Robert Sage, 1930

'The French weeklies are carrying my stories,' Wright reported in a letter to his friend back home, Owen Dodson, 'and I'm writing articles for some French dailies.' Writing them in English, he meant; they would then be translated into French. Several new short stories saw the light of day in this manner; it was a function of Wright's happy engagement with the literary circles of Paris. It was also a case of necessity, for, with the War only two years ended and austerity still the prevailing weather, there were no literary weeklies, monthlies, quarterlies, or anything else in English being printed in Paris, apart from the *New York Herald-Tribune*.

Had Wright presented himself at the house of Gertrude Stein twenty years or so earlier, she would have introduced him to Eugene Jolas and Elliot Paul, editors of *transition*; to Ford Madox Ford of *transatlantic review*, Ernest Titus of *This Quarter*. There were also *The Exile*, edited by Ezra Pound, *Broom*, *New Review*, *Boulevardier*, *Tambour*, and many others, most of them remaining in existence for about a year.

In 1947–48, there was nothing. The young writer stepping off the boat, with all the proper names of literary Paris sounding echoes of a grand society in his head, found that there was nowhere to take his work. Wright was unusual among anglophone artists in becoming actively involved in the French domestic literary scene.

Things improved between spring 1948 and spring 1949, when three literary magazines came into being. Two of them

21

were bilingual, with writing in both English and French. One of those was not even new, being a reincarnation of the 1920s magazine *transition*. Whereas the original *transition* had been a hotbed for American modernism, however, the revived version consisted mainly of translations of work by the French avant-garde. It was edited by a Frenchman who wrote in English, Georges Duthuit, to whom the title had been sold by Maria Jolas, and its connection with the generation of Joyce and co. was through an Irishman who wrote in French.

Samuel Beckett's contributions to Duthuit's *transition* were mainly in the role of (uncredited) translator. (On an occasion when some of his own poems were printed, Duthuit poked gentle fun at Beckett's poor spoken French, in the list of contributors; 'despite', he said, 'the undoubtedly original syntactical use of his adopted tongue, Beckett has contributed to such French reviews as *Les Temps Modernes*'.) Like its forerunner, Duthuit's magazine was open to the work of painters, and Beckett made one enduring contribution, a set of 'Three Dialogues with Georges Duthuit', an aesthetic manifesto in the form of conversations about painting.

B.　Total object, complete with missing parts, instead of partial object. Question of degree.

D.　More. The tyranny of the discreet overthrown. The world a flux of movements partaking of living time, that of effort, creation, liberation, the painting, the painter. The fleeting instant of sensation given back, given forth, with context of the continuum it nourished.

Not much of a welcome there for the fresh-faced young writer with his Hemingwayesque short stories in his satchel. For that he would have to wait until February 1949, when the magazine *Points* was born. *Points* was also bilingual and had two editors, one for each language, but it was more innocent than *transition* (note the upper-case 'P'). It also had more money, being owned and edited (in the English department) by Sinbad Vail, the son of

Laurence Vail, a Montparnasse 'character' of the 1920s, and the American heiress Peggy Guggenheim. So eager was Guggenheim for the published-in-Paris tradition to be extended, with her genes, that she bullied her son into it. The money she provided was sufficient for him to get on with doing the things he liked best – driving fast cars, playing billiards, drinking – and still put out regular issues of *Points*.

The result was a far cry from Duthuit's gnomic 'tyranny of the discreet overthrown'. According to one contributor, Vail's method of editing the magazine was to 'wait until he had enough manuscripts to fill up eighty-four pages and then take the lot down to the printer's, and that was that'. Try as he might, Vail could not rouse in himself an enthusiasm for literature. Poetry, especially, bored him. In an editorial written when the magazine reached five years of age, he looked back with weary languor on *Points*'s origins:

It was in the summer of 1948 that I first thought about starting a magazine. I was in Venice on holiday, a holiday from God knows what as I was not doing anything anyway . . . I vaguely thought about opening an art gallery in Paris, but I knew even less about art than literature. . . .

I often wonder why anyone ever starts a little literary magazine in the first place. There are vague ideas running around that they are created to publish writing that never has a chance in the commercial press, 'new' writing, 'experimental' writing and even 'good writing' . . . but I think the real reason is to give the editor and his pals an outlet for their own work plus an egotistical desire to acquire 'fame' or 'notoriety' which in other circles are achieved by eating goldfish in public.

At least now there was a space where the writer could write in English in Paris, and enough Guggenheim money ('I vaguely thought about opening an art gallery in Paris . . .') to ensure that it did not succumb – like almost every other little literary magazine – to a shortage of funds. Points even paid for the work it published – 3,000 francs for a short story (about £2

23

or $6), less for a poem. It wasn't much, but writers used to publishing their work in little magazines might have been surprised to be paid at all.

Vail continued to favour prose, eventually setting up a *Prix Points* and assembling a short-story anthology ('I once thought that all the stories in this anthology were very good. Now I think I'm bored with all of them'). He sacked his poetry editor in time for *Points* 16, and in the same issue cut out the French writing: 'We discovered that we hardly had any French readers,' he wrote in that favoured tone of things going from bad to worse. From having been bi-monthly, *Points* began to appear as a quarterly, and during some quarters did not appear at all, falling victim to the law of diminishing returns which affects all magazines of new writing – the 'newer' the writing, the greater the difficulties of survival.

What kept *Points* going for so long (it folded in 1955), apart from money, was Vail's easy-going manner, which attracted some more serious literary types to the magazine's offices on rue Bernard Palissy. Vail's high-born *ennui* ('I've been told to try and be original for once and not write an editorial; but then I do so little writing and it is so nice to see one's name in print, even in one's own magazine') concealed a knack for attracting contributors of genuine quality to his pages. In the first six months of its existence, *Points* published poems by David Gascoyne, Philippe Jaccottet, Nazim Hikmet; stories by Herbert Gold, René de Obaldia, Henri Thomas and Michael Hamburger; articles on French theatre (by Arthur Adamov) and on the phenomenon of Jean Genet, whose *Journal du Voleur* had just been published in French. Not a bad half-year for any new magazine.

*

Planted among the sparse advertisements for bookshops and restaurants at the back of the early numbers of *Points* was a notice announcing the birth of another magazine, *Zero*. It was based in rue Jacob, in the attic hotel room of a puckish American of Greek extraction, Themistocles Hoetis, who had arrived in Paris in September 1948. Although only twenty-three, he was officially a war veteran with a disability pension, having been shot down over Normandy. The magazine which he founded in partnership with a friend from Brooklyn, Asa Benveniste, can lay claim to being the first entirely English-language literary magazine in Paris after the War.

Hoetis and Benveniste went for a clutch of well-known writers – Christopher Isherwood and William Carlos Williams both contributed to the first issue – to bolster the efforts of the young Paris-based hopefuls. The début was planned for the end of 1948. Then it was advertised in *transition* and *Points* for early 1949, but had to be postponed again because of the usual shortage of cash. Hoetis located a printer near the Boulevard St-Michel who would print the magazine for $250, a sum well beyond the editors' reach. They eventually scrambled it together with the help of a third party:

A young seventeen-year-old American I met by chance when landing at Cherbourg the fall before was the key. I had helped him find a piece of lost luggage in the dockyards, and although he was travelling on to Switzerland by car and I to Paris by train, we exchanged addresses. He visited our scene in Paris several times, and was made aware of our printing problems and agreed to help out. When my next disability cheque came in early December, I sent it to him at his school near Lausanne, whereupon he cashed it for double the amount of the official French franc rate in Paris. He then smuggled it back to me by hollowing out a pocket in a thick old book and mailing it to my hotel. His name was Irving Thalberg, son of the actress Norma Shearer and MGM's famous producer Irving Thalberg – the subject I later learned of Scott Fitzgerald's novel *The Last Tycoon*. It was Irving junior who saved the day with smuggled cash for the first issue of *Zero*.

Zero was always going to need cash, smuggled borrowed or conned. Marlon Brando was the target of a later sting. Vail, who faithfully promoted Zero in his Points editorials, helped Hoetis out at one stage with an unreturnable loan. He reported in *Points* 18 that the *New York Times* stringer in Paris had 'suggested I merge with *Zero*, give them my money and let them do the work'. Vail promised to call the magazine 'Zoints'.

The first issue of *Zero* eventually appeared in the spring of 1949, with a moon-faced sketch of its editor on the cover in bold black and red strokes. In among the work of Isherwood, Kenneth Patchen and others, it included a significant pairing of writers, one famous and the other unknown, one rich, the other penniless, both living in Paris and both black.

Unlike Vail, Hoetis could offer no payment for the work he printed, but he had succeeded in coaxing a short story out of Richard Wright, which had previously appeared only in French. It was called 'The Man Who Killed a Shadow'; it reiterated the theme of *Native Son* in miniature (and of *J'irai cracher sur vos tombes*), and it was followed in the pages of *Zero*, as if by a policeman on the point of arresting it, by an essay called 'Everybody's Protest Novel', the first Paris publication – almost the first publication of any kind – by the twenty-four-year-old James Baldwin.

*

Baldwin's reasons for quitting New York were in essence the same as Wright's – in a letter written home he spoke of 'a violent anarchic, hostility-breeding' pattern, with race at the bottom of it, which was eroding the fabric of his identity – but the circumstances of his arrival could hardly have been more different. No chauffeur-driven car to meet him, no room reserved at the Trianon-Palace, no Gertrude Stein, no 'beautiful, absolutely beautiful' at the revelation of the wide boulevards and the quais. He had holes in his socks and $40 in his pocket. He was a ragamuffin with a big talent. His suitcase held a change of clothes, the manuscript of a half-finished novel, copies of the Bible and the works of Shakespeare, which he carried with him everywhere, and something by each of his more modern heroes, Dostoevsky and Dickens. He had not an ounce of Wright's success – in New York he had stumbled from one badly paid job to another, trying to help his widowed mother feed a family of eight – nor a cent of his healthy bank balance. His stepfather had died insane, he had lost the Christian faith which had sustained him through every crisis, and had, on the same day, so to speak, accepted the burgeoning of his homosexuality – not welcomed in Harlem, where he lived, nor in the church in which he had served as a young minister. About the only thing of value he carried with him to Paris was the address of Richard Wright.

Baldwin and Wright had met in New York. Too callow to aspire to approach the older writer on equal terms, Baldwin had nevertheless been helped by him to gain a fellowship in order to buy time to go on with his novel. It went under the provisional title 'Crying Holy'. When Wright saw the first fifty pages in 1944, it was a mess. But Wright was sufficiently convinced of the giftedness of its author, and of the promise of the work itself, for him to recommend Baldwin for an award from the Eugene F. Saxton Memorial Trust. That was five years ago; the money had long since been spent and 'Crying Holy' was still a mess. One of his reasons for quitting America ('I didn't go to Paris,' Baldwin would say later, 'I left New York.') was to try and turn the mass of pages into a novel. And yet another reason – though he shrank from admitting it – was that Richard Wright was there.

Baldwin arrived, by air, on November 11, 1948. A friend from New York met him off the connecting train and led him straight to St-Germain, where Hoetis was at the Deux Magots, engaged in the latest phase of the continuing *Zero* editorial meeting which was to last throughout that winter. Hearing of the imminent arrival of Baldwin, whom he knew vaguely from Greenwich Village, Hoetis arranged for Wright to be present. When Wright saw his protégé, he rose and welcomed him, as he always did in New York, with a smile and a paternal 'Hey, Boy!' These were the first friendly words that Baldwin heard in Paris, and just about the last he would hear from Richard Wright.

27

*

Baldwin was a noticeably tense young man, slight in stature, with extravagant hand gestures and a facial expression that could veer from tragic to comic, encompassing everything in between, in a moment's conversation. Immediately after his arrival, as he put it to a journalist who spoke to him about it later, he 'went to pieces', a process begun at home but hastened by his exposure to the chill of Paris. 'I'd gone to pieces before I left New York. But I really did go to pieces when I got to Paris.' Going to pieces was a part of Baldwin's defence against the world; and also, by now, a part of his style – something which, as a friend meeting him then for the first time noticed, 'explained everything and excused everything'.

Hoetis settled him into a cheap hotel – and for Baldwin it had to be cheap indeed – on the rue de Dragon, a few doors down, as he surely noticed, from a house in which Victor Hugo had once lived. After a few days, Hoetis returned with some other acquaintances and they parcelled Baldwin up and shipped him across the Boulevard St-Germain to a more agreeable abode on the rue du Verneuil, a pleasant street of ancient houses running parallel to the Seine. This was a small hotel, mainly for students and student types, run by a tolerant Corsican matriarch called Mme Dumont. The Hôtel de Verneuil was low in comfort – just one or two toilets, of the type that the French call 'à la Turque' but which the rest of the world knows as French, serving seven floors – but high in other benefits. It was international, friendly, and Mme Dumont was relaxed concerning the payment of rent.

She was relaxed about other things, too. Soon Baldwin was using his room – and, when his delay in handing over the rent exceeded even Mme Dumont's patience, other people's rooms – for a string of seductions, 'mostly young French boyfriends', according to Hoetis, 'a few of whom were shady characters'. He had spent the years between fourteen and seventeen in the pulpit, embracing the morality of the scripture he preached with extreme fervour. And when he broke free of the church, and renounced its Calvinist strictures, he did that with extreme fervour, too. 'In some deep, black, stony, and liberating way', he wrote, 'my life, in my own eyes, began during that first year in Paris.' And he determined to stay there until he had made himself a writer – or nothing at all. 'Go for broke' was Baldwin's motto; he virtually made a scripture out of *that*.

The architecture of Baldwin's everyday existence was totally ramshackle – he borrowed and couldn't pay back, took commissions and didn't fulfil them, made appointments and failed to keep them – yet somehow quite elegant at the same time. He was generous with his money on the rare occasions when funds allowed him to be, and with his time and sympathy when they did not. He offered wise counsel to friends in need; with a drink in one hand and a cigarette in the other, he was a wit, a talker of brilliance, a writer of potential genius.

Except that he never seemed to find the time, or the space, or the warmth (cheap hotel rooms were cold), to get much writing done. People went to cafés to keep warm, and sometimes to write; but in the cafés they would meet other people, and the one thing Baldwin never could resist was conversation.

One of Baldwin's new friends from the Hôtel de Verneuil was an American, even younger than Baldwin himself but with equally intense ambitions to write, called Otto Friedrich. He soon began to make a record of his encounters with the youthful literati in St-Germain. One evening in the summer of 1949, he had an argument with Herbert Gold, who also lived at the Hôtel de Verneuil, and one or two others, about Baldwin. A man called Newman was 'denouncing Jimmy', saying that the twenty-five-year-old Baldwin had never fulfilled himself.

Somehow this turned into an argument with Gold and his wife about Saul Bellow, now living on the rue de l'Université, and Edith Gold said Bellow is the most talented writer in America. . . . I said Jimmy had more talent than Saul Bellow would ever have, and they all glared at me. Edith said it was 'presumptious' of me

29

to compare someone who had published two novels with someone who hadn't published a single one.

A few nights later, Newman got into an argument with Baldwin himself, and Baldwin 'raged at him about all kinds of past history from Greenwich Village. Newman got very defensive. "Well, I may not know much about literature," he began one round, and Jimmy said, "Why, you know nothing *whatever* about literature."'

The hang-out for Baldwin and his crowd of writers, radicals, runaway youths and assorted patrons who helped provide him with food and beer, was La Reine Blanche, on the other side of the street – in every sense – from the Café de Flore. Cheap and seedy, it had a reputation of being a place for homosexuals, but it was popular with the Verneuil set, whatever their orientation happened to be. Otto himself was engaged to be married to a girl who had her own room at the Verneuil – in 1949, even when in Paris, respectable young Americans did not cohabit before marriage – and Baldwin was just as often seen in the company of one of his many 'girlfriends' as with another male. Paris was a magnet for young people from all over Europe after the War, some of them illegal, and one night La Reine Blanche was raided by 'two fat characters in raincoats' looking for foreign *rats-de-cave* without identity papers. Otto Friedrich (typically) had his papers in order, so there was no trouble for him, but Baldwin (typically) had forgotten to carry his with him.

So, they said, 'Ah-hah, and what do you do?' He said, 'I'm a writer.' They said, 'Ah-hah, and what do you write?' He said, 'Novels, stories, articles.' They said, 'Ah-hah, and who do you write for?' He said, '*Partisan Review* and *Commentary* and the *Nation*.' They said, 'Qu'est-ce que c'est ça?' They looked as if they were about to drag him away, but then he had an inspiration and said, 'And also for *Les Temps Modernes* – for Jean-Paul Sartre.' And then they said, 'Ah', and there was no further trouble.

He hadn't written anything for *Les Temps Modernes*, in fact, though Hoetis – 'the social lion', as Otto called him – had taken him to lunch with Sartre, at which Hoetis tried to inveigle Sartre into writing a piece for *Zero*. Sartre promised to think about it, and at the same lunch expressed an interest in republishing an essay Baldwin had written for the American magazine *Commentary*, entitled 'The Harlem Ghetto'. Nothing came of either project.*

Baldwin was now cut off from the New York journals which had sustained him – just – and was deeply involved in café life and in his own mostly desperate love-affairs. 'Crying Holy' took on the aspect of a prison, from which he frequently attempted to escape through new projects, new titles, new first chapters. 'The new novel is only on page 19,' wrote Friedrich in his ongoing commentary on the Verneuil scene at the beginning of October 1949, 'which doesn't look very promising';

> I was in his room this afternoon, and read what was in the typewriter, and it sounds just like 'Crying Holy' all over again – has a character called Gabriel who discovers the Lord, and whose mother was a slave. I said, 'Is this new novel just a new version of "Crying Holy"?' He said, 'Well, yes and no.'

'Crying Holy' was constantly being smoothed and rechiselled – taking different titles at different stages. It would eventually turn into *Go Tell It on the Mountain*, but that would take another three years.

One thing Baldwin did manage to complete, however, was the essay he had promised to give Hoetis for the first issue of *Zero*, 'Everybody's Protest Novel'. He finished it eventually, that is – while the rest of the issue was being printed, Baldwin's piece was still stuck in his typewriter. 'Everybody's Protest Novel' was surrounded by confusion, in fact. It had

*Sartre gave Hoetis a prose outline of his new play, *Nekrassov*, in 1955, which Hoetis, by then publishing books rather than magazines, included in translation in *The Zero Anthology*, together with an extract from *Le Diable et le Bon Dieu* (1951).

been started while Baldwin was still in New York, and was expected by *Partisan Review*. To the slightly disgruntled *Partisan* editor, William Phillips, a slightly apologetic Baldwin explained, as his essay came off the presses, '*Zero* was here and you were there.' (*Partisan* reprinted it anyway.) This tangle of intentions was nothing to what followed the essay's publication in Paris.

The bulk of the 4,000-word piece is taken up with a discussion of Harriet Beecher Stowe's pro-emancipation novel, *Uncle Tom's Cabin*, which Baldwin had read and reread obsessively as a child, but which he now pronounced 'a very bad novel'. For Baldwin, it was the function of the novel to reveal the human being in all his complexity; 'only within this web of ambiguity, paradox, this hunger, danger, darkness, can we find at once ourselves and the power that will free us from ourselves. It is this power of revelation which is the business of the novelist.'

Seven or eight years earlier, he would have said, 'the business of the minister', before going on to preach a sermon. Although he had stepped down from the pulpit, it was a theological energy that continued to activate his language, refined and redirected. 'Everybody's Protest Novel' is full of this energy: the words 'truth', 'freedom', 'revelation' resound throughout it with a sacred purpose, which is to affirm a devotion to the human being, 'not to be confused with a devotion to humanity which is too easily equated with a devotion to a Cause'.

When Baldwin said that Mrs Stowe's novel was 'very bad', he meant that while it may have succeeded as a pamphlet, it failed dismally as a novel. And it was precisely here, in his apprehension of the aesthetic merit of a piece of literature, and in his consideration of the supremacy of that aspect, that he differed most from Richard Wright. Wright was a social realist, and the fervour of the ex-Communist fired his pen as much as that of the ex-minister fuelled Baldwin's. For Wright, it was important that a novel, story or play have not so much a revelatory or spiritually improving function, as a socially improving one.

'Everybody's Protest Novel' is a remarkable piece of writing. One of Baldwin's first publications, it is already the product of a mature style. It not only contains all of Baldwin's current preoccupations, but suggests the totality of his potential. All his themes as a writer – with the exception of homosexuality, into which he was opening his investigation in a companion-piece for the second issue of *Zero* – are present here. Most pronounced is the theme which had exercised him, in a different realm, while he was still an adolescent – the choice between redemption and damnation:

> We find ourselves bound, first without, then within, by the nature of our [social] categorization. And escape is not effected through a bitter railing against this trap; it is as if this very striving were the only motion needed to spring the trap upon us. We take our shape, it is true, within and against that cage of reality bequeathed us at our birth; and yet it is precisely through our dependence on this reality that we are most endlessly betrayed. Society is held together with legend, myth, coercion, fear that without it we will be hurled into that void, within which, like the earth before the Word was spoken, the foundations of society are hidden. From this void – ourselves – it is the function of society to protect us; but it is only this void, our unknown selves, demanding, forever, a new act of creation, which can save us – 'from the evil that is in the world'.

For a twenty-four-year-old from a Harlem slum, with an education which had to be curtailed, for economic reasons, when he was seventeen, this is precocious. Towards the end of his discussion, Baldwin fulfils a promise he had made at the beginning, to show that 'those novels of oppression written by Negroes . . . raging, near paranoiac . . . [reinforce] the principles which activate the oppression they decry'. If Richard Wright did not recognize his own silhouette in that sentence, he had only to read to the end of the essay to find it fleshed out. Baldwin suggested that Bigger Thomas, the protagonist of *Native Son*, was nothing more than Uncle Tom's descendant, 'flesh of his flesh'. Beneath the subversive façade of Wright's protest novel lay a continuation, 'a complement of that monstrous legend it was written to destroy'. Baldwin portrayed the nineteenth-century crusader and the contemporary novelist 'locked together in a deadly timeless battle, the one uttering merciless exhortations, the other shouting curses'.

It was a subtle argument, but its conclusion left no room for doubt over Baldwin's feelings about the work of the man everyone had taken for his mentor. 'The failure of the protest novel lies in its rejection of life, the human being, the denial of his beauty, dread, power, in its insistence that it is his categorization alone which is real.' The protest novel was a ghetto; Baldwin would like to sweep it away – and, by extension, its architects along with it.

*

On the spring day on which *Zero* was published, Baldwin made a foray into the Brasserie Lipp. Whoever he was looking for, it was not Wright, but there he was, sitting at a table, and he called Baldwin over.

> Richard accused me of having betrayed him, and not only him but all American Negroes, by attacking the idea of protest literature.... And Richard thought that I was trying to destroy his novel and his reputation; but it had not entered my mind that either of these could be destroyed, and certainly not by me.

This is more than slightly disingenuous. The page and a half devoted to *Native Son* at the end of 'Everybody's Protest Novel' may be small-arms fire, but the aim is deadly. Then, hardly had Baldwin stepped back out on to the Boulevard St-Germain than he set to work on another essay, 'Many Thousands Gone'. It is a prolonged attack on *Native Son*.

> *Native Son* does not convey the altogether savage paradox of the American Negro's situation . . . . *Native Son* finds itself at length so trapped by the American image of Negro life . . . that it cannot pursue its own implications. . . . This is the significance of *Native Son* and also, unhappily, its overwhelming limitation.

By the time this essay was completed, in the following year ('Many Thousands Gone' was published in *Partisan Review*, November–December 1951), the rift between Baldwin and Wright had widened and was more or less unbridgeable. Hoetis's congenial notion of having 'the old black writer and the young black writer' at the same table, thrashing out ideas over *café au lait* and funnelling the results into *Zero*, was misjudged. The novel which Wright had looked through in 1944, was nearing completion, and Baldwin was launching it with high hopes indeed. He knew he was, as he said, 'smart'. He even knew he was smarter than Wright. 'All literature is protest!' Wright had snapped at him in the Brasserie Lipp, a copy of *Zero* lying on the table before them like the map of a disputed territory. All literature may be protest, replied the pupil who has learned so much he can outsmart the teacher, 'but not all protest is literature'.

*

> Unable to see it, I invented the biggest and loveliest prick in the world. I endowed it with qualities: heavy, strong and nervous, sober, with a tendency towards pride, and yet serene. Beneath my fingers, I felt, sculpted in oak, its full veins, its palpitations, its heat, its pinkness, and at times the racing pulsation of the sperm.

Jean Genet, *Journal du Voleur*, 1949

Before getting down to work on the essay in which he would take direct aim at Wright, Baldwin had a second commission to fulfil for *Zero*. 'Preservation of Innocence' was published in *Zero* no. 2, Summer 1949. Its theme, like the theme of 'Everybody's Protest Novel', is 'know thyself', though this time the subject of the sermon was not race but homosexuality. And the young ex-minister was preaching the virtues of that tendency, not the vices. It exposes the repressions implicit in the approved image of American machismo, as exemplified in the novels of James M. Cain and Raymond Chandler. And it shows the young homosexual to have been a feminist:

> In the truly awesome attempt of the American to at once preserve his innocence and arrive at man's estate, that mindless monster, the tough guy, has been created and perfected, whose masculinity is found in the most infantile and elementary externals and whose attitude towards men and women is the wedding of the most abysmal romanticism and the most implacable distrust. It is impossible for a moment to believe that any Cain or Chandler hero loves his girl; we are given overwhelming evidence that he wants her, but that is not the same thing and moreover, what he seems to want is revenge. . . . The woman, in these energetic works, is the unknown quantity, the incarnation of sexual evil, the smiler with the knife. It is the man, who, for all his tommy-guns and rhetoric, is the innocent. . . . Men and women have all but disappeared from our popular culture, leaving only this disturbing series of effigies with a motive power which we are told is sex . . . .

Sexual difference was not something Richard Wright had ever had cause to deal with at close quarters. It existed outside his nature, outside nature itself. It was linked to perversity. A friend wrote to Wright about Baldwin, using the word 'filthy'. Yes, Wright replied, that was the word. He felt uncomfortable in Baldwin's presence. 'It's always the same with homos.' Another friend told him: 'Behind all that Baldwin says is a kind of useless, quiet, shameful weeping.' Wright agreed with that, too. Unbowed by the worst that American racism could aim at him, homosexuality still presented itself as a threat. 'Yeah, he can write,' a friend of Baldwin's recalled Wright saying at the time, 'but he's a faggot.'

'Faggot', with its overtones of camp cliquishness, was precisely the wrong term for Baldwin's still developing, still exploratory, relationship with his own sexuality. The investigation of the self was a mission he undertook with displaced religious zeal. The pure in spirit, in Baldwin's lay theology, were those prepared to accept, not resist, the foul rag-and-bone shop of the heart. 'Preservation of Innocence' is not as subtle a piece of writing as 'Everybody's Protest Novel'. But although the two essays share a set of overlapping concerns, 'Preservation of Innocence' is distinct in a particular way – there is nothing in it about race – and Baldwin surely would not have written it had he stayed at home. This was a subject which, as Hoetis says, *Partisan Review* (which had reprinted 'Everybody's Protest Novel' without stating where it had been first published) would not touch 'with a ten-foot pole'. Paris was freeing his pen and nourishing his ambition; the subtitle he gave to this, the second chapter of his search for the American soul, was 'Studies for a New Morality'.

III

Spent yesterday evening at the Geists. The Sarrautes were there as well. The latter started showering with praise that sod Jean Genet, who boasts (with talent, I must confess) of being a thief, a scoundrel and a prostitute. . . . Who dares to speak of goodness here? Goodness has nothing to do with it.

Jean Hélion, *Journal d'un peintre*, c. 1950

Where but in the pages of *Zero* (circulation: approximately 1,000) was the new morality to be studied? Baldwin snatched his subtitle out of the Parisian air, which was thick with talk of ethics, values, old and new moralities, the non-existence of God. 'Man is nothing else than what he makes of himself.' If there had been certainty in shared values before the War – in the nineteenth century, as Gertrude Stein put it in *Wars I Have Seen* – then the War itself had shattered it. The intellectual world was in a crisis of conscience. Whom to write for? Whom to condemn? How to define resistance and collaboration? Some, like Camus, had worked fearlessly for the Resistance; others had joined the day the peace broke out. The definition of collaboration widened to the point where it appeared to trap anyone who had not actively resisted, and often the fiercest accusers were those whose own hands were not spotlessly clean. Simone de Beauvoir endorsed the purges carried out after the Liberation – 'there were certain men who could have no place in the world we were trying to build' – while people whispered about her own behaviour before it (among other 'lapses', she had produced programmes for Radio Nationale, which supported the Vichy government). Camus and Jean Paulhan, on the other hand, men with impeccable reputations, spoke out against the purges and sought forgiveness for writers whose behaviour had been foolish rather than wicked. 'We are all responsible for an absence of values,' wrote Camus.

Sartre promised a set of 'existentialist ethics', but meantime, swinging between the forces of Left and Right, showed a lack of resolve which resulted in passages such as this appearing in *Les Temps Modernes*:

> In no country in the world is the dignity of work more respected than in the Soviet Union. Forced labour does not exist because the exploitation of man by man no longer exists. The diverse measures applied in American prisons contrast singularly with the equitable dispositions of collective work in the Soviet Union.

Even Richard Wright must have questioned his loyalty when, at an introduction he himself had brought about, he beheld Sartre and de Beauvoir publicly snubbing the American ex-Communist Louis Fischer as Fischer tried to enlighten them about the horrors of the Stalinist regime.

Nineteen forty-nine was the year in which Gallimard published Genet's autobiographical novel, *Journal du Voleur*, which contained, amid a wealth of jewelled obscenity, loving, lingering descriptions of other men's penises, their smells, sizes, crooks and bumps. So enthusiastically did literary Paris embrace the author of this eulogy to the decay, not the preservation, of innocence, that it is tempting to see him as a demonic force absorbing the guilt which pervaded the city. Genet felt neither the need to deny the suggestion of collaboration, as so many did, nor to puff up dubious credentials as a *résistant*. On the contrary, he admired the Germans and was given to praising Hitler – anything to keep alive the happy memory of French humiliation, or to shock bourgeois society into a sense of its own moral emptiness.

The scandalized pleasure with which Paris and the larger world at once reviled Genet's lyrically obscene novels, poems and plays, helped keep the existentialist vaudeville in business. 'Philosophy as farce' would have been as good a billing as any. Vian drew up a list of signs by which the uninitiated could recognize the existentialist in the St-Germain night:

> Dishevelled hair, falling in curls over the forehead. (See the famous portrait of Arthur Rimbaud, patron of all existentialists.)
> Shirt open to the navel, winter or summer.
> The existentialist, not having a pillow, goes everywhere with the book by Sullivan, *J'irai cracher sur vos tombes*.

The cheap press – *les torchons* – made the most of it. The weekly *Samedi-Soir* took to reporting every statement made by the godless thinker as soon as he said it (and sometimes before he said it) and satirized the pilgrimages to the Flore by tourists in the hope of glimpsing Sartre (who anyway had since decamped to another bar, the Pont-Royal). 'Monsieur Boubal,' *Samedi-Soir* reported, in July 1949,

> manager of the most famous café in the world, started a revolution in St-Germain by installing a fridge where Jean-Paul Sartre used to sit.
> At first sight, there is nothing to make a fuss about. But this outrage of 'Lèse Sartreté' would have been unthinkable only six months ago. The bench where 'The Sartre' – as Boubal calls him – used to place his then unknown behind had remained untouched until now. And suddenly Boubal, in spite of his reading of the Blue Guide classics, has shamelessly pushed aside the historic bench and put a fridge there instead.

After midnight, *Samedi-Soir* claimed, 'Existentialists hide in the Club du Tabou. . . . On certain nights, the existentialists throw themselves screaming into frenzied jitterbugs and boogie-woogies.'

This conflation of youthful hedonism with existentialist ideology appalled de Beauvoir, who recorded Sartre's irritation with the attacks: 'Wandering about, dancing, listening to Vian play the trumpet – where was the harm in that?' How was the world to be expected to have confidence in a philosopher 'whose teachings inspired orgies'?

One youthful hedonist who was welcomed into Sartre's inner circle, given pages and pages to play with in *Les Temps Modernes*, and yet remained outside it, refusing to sit stony-faced at the master's feet, was Vian himself. Making free with all the materials of his daily life for his unending stream of writings, he invented for one of his novels a philosopher called Jean-Sol Partre, author of *La Lettre et le néon*, a study of neon lighting.

TWO

We Are Outlaws

I

The gloom which had depressed Paris year upon year lifted on Easter Sunday, 1949. Not just the gloom of guilt and austerity, though that was ending too, but the actual gloom of having no lighting. The lights of Paris, for almost ten years 'dimmed with humiliation', as one journalist put it, were turned back on. The City of Light was relit.

Great monuments, reduced to vague, ghostly shapes in the blackout, had their pre-war floodlighting restored. The transformation of the Arc de Triomphe and Notre Dame Cathedral was not only dramatic but revitalizing. Elliot Paul, an editor of the original *transition*, described how Parisians bathed in the free-shining light, now that regulations curtailing the supply of electricity had been suspended. There was 'light in their houses, homes, hotels and little shops every day . . . permission was given for all and sundry to turn on electric advertising signs and illuminate window displays'. The relighting of Paris was celebrated in a night of festivity.

The Marshall Plan to help in the reconstruction of Europe was under way, and France was its main beneficiary. The Minister of Economic Affairs spoke on the wireless of France's gratitude (he meant the French government's gratitude) to the United States: 'All this merchandise has been given to us by the American government,' he said. 'A great lifting of the heart goes up from the French towards the generous American people.' For the moment, the painted graffiti on the walls of Paris saying 'US Go Home', the workers' demands for 'trade not aid', the complaints in the fashionable cafés about 'loud Americans' with too much money, the official crackdown on the sale of Coca-Cola – for the moment, those feelings were forgotten, as austerity ended in the flick of a switch.

The city, which had been running smoothly, if slowly, on bicycles, was now fuming with automobiles, hurtling through the narrow streets of St-Germain, causing an ear-splitting racket and giving rise to the neologism *embouteillage*: 'traffic jam'. The food markets were also full and tempting again, and the invidious 'black traffic', no longer needed, ran into the ground.

'The hucksters shout their prices and the shop apprentices have become barkers,' wrote Janet Flanner in the *New Yorker*:

> standing at the shop doors and bawling about the luscious wares inside. In the *charcuteries* there is a mosaic of every known dainty – turkey paté, truffled pigs' trotters, chicken in half mourning, whole roast goose livers, boar's snout jelly, and fresh truffles in their fragile bronze husks. In the poultry shops, there are Strasbourg geese and Muscovy ducks. In the entrail shops, there are indescribable inner items and blood sausages. At the fish stalls, there are costly deep-sea oysters and enormous hairy sea spiders, to be buried in mayonnaise. The street barrows are filled with bearded leeks and potential salads. Food is still what Parisians buy if they can.

An American journalist working for one of the international news services calculated that during the first half of 1949, he and his colleagues filed only 60 per cent as many stories as they had during the previous six months. The news was that France was only three-fifths as newsworthy as it had been, which was good news.

Coincidental with the diminishing crisis was a swelling of tourism. The back pages of the *New York Herald-Tribune*'s European edition, published in Paris, took on the appearance of a social circular, giving details of the boat-trains to Cherbourg and Le Havre, the best way to get to the Riviera, and how to fly direct from there to America. There were Travel Notes, with helpful hints on how to get by in Switzerland, if you happened to fancy a skiing break, or needed to know the best hotel for a weekend in Rome. The *Herald-Tribune* also gave news of 'Paris Arrivals. . . . Ile de France puts 1,879 Ashore at Le Havre. Passenger lists included Myron C. Taylor and Gian Carlo Menotti. . . . The following persons have registered at the offices of the American Express Company, 11 rue Scribe' – followed by a list of names and the hotels at which newcomers could be contacted. The paper also helpfully informed readers of new books 'now available at the American Library, at 9 rue de Téhéran'.

Not much fuss was made in the paper about the ending of one decade and the beginning of another. On December 31, the *Herald-Tribune* ran a lengthy piece under the headline: 'The Half-Century: An Accounting', which proposed that the 'major forces' that had changed civilization in the past fifty years could be summed up in three names: Lenin, Hitler, and Einstein. Had the writer waited a week or so, he could have included, as a coda to the article, the 'major force' which would dominate the second half of the century: at the beginning of January 1950, President Truman ushered in the new decade by announcing that the H-bomb was going into production in the United States. 'The fear it engendered became cosmic,' wrote Simone de Beauvoir. The new weekly, *Paris-Match*, entertained its readers by illustrating the effects of such a bomb landing on Paris: eighty square kilometres reduced to dust.

There is a clue here to the change occurring in the consciousness of the generation which came of age after 1945. For the writers who grew up before the War, and for those whose maturity was forged during it, the enemy of sane and civilized life was clearly identifiable, in the other camp, on the foreign side of the border, 'over there': the Nazis. The Cold War presented a different type of enemy – this one, which threatened to destroy us as well as our adversaries in the cause of combating Communism, was in our own government, at home. Visualized in simple geographical terms, the inevitable war between the eagle and the bear would take place over Europe's head – eighty thousand square kilometres reduced to dust.

II

If, at the beginning of 1950, some clairvoyantly gifted editorialist had wanted to pin a label on to the decade just beginning, he or she might have tagged it 'subversive'. During the 1940s, we were liberated from the threat of tyrannical domination; during the 1950s, the fight will continue, but it will be liberation from convention, from the tyranny of form, in society and in art.

It sounds like the opening shot of an artistic manifesto. So let him hammer out some *dicta* for the writing of the 1950s:

> Most of the traditional categories in literature are merely distinctions, hallowed by antiquity, which have been allowed to harden . . . .
> All categories are utilitarian; when they cease to be recognized as such, they become obnoxious . . . .
> We are for any innovation in creative writing which renders creative writing more expressive . . . .
> We will hit at all clots of rigid categories in criticism and in life . . . .

These statements of earnest intent are drawn from the pages of an actual magazine, published in St-Germain, in English, called *Merlin*. In 1950, it did not exist. Its guiding intelligence was just about to arrive on French soil for the first time, from Scotland, but on a meandering, aimless visit in a 1924 Ford Talbot, with family in tow, and little money, which ended badly with him back in Glasgow, wondering what to do next about his writing and his marriage. A typical journal entry made by Alexander Trocchi at the time reads: 'Camped outside Paris, mud, dripping water, mosquitoes and the rain. Money short as usual . . . .' Trocchi did not settle properly into St-Germain until January of the following year, having by then off-loaded the wife and two young children he felt had become such a drag on his future and his potential.

Like Baldwin, like Wright, Trocchi was impelled from his native land as if by an independent force. The weight of oppression he had to struggle free of was not racial, it was provincial. Scottish prose literature of the post-war years contained little to stimulate a mind like Trocchi's, which had looked into *Ulysses* and been modernized. For him, the art was the man. You are what you write. Live it, die for it.

Temperamentally, Trocchi was a revolutionary, and when he looked up at the slate skies of Glasgow, a great industrial city with an industrial pride but little revolutionary ardour, where the main philosophical debates were between Catholic and Protestant, and then thought about the new forms that had come to his notice from across the Channel – in philosophy, in fiction, in the sexual autobiographies of Henry Miller, which he had read, and Genet, which he had only read about – he knew he must propel himself outward. He struck out into cosmopolitanism, and with a grand project: nothing less than a total revolution in the consciousness of his time.

In years to come, Trocchi would shift his field of action away from literature, as he chased more and more ambitious, change-the-world shadows, overreaching himself in the process; but for the time being, his tool was the written word and his goal was the subversion of conventional – now that he was in Paris he would say 'bourgeois' – values. He skipped London, the traditional centre of attraction for literary talent from Scotland, and made straight for St-Germain-des-Prés. Trocchi did not come to Paris intending to edit a literary magazine, but to write novels, poems and essays. He had already written some fiction, though none of it had been published. He was given to a number of bad habits, but not to underestimating his own potential. A glance at some of the uncompleted work he wrote while still in his mid-twenties suggests that he was entitled to value himself highly. The city is Glasgow in the 1940s, and the picture surface reflects a writer already planning his escape:

> Faded now. The lost gentility of another century. A street of old houses, respectable in its location towards the west of the city. A street of bank-clerks, insurance agents, shopkeepers. The women of the street, tired, genteel, dignified, poor. Husbands, for one reason or another, not quite unsatisfactory. Their sins abroad in conversation. An affair of rumour and unfinished sentence, because outside their respective houses they were neat men, dandy men, polite in conversation. And no man collarless. As the years turned the faces of the younger women became more hollow, tongues sharper, lips less red and soft. The ruin of women's faces in a street of surprised indignant men. To a stranger the street must have given the impression of peace. Underneath passed a procession of sad days, plagued by the curse of respectability on a small income.

Trocchi was an unusual Scotsman – in fact, he was only three-quarters a Scot. His father's father was Italian, and it was family pride that there were connections all the way to the Vatican. True or not, Trocchi stood aloof from religious warfare in a city where allegiances are staked out on sectarian grounds. His oppositions were to be dramatized on a larger scale.

Aged twenty-six, he had only recently left Glasgow University, his studies in philosophy having been interrupted by war service. His professor in the department described him as the best philosophy student ever to sit in his tutorials. Trocchi had recently been awarded a £400 travelling scholarship by the university, which had financed his travels to Paris in the first place. Of all his contemporaries in St-Germain, with the exception of Baldwin – who didn't like him and who saw him only passingly during the five years that they shared the same cafés and hotels – he was the most precociously gifted.

With a grounding in the classics and a capacious memory for verse, Trocchi seemed to his contemporaries to move with enviable ease among cultures of diverse ages and orientation. He possessed an Olympian regard, which, tempered with a generous manner and a way with people of every class and type, made him a natural leader in the literary coteries of the Left Bank. Or, if you chose to see it from a different point of view, as some people did, a born manipulator.

Over six feet tall, with a hawk's nose and brooding eyes set in a craggy face, he was a man of large enthusiasms. Trocchi would sweep through Paris in a taxi, even though it consumed his last few francs. 'Alex always had money on his person, somewhere, in his sock or something,' says the poet Christopher Logue, a colleague on what was to be *Merlin*, and one of Trocchi's closest friends. It was not easy to get Alex's goat, he says; but Logue, liking nothing better than an argument, would try. He might start by traducing Trocchi's favourite philosophers. Then he would get his come-uppance:

'Very well old man. I would not want it said I invited a friend to lift his head on to the block; but nor is it wise to keep so fine a communications centre in the sand. True, the chief use of logical discourse is highlighting fallacy. But to spot the dotty upshot in fair, or maybe wicked words, is just as useful as to invent King Kong. And what's more – evil men fear it. They do not fear poetry. They quote it.'

'I want to do it like Keats,' I said, anxious to change ground. 'He did not bother with argument.'

'The only evidence for that is his failure to talk Fanny Brawne into bed. With respect, old man, if you can do it like Keats, so much the better for us both. But can you? Is this', putting his finger on my manuscript, 'as good as

"O latest born and loveliest vision far
    Of all Olympus' faded hierarchy!
Fairer than Phoebe's sapphire-regioned star
    Or Vesper, amorous glow-worm of the sky . . ."

because if you think it is, let us say no more – except that I might be wrong – and as you are not in love at the moment, see if you can get to know that young lady over there.'

*

'Be careful you don't become notorious instead of famous,'
someone warned Trocchi. It was a remark which disconcerted
the outwardly imperturbable Scot, for it exposed an aspect of
his nature he was not happy with, an emotional loose wire, a
likelihood of spiritual damage. Another thing about him that
struck Logue was that he had a talent for surrounding himself
with people who hovered between being admirers and disciples. 'Alex didn't mind fools. He could be surrounded by
them, quite happily. He was the sort of person who could have
been the leader of a cult, you know, sleeping with all the
women and what not. He could convince anybody to do just
about anything.' One day while they were sitting together at a
café in the rue de Tournon, Trocchi talked about bloodshed
with such force that Logue fainted. 'Just by the power of
words.'

By that time, Trocchi had read the works of Genet, and was
trying to draw from him the secret of investing the written
word with kinetic energy. Early attempts show him more given
to superficial scatology than capable of breaking into the hidden purity of the poet-thief. In a poem of the time (later published in *Merlin* under the pseudonym 'James Fidler'), he
writes of a woman's 'gut open like Christ's wound', and of
'more wars in that vast vagina of hers/than candles lit for the
virgin'. It is not surprising that a diaristic scribble concerning
Genet's *Notre-Dame-des-Fleurs*, made in the spring of 1951,
links sex and cruelty: it refers to the moment at which Genet's
transvestite heroine seals her fate, which is to be guillotined:

> The words which decapitated Our Lady of the Flowers were very
> amusing:
>> 'L'vieux était foutu. Y pouvait seument pu bander.' (The old
>> guy was totally fucked. He couldn't even get it up.)

Trocchi was reading Genet's novels in the French he had
learned mainly by osmosis. Although *Notre-Dame-des-Fleurs*
had been translated and published in a limited edition in the

United States in the 1940s, Trocchi himself would be the first to make Genet widely available in English, initially by including extracts from *The Thief's Journal* in *Merlin*, then by issuing the complete novel under the magazine's publishing imprint.

Merlin would provide a vehicle for Trocchi's activity – or, as another colleague puts it, 'his ego' – over the next four years. During his first few months in Paris, however, he tried to get to grips with the philosophical jousts which were enlivening the French scene. Jotting his impressions in a notebook, he imperiously predicted that he would have 'something no doubt to say about existentialism'. It amounted to a twenty-page critique of Sartre's ideas. It never went into print. The fundamental reason why is made plain by another diary entry, which represents the two sides of the Scotsman's nature quite neatly, the Calvinist and the hedonist, each continually unbalanced by the other. He opens his sentence with a typically arrogant and challenging declaration: 'I had hoped to avoid an all-out onslaught on existentialism, especially as there's much in it that appeals to me'; and closes it, 'including white curves in black ski-trousers'.

*

To Trocchi, Paris was the city of Joyce. He had scant interest in the doings of the Lost Generation. Hemingway had admired Joyce, therefore Trocchi might have admired Hemingway for that, but not much else. Aleister Crowley, the Great Beast and black magician, had had a spell in Paris in the 1920s . . . . Trocchi might have been thinking about *him* on the boat from Dover to Calais. But F. Scott Fitzgerald? No.

There was already a writer in Paris, a disciple of Joyce, who 'interrogated' form, questioning the status of literary categories, even the nature of the word and its relation to breath: Beckett. He turned away from most art 'in disgust, weary of puny exploits . . . of doing a little better the same old thing'. Preferring what, then? his interlocutor Duthuit asked in one of their 'Three Dialogues' in *transition*. Replied Beckett: 'The expression that there is nothing to express, nothing with which to express, nothing from which to express.' Beckett's method was to write and write and write at a subject, until the subject disappeared and only the writing remained.

He had come to Paris as a teacher from Dublin in 1928. He met Joyce and helped him with some mundane tasks while Joyce concentrated on *Finnegans Wake*. Beckett had played a part in the Resistance during the War, although he was reluctant to reveal what his part was – a restraint which harmonizes his modesty and integrity. His feet felt secure on French soil, as did, increasingly, his pen in the rarefied French language. In English, he was already a considerable stylist, but he felt distracted by the ornamentation English proffered. Writing in French enabled him to rewrite himself, plainer than before. In French, he said, 'It is easier to write without style.'

Beckett had a coterie reputation in 1950, made up in part of his having been Joyce's friend, and of his skill as a translator of difficult texts from both French into English and English into French. He had even rendered himself into French: his translation of *Murphy*, which had been published in London in 1938, came out in Paris in 1947 – and went again, unnoticed. Since the mid-1940s, he had been writing directly in his adopted language, funnelling his 'nothing to express . . . together with the obligation to express' into a series of novels.

The first discussion of Beckett's work in a Paris-based English-language journal came in *Points*, at the end of 1951, in the course of a review of *Molloy*, which had lately appeared in its original French edition. As was the case with many things which happened in the pages of *Points*, the decision to review *Molloy* came about as a result of serendipity. Beckett's novel was published by Les Editions de Minuit, which happened to share an address – 7 rue Bernard Palissy – with *Points*. A review copy found its way upstairs to the magazine's disorderly office, and an article was put into preparation.

The review was the work of one Jared Shlaes, making his

first appearance in print. It displays a certain prescience in introducing Beckett to the anglophone readership in Paris, despite a tendency to be flippant:

> Beckett is a saint, but he is not yet a very great saint. He may come to be that if enough people begin to write and talk about his books and if one day they begin to publish annotated and critical editions and argue about the grammar school he went to and the number of cups of coffee he drank a day and the long and bitter fights in the literary journals and back rooms of bookshops about what *Molloy* really means . . . .

Beckett has everything it takes to make a 'saint', Shlaes concluded, confusingly, 'except publicity'.

It's unlikely that Beckett ever read this, or any other of the reviews of his first work. He disdained critical comment. He would have abhorred the description of himself as a saint, and publicity was the last thing he was seeking. But in his own reluctant fashion, he did seek publication, in English as well as in French. That was on its way, in the form of Trocchi and *Merlin*.

*

Merlin took itself extremely seriously. The editors' aspiration was to create a *Temps Modernes* in English, to give, in the words of the latter journal's first editorial, 'an account of the present'. Richard Seaver, a young American who was writing a thesis in French, and who was to become closely involved with the magazine, described the ways in which he and his colleagues differed in their approach to life and literature from the 'so-called Lost Generation':

> Paris may have been our mistress, but the political realities of the time were our master. This was the dawn of the Atomic era. . . . The first issues of *Merlin* could not have exceeded sixty-four pages, but each bore the weight of the early Cold War world on its meagre shoulders.

The journal was the progeny of Jane Lougee, a long-haired, beautiful New Englander who had come to Paris, aged twenty-five, with the intention of studying the fine arts. She had a private income, modest by Guggenheim standards but large enough to enable her to pursue her studies in comfort and to take seriously the suggestion, when it was put to her, of part-funding a literary magazine. During the winter of 1950–51, while living on the Boulevard Montparnasse, she met a Chicagoan named Victor Miller. Unimpressed by the current outlets for writers, and seeing an increasing amount of literary talent in the quarter, Miller planned to set up a new magazine to rival *Points* and *Zero*.

The magazine was to be called 'Mss' (as in 'manuscripts'). Miller was to be the publisher, Jane his assistant. Trocchi got involved more or less by accident. 'Word got about that there was this Scottish fellow in town', says Jane Lougee, 'said to be very bright, over from Glasgow on a scholarship, who might be interested in doing something for the magazine. The idea at first was just to get him to write for it, but as soon as we met him it was clear that here before us was the editor.'

Victor Miller dropped out of the scheme shortly afterwards, and left town with Trocchi snapping at his heels and announcing to anyone who would listen – Trocchi had the gift of making people listen – that Miller had 'behaved very badly'. All through his life, in every situation he created, Trocchi would at some point pause in order to announce, with a grand affectation of disappointment, that someone, or indeed everyone, had behaved *very badly*.

Apart from the financial problem it caused, Miller's departure did not trouble Jane. She was quite attached to her 'Scottish fellow', and now she had found her niche: she became the magazine's publisher, scraping from her allowance to pay its expenses, and made Trocchi her editor.

By the time of accepting his (unpaid) post, Trocchi had come into contact with Logue, who had apprenticed himself, by proxy, to Ezra Pound. He had come to Paris for basically the same reason as Trocchi, 'out of a complete failure to be interested by what was happening in London at the time. It was so drab. There was nowhere to go. You couldn't seem to meet any girls. If you went up to London in 1951, looking for the literary scene, what could you find? Dylan Thomas. I thought that if I came to the place where Pound flourished, I might flourish, too.'

Logue was in most outward ways the opposite of Trocchi: small and fiery, with a tendency to be over-emotional, he lacked the big man's proprietorial confidence. Currently preoccupied with all things medieval, including the arts of falconry, Logue supplied the magazine's name: the female merlin is a hawk known to falconers as keen-eyed, bold and formidable – just the attributes to be found in the partnership of Trocchi and Jane Lougee, in fact. The first issue was conceived and laid out in Jane's studio apartment. As an editorial address they used the Librairie Mistral, an English-language bookshop on the Left Bank, opposite Notre Dame, recently set up by George Whitman. (It would later change its name, in homage to Sylvia Beach, to Shakespeare and Company.) Copies were available on May 15, 1952.

*

The contents of *Merlin* no. 1 consisted of short stories by Trocchi and Alfred Chester, a critical article on existentialism by A. J. Ayer – the nearest thing English philosophy had to a *vulgarisateur* like Sartre – and some twenty pages of poems by Logue, William Burford, Patrick Brangwyn, Charles Hatcher – each part of the *Merlin* coterie – and 'James Fidler', aka Alexander Trocchi.

The pieces by Chester and Ayer were the best things in the issue; though the latter's had been published already, it was expert and timely. Chester's story was an effective tale of unrequited love narrated by a woman. The poems were, for the most part, more Poundian than Pound. If, as is likely, Baldwin borrowed a copy of *Merlin* from one of his better-off friends at the Hôtel de Verneuil or La Reine Blanche, what did he make of this:

Yet it was Chepren, recumbent Lion, guardian of Giza,
Who knotted the waters Cheops loosed
From Abydos to the Fayum,
Made Nile obey his miracles
And fed White Wall Memphis . . . .

And so on, for two pages, forcing twenty names into as many lines.

The next issue contained the first of the magazine's editorials, with their mix of bombast and *bizarrerie*:

For the poet, *qua* poet, time is not a concept; it is something in which he is emotionally involved. . . . The poet is situated beyond the problematical in a personal cosmos whose vital centre he is and which grows away from him on all sides into the warm flanks of mystery.

The article is unsigned, but those 'warm flanks' bear the unmistakable imprint of Trocchi. His prescriptiveness at times hits an almost comical note of high-minded banality – 'To say that *Merlin* is against obscurantism in criticism is not to say that it is against obscurity in poetry' – but what he was getting at was simple and serious enough: that *Merlin* was situating itself in the post-war European avant-garde; that it was declaring itself *engagé*.

The competition was hardly stiff. *Zero* had temporarily suspended publication, while Hoetis sought out different forms of adventure in Tangier, then in Mexico, and finally back in New York (from which base *Zero* did resume publication). *Points* trundled along; it had the virtue of continuity, if not much else. Vail's commitment was not to the Left or to the Right, it was to the good life, and although *Points* put out many more issues than *Merlin*, it had neither the intellectual seriousness nor the international outlook of the younger journal.

Trocchi, on the other hand, had the ambition and the personality necessary to orchestrate a literary scene, and he was beginning to attract some talented people to his camp. Each issue of *Merlin* is better than the one that went before. Over the next two years, it would publish, among much else, Genet and Ionesco (the latter for the first time in English, with *The New Tenant*); Sartre writing on Genet; poems by Nazim Hikmet, W. S. Graham and Paul Eluard; artwork by Brassaï and Ernst Fuchs. By the second issue, Richard Seaver, who was studying French at the Sorbonne, had become Trocchi's second-in-command, and his influence began to show. *Merlin* no. 2 contained an article by him, 'Samuel Beckett: An introduction', the longest and most serious appreciation of Beckett yet to have appeared in English or French. There were also critical commentaries on Ionesco, the Marquis de Sade, Malaparte, and of course Pound. Seaver went to visit Sartre at the rue Bonaparte and negotiated an agreement – in principle, but not in practice, an exchange agreement – with *Les Temps Modernes* to take articles from the French magazine's pages, translate them and publish them in *Merlin*. The main fruit of this initiative was a two-part article, 'SS Obersturmführer Doktor Mengele' by Miklos Nyiszli, the first of the concentration-camp memoirs to expose the diabolical experiments which took place at Auschwitz.

Another quality which is useful to an editor is ruthlessness, and Trocchi had ruthlessness in abundance. Nothing displays it more vividly than the letter he wrote to the Scottish-based poet Alan Riddell, who had been employed by Victor Miller to scout for talent in England and Scotland. Wishing to purge the magazine of the last traces of his predecessor, Trocchi sacked Riddell even before the first issue of Merlin had appeared.

28th April 1952

Reluctantly, following a general vote of no-confidence in you on the part of our contributors, I ask for your resignation as Assistant Editor. At the same time I must ask you not to represent yourself as officially connected with *Mss* in London or elsewhere. The question only arose a few days ago when it was pointed out that while you were in Paris under my wing no harm, and possibly good, could come out of your being associated with *Mss*, but that, alone in London and representing the magazine there, you might do considerable damage.

Personally, I believe that the danger was overestimated but unfortunately I could not honestly say that it was non-existent. I do have doubts about your character and capabilities in relation to an international review, but, while you were in Paris, was able to defend you against criticism by pointing out that you were 'teachable'. After you had left, and your critics came round against you in force, recourse to that defence was impossible. I swithered for a long time over the problem . . . are you in London the right man to be going round saying 'I am the Assistant Editor of *Mss*', and, putting personal feelings aside and considering the question solely in my capacity as Editor, I decided that you were not. Logue, Burford and Chester were unanimous in saying that if you approached them they would not think of contributing, nor can I think that you would have met with any success with Ayer. It was pointed out, undeniably, that, apart from the Scots poets (none of whom we now intend to use), you had got hold of nothing. Anyway, there it is, and *qua* editor that is my final decision.

As for his personal feelings, Trocchi added by way of consolation, he felt 'lousy' about it, 'the more so because I realize what a difficult position I have created for you in Scotland'. Riddell would have been cheered to receive the advice to 'get on with your own writing', and to know that his boss, who had sacked him before the enterprise had got under way, would be at all times 'pleased to hear from you'.

Trocchi was at work on a novel, *Young Adam*. The stories of his own which he published in *Merlin* are written in a clean-limbed, highly visual style, which is obsessed by the surfaces of things. It would reach greater maturity in *Young Adam*, a taut murder story which shows the influence on the author of the philosophical novelists who were his neighbours.

I looked in the mirror. . . . Nothing out of place and yet everything was, because there existed between the mirror and myself the

56

same distance, the same break in continuity which I have always felt to exist between acts which I committed yesterday and my present consciousness of them. . . .

I don't ask whether I am the 'I' who looked or the image which was seen, the man who acted or the man who thought about the act.

Although it is set in Scotland – on the stretch of canal connecting Glasgow and Edinburgh – *Young Adam* has nothing in common with other Scottish writing of the time. It actually has the feel of a French novel written in English. It was a deliberate divorce, as much as it was the natural effect of continental air and new vocabularies. Having begun the process of freeing himself of his cultural background, Trocchi set about getting rid of his domestic baggage, too. He was becoming increasingly involved with Jane, whose new-world attractiveness and ambition must have seemed irresistible. The effect of meeting Jane and of encountering 'white curves in black ski-trousers' was to put his marriage *en panne*. His Scottish wife Betty had come to Paris to visit him but had had to return home to earn money to support the family (there could be no money expected from Trocchi), leaving him in charge of their two daughters. Not having time to care for them, in between literary and romantic commitments, however, he farmed them out to a French foster mother, who spoke no English.

*

Nineteen fifty-two, the year of *Merlin*'s launch, was also the year of the most talked about literary dispute in post-war France. A quarrel between Camus and Sartre had been ignited by a devastating review in *Les Temps Modernes* of Camus's philosophical work *The Rebel*, written by a young disciple of Sartre's, Francis Jeanson. Camus replied in haughty terms, and received, as a counter-thrust, a further rebuke, this time from Sartre himself. The disagreement was more political than philosophical. Sartre was growing ever closer to the USSR and to living Marxism. Camus distrusted all forms of socialism; he was an idealist, a moralist; 'sensitive to the misfortunes of man,' wrote Simone de Beauvoir, with the sneer of the convinced Utopian, 'he blames nature'. There was no longer any basis for friendship between the two men. As for de Beauvoir – who on all things followed not just the party line but what *Samedi-Soir* might have called the 'Sartreté line' – Camus 'who had been dear to me . . . no longer existed'. The *Merlin* crowd, looking on in wonder at the amount of attention this quarrel commanded in comparison to how it would have been regarded in Britain or America, dutifully sided, as Seaver put it, 'with the political scrapper over the detached philosopher'. Seaver wrote about the argument in *Merlin* and Trocchi reported on it at the request of a London-based magazine, *Nimbus*, whose readers would not have had the advantage of witnessing the dispute at close range. Curiously, he anticipates that fearsome phrase of de Beauvoir's about Camus no longer existing:

> Camus has withdrawn into a largely emotional isolation, into the position of non-participation outlined in his *L'Homme révolté*, and since Sartre and Jeanson combined to attack him his public utterances have been few. Sartre, the pamphleteer, the man of action, flies to Vienna with a new, as yet incomplete manuscript on his lap: for him Camus is a thing of the past.

Sartre was your man, if 'hitting out at clots of rigid categories' was your game. According to Seaver, politics was of greater moment to *Merlin* than 'experimental writing', but to have given precedence to radical politics over radical writing would have been to go against the collective spirit of the group, and anyway the evidence does not suggest that this was the case. What Seaver meant, perhaps, was that it was not *Merlin*'s aim to give priority to literature over politics, but that the one should respond and reflect the other, that literature, in particular, should swim in the political current – with or against it, so long as it did not stand outside it – and that the magazine should reject the simplicities of art for art's sake. Politics, at the same time, ought not to neglect the manifestations of artists. In this, as in other things, *Merlin* was taking a lead from *Les Temps Modernes*.

When it comes to situating *Merlin* in literary history, however, it is for its championing of an ostensibly apolitical 'experimental' writer that it will be noted, and Seaver who will gain much of the credit. Not only did Seaver translate for the magazine and write articles of his own, he also allowed his home in an abandoned warehouse at 8 rue du Sabot to be used as the group's headquarters. On his way home from the cafés in St-Germain to the former banana-skin-drying depot where he lived, Seaver often passed through the street adjoining the rue du Sabot, rue Bernard Palissy, which housed Les Editions de Minuit. Minuit had been famous during the Occupation as a clandestine publisher of mainly Resistance texts – the most famous of which was *Le Silence de la mer* by Vercors – but it had recently been sold to Jérôme Lindon, who specialized in work of a more modernist sort. The window display intrigued Seaver as he cycled by, for it showed only two books, both by Beckett: *Molloy* and *Malone meurt*, newly published in French:

> I passed that window several times before I made the connection. I was then very deeply into Joyce, and remembered that it was Beckett who, twenty-odd years before, had contributed the opening essay to *Our Exagmination Round His Factification for Incamination of Work in Progress*. It was Beckett, too, I recalled who had with the French writer Alfred Peron translated the 'Anna Livia Plurabelle' episode of *Finnegans Wake* into French. What was this Irishman . . . doing writing in French?

Six publishers had rejected *Molloy* before it landed on Lindon's desk. Aware that it was the first novel of a trilogy, Lindon wanted to publish it, but he felt the need to be cautious. He informed Beckett that in the meantime he would prefer to offer a contract for this book alone. The unpublishable, unsellable Beckett replied that it was all or nothing at all. Lindon, reconsidering, thought he might have a masterpiece on his hands – well, you never knew – and agreed.

Seaver bought both the books direct from Minuit, and read them. When he had finished, he reread them. He found them 'stunning'. He enquired at the Bernard Palissy office if Minuit had published any more books by Beckett. The answer was no, though another novel, *L'Innommable* (*The Unnameable*), was in preparation. However, Seaver was directed to a different publisher, Bordas, which had a few years ago put out the French version of *Murphy*. Seaver thanked his informant, then went straight over to Bordas, just a stone's throw away on rue de Tournon. Was *Murphy* still in print? Yes, it was.

> By the look of the stock in the back of the shop, the original printing was all but intact. According to A. Alvarez, ninety-five copies had been sold by 1951. I presume, by the delighted reaction of the clerk to my request, that my copy was ninety-six.

Murphy offered the same comedy, the same sense of the grotesque, as did the other two novels. Over the next few weeks, Seaver tracked down everything he could find by Beckett. There wasn't much: a short story entitled 'La Suite' in *Les Temps Modernes* in 1946 (unaccountably, the magazine published the first part only – the finished work was to have been called 'La Fin'); and another, 'L'Expulsé', in *Fontaine*, which had come out in 1947. What Seaver held in his hands was Beckett's complete published work in his adopted language.

Seaver set to work writing an article about his discovery, which he intended to submit to *Points*. But then he fell in with Trocchi, who shared his interest in Joyce and was willing to believe that the man frequently (but erroneously) referred to as 'Joyce's former secretary' was worth taking note of. In 'Samuel Beckett: An introduction', published in the second issue of *Merlin*, Seaver predicted that Beckett would be unlikely ever again to write in his first language (which turned out almost to be true), and that his work would 'ultimately be judged as a part of twentieth-century French literature'.

With youthful presumption, Seaver sent a copy of the magazine to Beckett himself. He received no reply, but from the author of 'I could die today, if I wished, just by making a little effort', this was not altogether surprising. He also sent his article to Lindon, owner of Les Editions de Minuit. The publisher was more forthcoming than his author. He tipped Seaver off that Beckett was sitting on a novel in English, which might one day be translated into French for release in Paris, but so far was unpublished. Seaver wrote again to Beckett, mentioning the bruited novel and politely informing him that the magazine with which he was associated (with typical grandiloquence, Trocchi had styled him 'Advisory Editor and Director') would be deeply honoured, highly delighted, eternally grateful, to have the opportunity, if a way could be found, of considering, for possible excerption, or serialization, if permission were to be granted, etc.

Again, there was no reply. But, says Seaver, 'I had rather expected that.'

> We had all but given up when one rainy afternoon, at the rue du Sabot banana-drying depot, a knock came at the door and a tall, gaunt figure in a raincoat handed in a manuscript in a black imitation-leather binding, and left almost without a word. That night, half a dozen of us – Trocchi, Jane Lougee, Christopher Logue, Patrick Bowles, Charles Hatcher and I – sat up half the night and read *Watt* aloud, taking turns until our voices gave out. If it took many more hours than it should have, it was because we kept pausing to wait for the laughter to subside.

Beckett had not been cavalier in handing over his manuscript to the young editors; in fact, he was very particular about which section of the novel the magazine could print, if it wished to print any. Beckett had specified a portion characterized by monotony and repetition, beginning 'Watt had little to say on the subject of the second closing period in Mr Knott's house.' It went on for fifteen pages in this vein:

> Here he moved, to and fro, from the door to the window, from the window to the door; from the window to the door, from the door to the window; from the fire to the bed, from the bed to the fire; from the bed to the fire, from the fire to the bed; from the door to

the fire, from the fire to the door; from the fire to the door, from the door to the fire; from the window to the bed, from the bed to the window . . . .

Most readers, even the few who had heard of Beckett, would have been scratching their heads over this. But *Merlin* had found the figure who in later years would justify the magazine's existence. Other contributions by Beckett followed: a portion of *Molloy* in the Autumn 1953 issue, translated into English by Patrick Bowles, in collaboration with Beckett himself; and in the next issue, 'The End', being a complete rendering into English of the story which *Les Temps Modernes* had published only half of, translated this time by Seaver, again with Beckett's help.

We met at Le Dôme at Montparnasse, ensconced ourselves at an isolated table near the back, and began to work. Or rather: Beckett began to read. After a few minutes of perusing my translation, then the original, his wire-framed glasses pushed up into the thick shock of hair above – the better to see, no doubt – he shook his head. My heart sank. Clearly the translation was inadequate. 'You can't translate that,' he said, fingering the original with utter disdain. 'It makes no sense.' Again he squinted at the two texts. Several more minutes of ruminations and cross-checking produced a more optimistic report. 'That's good,' he murmured. 'Those first three sentences read very nicely indeed.' The opening passage to which he referred went, in my translation:

They dressed me and gave me money. I knew what the money was to be used for, it was for my travelling expenses. When it was gone, they said I would have to get some more, if I wanted to go on travelling.

'What do you think of the word "clothed"', Beckett said, 'instead of "dressed"? "They clothed me and gave me money." Do you like the ring of it better?'

Yes, clearly: 'clothed' was the better word.

'In the next sentence', he said, 'you're literally right. In French I spelled it out, said "travelling expenses" all right. But maybe we can make it a bit tighter here, just say something like, "it was to get me going" or "it was to get me started". Do you like either of them at all?'

On we went, phrase by phrase, Beckett praising my translation as a prelude to shaping it to what he really wanted, reworking here a word, there a whole sentence, chipping away, tightening, shortening, always finding the better word if one existed, exchanging the ordinary for the poetic, until the work sang. Never, I am sure, to his satisfaction, but certainly to my ear. Under Beckett's tireless wand that opening passage soon became:

> They clothed me and gave me money. I knew what the money was for, it was to get me started. When it was gone I would have to earn more, if I wanted to go on.

*

Subscribers to *Merlin* were accustomed to long intervals between consecutive issues. Between numbers five and six of the magazine, for example, there was a gap of almost a year. But members of the group did not sit around idly during these pauses. Christopher Logue had gathered his poems together and given the collection a title, *Wand and Quadrant*; all he needed now was a publisher. Patrick Bowles had been working with Beckett on the English *Molloy*. The assiduous Seaver had also devoted himself to Beckett, while at the same time taking a teaching job to help finance further issues of the magazine. Jane Lougee was happy in her role as the mother of *Merlin*, and Trocchi laboured over the novel he had started in Glasgow, *Young Adam*. While writing and most other things came more easily to Trocchi than to the rest, he had difficulty in closeting himself in a silent study. He was getting known as a big man in town, and he needed to be out and about, exercising his big personality.

The main problem which bedevilled *Merlin* was the usual one – a lack of money. Its circulation was limited, and was unlikely ever to rise above 2,000 copies. Not only were printing bills expensive, but mailing costs were too, and the editors had run into trouble with the French authorities, who had refused to grant postal-rate privileges, on the grounds that

Merlin appeared too infrequently and was not a legitimate business; and by the way, did not the young gentlemen know that French law required them, as publishers of a magazine, to find a French *gérant*, or manager?

Distribution in London and America, where they had hoped to sell most of their copies, was a time-consuming task, difficult to organize and unrewarding in its results. To make things worse, a deal with the American Embassy, whereby 600 copies of each issue were to have been purchased and distributed as part of a cultural exchange in French *lycées* (at the Embassy's expense) collapsed after the publication of Sartre's piece on Genet in Vol. Two, no. 1. 'That is why I do not fear to call this book, the most beautiful that Genet has written, the *Dichtung und Wahrheit* of homosexuality' – not quite the type of culture the American Embassy had in mind when it first agreed to the exchange. Compounding this disaster, according to Jane Lougee, 'Whenever we sent large numbers of copies to England afterwards, or if they were printed in Spain and had to be shipped to Paris, they were always held up and investigated – all because of the names of Sartre and Genet.'

So, as if it might relieve the pressure of putting out a loss-making magazine at irregular intervals for a handful of ungrateful readers (several subscribers had cancelled after reading the unreadable portion of *Watt* – and there were not that many subscribers anyway), and of dealing with pig-headed bureaucracy, they decided to expand their business activities and start publishing books as well. The imprint, under Trocchi's directorship, was to be called Collection Merlin.

*

What was attractive to Trocchi in Beckett can be summed up in one word, or half a word: 'anti-'. He was the author of the 'anti-novel', and, coming up, the 'anti-play'. He was a man who had withdrawn from most forms of social obligation, who was uncompromising in his dealings with publishers and editors, who was dedicated to casting a literary form in the image of the word which was a key to existence: nothing.

Beckett wrote about creatures in a variety of absurd and alien postures and situations – living in a cave or in a swamp, motionless in a chair or stuck in a dustbin. Beckett was himself a defiance. Disregarding all that went before, he was the writer at point zero, refusing to budge, yet, by force of nothing more or less than breath itself – just the breath required to insist 'I will not budge' – inevitably in motion. His writing he described to a friend as 'fundamental sounds . . . made as fully as possible'. I will not budge; I budge.

What Trocchi perceived stirring in this zone of impotence was a reflection of his own motivation: Beckett's characters, he wrote, 'are so inactive, so vegetable, that they are also in a queer and disquieting way in revolt'. Trocchi saw Beckett as being in the position in which he wished to place himself – outside of history. The Scotsman was already given to describing himself in notebooks and letters as an 'outcast', a 'nomad'. He had envied Genet his capacity for subversiveness, which seemed to him at first unsurpassable. How much farther out can a man go? he wondered. Beckett gave him his answer. Beckett was beyond the attitude of social revolt that defined Genet. Beckett's absurdity was not social – that was merely an effect of it. Nor was it even philosophical: God was not dead (the popular storm blowing around existentialism was more concerned with its atheism than with its being a philosophy which inspired orgies), for he had never existed. Man? Nothing more than a figure in the primeval mud, struggling with the fact of his own existence. The redeeming chink of light was that in his shadow sits a figure with pen in hand, refusing to lift it yet inexorably propelled towards the act of doing so. A man of action for the 1950s.

As someone who was always trying to convince himself that he had a mission to reject and revolt, Trocchi found in Beckett a ripe aesthetics for an outcast. When it came to drawing up the publication list for Collection Merlin, then, the choice of book to launch the imprint was *Watt*.

Since the War, and his relocation to a different language, Beckett had been extraordinarily prolific. Between 1945 and 1950, he wrote (all in French) *Mercier et Camier*, *Molloy*, *Malone meurt*, *L'Innommable* (novels); 'L'Expulsé', 'La Fin', 'Le Calmant', 'Premier Amour' (short prose); and the plays *Eleuthéria* and *En Attendant Godot*. By the beginning of 1951, all that had been published of this was some of the shorter prose. He had written *Watt* during the war itself, hiding out on a farm in an unoccupied region, to keep his hand in, as he put it, in English.

Once settled back in Paris, Beckett wrote his two plays, but he met with as little success in drama as he had in fiction. After several rejections, he put *Eleuthéria* away (it remains unperformed and unpublished); *En Attendant Godot*, written in 1948, took five years to reach the stage.

During that half-decade, something which later became known as the Theatre of the Absurd stirred into life in the collective consciousness of a few writers. The Absurd is commonly regarded as a French theatrical movement, but while all three of its principals wrote in the language, none was actually French. In addition to Beckett, there was Arthur Adamov, a Russian-Armenian who came to Paris in his teens, and Eugene Ionesco, a Romanian who had been brought up in France. (All three had connections with *Merlin*.)

In this linguistic dislocation can be glimpsed the illogic of the absurd itself. The writers whose works laid the foundations for the Theatre of the Absurd in the late 1940s (they had little to do with one another, and, to their annoyance, were often grouped with the existentialists) could only have arrived at the station they did by moving away from their first languages. Absurd theatre emerges from a distrust of the language, a rejection of the faith bestowed by a native tongue in the connection between word and object. Absurdism places a human-being-sized question mark over that connection. This question mark is at the end of every Beckett sentence. In *Mercier et Camier*, the first novel Beckett wrote in French (but the last to be published), he uses an element of Irish vaudeville farce to point up the difficulties which two ordinary Irishmen might encounter simply in ordering a drink at the bar:

> What will it be? said the barman.
> When we need you we'll tell you, said Camier.
> What will it be? said the barman.
> The same as before, said Mercier.
> You haven't been served, said the barman.
> The same as this gentleman, said Mercier.
> The barman looked at Camier's empty glass.
> I forgot what it was, he said.
> I too, said Camier.
> I never knew, said Mercier.

Both Beckett and Adamov were writing in a way which could be retrospectively described as absurdist during the 1930s and '40s, but the War hardened those elements in their imaginations. It was the gas chambers which led Camus to talk of an 'absence of values', and the Theatre of the Absurd was forged in honour of absent values. 'The words in our ageing vocabularies are like very sick people,' Adamov wrote in 1938. He was looking ahead: what words are sicker or more absurd than the words which met the newly arriving prisoners at Auschwitz, 'Arbeit Macht Frei'? After this, the exchange between Hamm and Clov in Beckett's *Endgame* –

> *Hamm*: We are not beginning . . . to . . . to . . . mean something?
> *Clov*: You and I *mean* something?

– makes perfect sense.

The authors of the texts called 'absurdist' recognized that once the seed of distrust has been sown in language, everything else falls apart, including religion (the Word) and faith in a coherent objective reality. Absurd theatre moved as far as it was possible to move from representations of conventional reality, and yet still makes sense. Absurd plays achieve the status of 'anti-plays'. In one of the first pieces of absurdism, Ionesco's *La Cantatrice chauve* (*The Bald Prima Donna*), husband and wife address each other using affirmative statements of banality.

> *Mr Martin*: I live at Number 19, dear lady.
> *Mrs Martin*: How very extraordinary! I too live at Number 19, Sir!
> *Mr Martin*: But then, but then, but then, but then, but then, perhaps it's in that house that we met, dear lady.
> *Mrs Martin*: It's quite possible, Sir, but I have no clear recollection of it.
> *Mr Martin*: I have a flat on the fifth floor, flat Number 8, dear lady.
> *Mrs Martin*: How very extraordinary! Oh goodness gracious, how very amazing and what a strange coincidence! I too live on the fifth floor, Sir, in flat Number 8!

And so on, until:

> *Mr Martin*: Goodness, how strange, how amazing, how extraordinary! Then, Madam, we must live in the same room and sleep in the same bed, dear Madam. Perhaps that is where we have met before!

Friends to whom Ionesco showed his script apparently thought it very funny; the playwright considered *La Cantatrice chauve* a tragedy, 'the tragedy of language'. According to Ionesco, the idea for the play came from a how-to-learn English course, *L'Anglais sans peine*, which involved two imaginary couples, Mr and Mrs Smith and Mr and Mrs Martin.

> To my astonishment, Mrs Smith informed her husband that they had several children, that they lived in the vicinity of London, that their name was Smith, that Mr Smith was a clerk, that they had a servant, Mary – English, like themselves. . . . What was truly remarkable about [the English primer] was its eminently methodical procedure in its quest for truth. In the fifth lesson, the Smiths' friends the Martins arrive; the four of them begin to chat and, starting from basic axioms, they build more complex truths: 'The country is quieter than the big city . . .'

While writing his 'parody of a play', as he calls it, Ionesco said that he had to break off from his work occasionally and rest on the sofa, 'for fear of seeing my work sink into nothingness, and me with it'. And yet *La Cantatrice chauve* seems to audiences instinctively familiar with the terms of its meaninglessness to be quite coherent.* Adamov (whose first play was called *La Parodie*) seemed to be making precisely this challenge the central concern of his work. 'Man,' he wrote, 'suddenly realizing that he does not understand, will begin to understand.'

*

Suddenly, in the same way, the Theatre of the Absurd, where nonsense makes sense, begins to take place. In April 1950, a play with one foot in the Absurd, Boris Vian's *L'Equarrissage pour tous* (*The Knacker's ABC*), was staged at the Théâtre des Noctambules. It was followed, in May, by *La Cantatrice chauve*. In the same month, unable to get his plays put on, Adamov published a pair of them in a book, and by November had two plays running at the same time in small Left Bank theatres.

Beckett would not have had the opportunity to read either Adamov or Ionesco when he came to write *Godot* in 1948, for their work had been neither published nor performed, and it's unlikely that they knew much about him. But during that same spring of 1950, Beckett submitted the script of *En Attendant Godot* to Roger Blin, who was well known in Paris as an actor and director. The two men had never met. What prompted Beckett to ask Blin to read his scripts was a production of *The Ghost Sonata* by Strindberg which Blin had mounted at the Gaîté-Montparnasse at the end of the previous year. For his part, Blin had already heard of Beckett from the surrealist Tristan Tzara, who, Blin recalled, 'greatly admired *En Attendant Godot*', and had spoken to him at length about it.

---

*La Cantatrice chauve is one of the longest-running plays in history; it opened a run at the Théâtre de la Huchette in Paris in 1957, and was still going in early 1994.

Beckett submitted *Godot* and *Eleuthéria* to Blin, who became seriously interested in both as soon as he read them. In fact, he was at first more tempted by *Eleuthéria*, but the play had seventeen characters. 'In *Godot*, on the other hand, there were only four, plus a child and a tree. It made things easier. . . . I was quite mad about Keaton, Chaplin, above all Harry Langdon – those early American comics. When *Godot* first came into my hands, that's what I thought of.'

Blin informed Beckett that he wished to mount a production of the play. He felt obliged to warn the author, however, that he had no theatre, no ready troupe of actors, and no ready cash. *Waiting for Godot*, which had waited a long time for someone even to want to produce it, would have to wait another three years.

*

Rehearsals finally began at the end of 1952, at the Théâtre de Babylone, a small place hidden in a courtyard behind an apartment block on the Boulevard Raspail. The parts of Vladimir and Estragon were taken by Lucien Raimbourg and Pierre Latour. Blin himself wished to play Lucky, who delivers the furious speech at the close of Act One – Blin had a bad stammer, which did not, however, afflict him when he spoke onstage. But in the middle of rehearsals, the actor who was to play Pozzo, the squire-like master who drives his servant Lucky with a whip, declared that he was ill at ease in his part, and left the company. Blin called in an actor whom he had originally thought of for the part of Lucky anyway, and took over Pozzo himself.

The actor Jean Martin recalled entering the theatre for the first time, seeing Blin standing in the front row, and 'a little further back a thin, silent figure, looking keenly at the stage, sitting there with his glasses pushed up and a text in his hand'. Blin had some difficulties in becoming Pozzo, Martin noted,

as Pozzo is fat and extrovert. Blin was very thin and reflective, and had to use padding and a false stomach, which made him feel uneasy. He also had to alter his voice as a fat man's voice is different from a thin man's. The voice he was searching for had to be deeper, bringing with it a rumbling noise, which made it all the more surprising. He also had to be bald, so he wore a skull cap.

The costumes were designed by Blin. Those of the tramps were decrepit. Vladimir had a very, very old tailcoat, frayed, used and mottled. Estragon also wore an old pair of velvet trousers held up with string. A collarless shirt for one, a dicky-bow without shirt for the other. Both wore bowler hats.

Contrarily, Pozzo was a 'Gentleman Farmer' (or at least how we imagine one), sporting jodhpurs and leggings, a tweed jacket, a grey bowler, monocle and pipe. Lucky wore torn cord trousers, cut off at the calf, a blue and white striped sailor's jersey and, over all this, the red and gold jacket of a French liveryman. He also wore an unlikely long white wig held on to the top of his head by a hat. All this belonged to the circus. That's what Blin wished . . . .

The leaves on the trees at the beginning of Act Two were represented by green ribbons tied to the branches. To a journalist curious to know about his new project before it opened, Blin described it as 'a play that contains no action and characters who have nothing to say to one another'. It opened on January 5, 1953, and the audience, despite some bafflement, was not bored. *Godot* became the surprise hit of the season, the opening night a legendary occasion. 'I must have met a thousand people who are very proud to have been in the audience for the first night,' said Jean Martin. 'The problem is that the Théâtre de Babylone seated only two hundred.'

The critics, who were there, were not bored either. 'In my opinion, Samuel Beckett's first play will be spoken of for a long time,' wrote the first reviewer of *Godot*, Sylvain Zegal, in *Libération* (January 7, 1953):

These two tramps are feeble and energetic, cowardly and courageous; they bicker, amuse themselves, are bored, speak to each other without understanding. They do all this to keep busy. To pass the time. To live or to give themselves the illusion that they are living. They are certain of only one thing: they are waiting for Godot.

71

Jean Anouilh said that *Godot* was like 'a music hall sketch of Pascal's *Pensées*', as played by clowns. The 'anti-play' ran for 400 performances at the Babylone, before transferring to a larger theatre.

Nineteen fifty-three, then, was the year when the writer whom Blin described as 'unknown, but curiously already celebrated', became well known and celebrated. *Godot* was on. The final volume of the trilogy, *L'Innommable*, was published in French. And the editors of *Merlin*, having first championed him in their magazine with translations, were now about to relaunch him in English with his last English novel.

IV

In the spring, on a day between the appearance of issues four and five of *Merlin*, another literary magazine came into existence, the *Paris Review*. Its founders looked back more self-consciously to the golden age of Americans in Paris. The very title was a cast-off from a 1920s journal, the *transatlantic review*, edited by Ford Madox Ford and occasionally Hemingway, which had originally intended to call itself 'Paris Review'.

The founders of the 1950s *Paris Review* were all American and all fresh out of Ivy League universities. They were a better-off lot than their rivals down at the banana-skin-drying depot which, in addition to being *Merlin*'s HQ, now served as Alex and Jane's pad as well as Seaver's. The editor-in-chief of the new magazine, George Plimpton, was the son of a prominent New York lawyer and diplomat; fellow editor Peter Matthiessen's father, an architect, counted equally among the East Coast's top people, as did the family of the *Paris Review*'s business manager, John Train.

The novelist Irwin Shaw, who was of an older generation but who enjoyed acting as host to the group whenever he stayed at the apartment he kept in Paris, later spoke about them with the gruff affection of a paterfamilias:

The literary hopefuls of the Paris contingent spoke in the casual tones of the good schools and could be found surrounded by flocks of pretty and nobly acquiescent girls, in chic places like Lipp's on the Boulevard St-Germain or on the roads to Deauville or Biarritz for month-long holidays. They were mild-mannered, beautifully polite, recoiled from the appearance of seeming ambitious and were ready at all times to drop whatever they were almost secretly composing to play tennis (usually very well), drive down to Spain for a bullfight, fly to Rome for a wedding or sit around most of the night drinking. As far as I could see, none of them had a job and although they lived frugally in cheap rooms they gave the impression that they were going through a period of Gallic slumming for the fun of it. One guessed that there were wealthy and benevolent parents on the other side of the Atlantic.

A silver thread ran through the pages of the magazine. Produced in book format, by arrangement with the French publisher La Table Ronde, it was printed on good-quality paper, with a decorative cover, an elaborate frontispiece depicting the Louvre, and original illustrations, often by young artists but occasionally by not so young artists, such as Picasso. Even the *Paris Review*'s address was good: the magazine had its office in the palatial buildings of the French publisher Plon on rue Garancière.

Such a smartly turned-out boy was bound to arouse a grudge in the breasts of the tearaways on the other side of the street. William Burford, one of *Merlin*'s associates who had recently left Paris, wrote to Trocchi on hearing of the plans for the new magazine:

The news from Paris is exciting and challenging. Wish I were in the thick of it. Always love a contest. And you'll have one with the *Paris Review*. Same old crowd that's been dictating to American literature for twenty years. I remember Matthieson [*sic*] as a typical bright young man, which means dull young man. Ridiculous way of looking down his nose and seeming solemn. So let's make some mincemeat this time.

The editorial in the first issue of the *Paris Review* set out its principles. It was quite clear about the fact that the magazine did not intend to dabble in politics, not even literary politics. This would have been evident in any case from the list of contents, which included the name of Henri de Montherlant, who had recently been shunned in France for having been a supporter of the collaborationist Vichy government during the War. The author of the editorial, William Styron ('advisory editor'), stated that the *Paris Review* would have 'no axe to grind' and stressed the preference for fiction and poetry over criticism. They intended to give space to the creative work of 'both new and established writers rather than people who use words like *Zeitgeist*'. Styron mentioned Ezra Pound's magazine *The Exile*, but only in order to contrast its 'powerful blasts' of literary polemic with the *Paris Review*'s neutralist position. The issue also showed that the founders continued to recognize the advantages of keeping good connections; while the first number of *Merlin* stated simply 'Edited by Alexander Trocchi', the names on the masthead of the *Paris Review* outnumbered those on its contents list.

The main feature of the première issue was a lengthy interview on 'The Art of Fiction' with E. M. Forster. Plimpton had made the acquaintance of the English novelist while studying at Cambridge. After crossing the Channel, when his studies were finished, to join his co-founders and become editor-in-chief of the magazine, Plimpton suggested to Forster that he inaugurate the series which was to grow into a genre of its own, the *Paris Review* interview. He agreed, and the interview was conducted by P. N. Furbank (later Forster's biographer) and F. J. H. Haskell, one of them asking the questions while the other jotted down the answers in pencil. Graham Greene, Alberto Moravia, Georges Simenon and James Thurber were among the others interviewed in the first years of the *Paris Review*'s existence.

Certain writers declined to be interviewed. Beckett was one, which puzzled Plimpton: 'A few questions about the craft of writing', for goodness' sake. They tried going through Patrick

Bowles, but got nowhere. Meanwhile, Plimpton, whose gifts were for the witty article and the generous good time, looked on in bafflement as Beckett and Bowles worked together on the translation of *Molloy*: 'The two sat together at a café table and argued about the correctness of a word as if they were scholars working on a medieval manuscript by a Flemish monk.'

Not every candidate for a grilling on how to write a novel had to be as eminent as Greene or Forster. The subject in *Paris Review* 5 was one of the magazine's own, William Styron, then aged twenty-seven and with just one novel behind him, *Lie Down in Darkness*. His interrogators were Plimpton and Matthiessen – two of the editors interviewing another editor. It sounds as if they had difficulty keeping a straight face.

Interviewers:	You were about to tell us when you started to write.
Styron:	What? Oh yes. Write. I figure I must have been about 13. I wrote an imitation Conrad thing, 'Typhoon and the Tor Bay' it was called, you know, a ship's hold swarming with crazy chinks. I think I had some sharks in there too. I gave it the full treatment.
Interviewers:	And what time of day do you find best for writing?
Styron:	The afternoon. I like to stay up late at night and get drunk and sleep late. I wish I could break the habit but I can't. The afternoon is the only time I have left and I try to use it to the best advantage, with a hangover.

Imagine the head-shaking that went on over at *Merlin*! There they insisted that writing could not hold itself aloof from politics; they made deliberate efforts to air the cries of rebellion, in content and form, and to link, as the *Times Literary Supplement* put in an article on the Paris scene, 'the strictly creative aspects of the magazine to the day of the week'. And here came a presumed rival, carrying on a cosy chat about booze and 'chinks', and making the centrepiece of the first issue an interview with a septuagenarian novelist who hadn't written a novel for thirty years.

Not that the *Paris Review* people cared. As if deliberately distancing themselves from the *enfants terribles* on the rue du Sabot, they made the second in their series 'The Art of Fiction' an interview with the arch anti-Sartrean François Mauriac. On the inside back cover, the editors smoothly announced that authors from whom contributions to future issues of the *Paris Review* were expected included Jean Anouilh, Jean Cocteau, T. S. Eliot, William Faulkner, Thomas Mann and Evelyn Waugh. (All of those writers did appear in the magazine, but mostly in the role of interviewee.)

The *Paris Review* kept up the spruce, well-tended appearance of a literary society, publishing a mix of the established and the new which managed usually to be of good quality without being exciting. 'The significance of the magazine is limited', the anonymous *TLS* writer commented, 'to those who will eventually fit into the suave pages of the *New Yorker*. It is too much like a chic miscellany: there is no sign of a fresh development of writing to express our very changed conditions.' Which, he concluded, was just where *Merlin* looked like succeeding, if it could survive.

*

Some people envied the *Paris Review* its fine connections, while others, as is to be expected in literary society, despised them. Yet others were moved to ask: just how good are they? Where exactly did the money come from to produce a handsome magazine of a couple of hundred pages four times a year, at regular intervals, able to afford payments to contributors, with fancy artwork, from a fancy office? Did the connection, by any chance, go all the way to the US Embassy, to the office of cultural affairs there? To the CIA, in effect?

As a further effect of the Cold War, the CIA had a large and ever-increasing presence in Europe, Paris in particular, and was already spying on the activities of troublesome expatriates such as Richard Wright. From time to time, it approached young men and women from among the expatriate community, offering to pay them to do its spying for it.

The *Paris Review*, a literary magazine devoted to poems, short stories and long conversations with novelists, seems at first sight an unlikely recipient of ideologically determined disbursements; but the other side of the bill says that publications generally reflective of 'American values' and broadly in line with the American government's hatred of Communism might be looked on favourably if a request for funding were to be made. That the CIA had an arts grant is a fact – look upon it as an arts foundation with a subtle political slant and it doesn't seem so unlikely, after all.

The CIA was certainly in the business of sponsoring literary publications. In the same year as the *Paris Review* was founded, a front organization was set up, the Congress for Cultural Freedom, with its head office in Paris. It set about the task of establishing a network of anti-leftist magazines throughout the world: *Preuves* in France, *Encounter* in England, *Transition* in Uganda, and several others. But the *Paris Review*?

Otto Friedrich, Baldwin's friend from the Hôtel de Verneuil who contributed to the exposure of the connection between the CIA and the Congress for Cultural Freedom in the 1960s, is candid about the link, which he believes existed:

> The *Paris Review* was funded by the CIA, no doubt about it. Plimpton, after all, was the son of a top diplomat. The money might have come through that channel, but there would have had to be a return somehow. It might have been just a matter of the CIA asking these people to keep an eye on things around their café tables and in their hotels. There was lots of it going on at the time. There wasn't even anything particularly sinister about it.

Plimpton, admitting that rumours of a link have been hard to shake off, is adamant that there were no government favours done for favours returned. 'The *Paris Review* was started with private money. The families of Peter Matthiessen, John Train and myself each gave $500. That got the magazine off the ground.' He freely admits, however, that one prominent member of the *Paris Review*'s editorial team was actually working for the CIA at the time, as he confessed to colleagues in later life. He resigned his security position, Plimpton claims, after being asked to spy on the expatriate community.

If suspicion lingered of CIA favours at the rue Garancière offices of the magazine, across from the Jardin du Luxembourg, it should have been all but banished by the Fall–Winter issue, 1954–55, for it was then that the name of the *Paris Review*'s new publisher appeared on the masthead for the first time. Connections were still good. It was the Aga Khan.

*

'Tiens-toi bien,' wrote Samuel Beckett to his friend and former agent George Reavey in July 1953:

> our old misery *Watt*, with the Merlin juveniles here in Paris who are beginning a publishing business.

Reavey had been totally unsuccessful in acting as an agent for the Irish writer, but it's unlikely that anyone else would have had more success. Beckett seemed to most publishers to be unreadable; and, when readable, to be unsellable. The A. P. Watt agency in London had tried acting for him after the War, but had failed to earn anything more substantial than backhanded flattery. When returning the manuscript of *Watt* to the agency in 1946, the publisher Frederick Warburg felt it necessary to place the word 'novel' in dubious quotation marks. This was clearly a writer to be watched, he wrote (Beckett had started publishing in the 1920s!), and the firm would be interested in seeing his next book – but as for *Watt* . . . . Warburg deliberated for a line or two before finally landing on the word he wanted: 'perversity'. Still, he had an inkling. It may be, he said, 'that in turning this book down we are turning down a potential James Joyce'. *Watt* would have to wait another seven years.

In the meantime, there had been a relatively healthy reception for the first two volumes of the Trilogy. Neither book caused a sensation, but nor did they appear in total silence. *Molloy* received a healthy score of reviews in the French literary press, most of them intelligent and comprehending, and some longer articles on Beckett were in preparation for the following year's intellectual journals when Richard Seaver, passing by the tiny display window of Les Editions de Minuit on his bicycle, had his curiosity aroused to such an extent that it resulted at last in his procuring a Beckett manuscript of his own.

In the late summer of 1953, the *Merlin* juveniles issued a flyer:

COLLECTION MERLIN

is pleased to announce the publication of

WATT

a novel in English by

SAMUEL BECKETT

The original edition consists of 1,125 copies, the first 25 of which printed on luxury paper signed by the author will be lettered A to Y and will be sold at 2,500 frs, £2.10 or $7.00. The remaining copies will be sold at 850 frs, 17/6d or $2.50.

Beckett wrote to his friend Reavey: '*Watt* is just out in an awful magenta cover from the Merlin Press.'

*

The advance paid to the author for the right to publish *Watt* in its original English was 50,000 francs, about $100 or £35. It wasn't much, but *Merlin* immediately signed a contract with Les Editions de Minuit, giving Lindon the French translation rights, which brought the author a similar sum. To add to that, there was a third contract, this one giving Collection Merlin the right to publish the English translation of *Molloy* (advance: 30,000 francs). It still was hardly a fortune, but it would have been something – if Beckett could have got his hands on it.

On November 6, 1953, some two months after publication,

Beckett received a letter on Collection Merlin headed notepaper, concerning the translation rights for the French edition of *Watt*:

> A check or *mandat* ought to be accompanying this letter. We should like to postpone this payment . . . which we very simply haven't got. . . . Our affairs should definitely improve this month . . . .

Beckett's reply is not known, but it's likely that he received the news with his customary tolerance. Nine months later, another letter followed:

> The whole thing is not difficult to explain. The money would have been paid to you precisely on those dates indicated in my letter of 29 May had you been in Paris or had you left instructions how we were to get the money to you in Ireland. Believe me it is as simple as that.

Beckett wrote back within three days ('My dear Trocchi'), giving the number of his Paris bank account. A month later, however, he was writing again ('Dear Mr Trocchi'), complaining that the excerpt from *Molloy* printed in the latest issue of *Merlin* was full of errors, and what's more

> I am still waiting for you to begin payment of the royalties you owe me. I begin to weary of your treatment of me.

Trocchi was unfazed. Grand as ever, he drew up a letter of indignant response: 'The whole complication arose because you were in Ireland,' he wrote, a case of the debtor unloading the blame on to the creditor;

> That you were able to get so many recriminations on one small page does credit to your literary ability but says little for what I believed was our friendship.

The affection between the generous Irishman and the *Merlin* juveniles survived this storm, however; resisting the suggestion of an American publisher, who wished to render *Molloy* into English using a 'first-class man', Beckett fixed 'stubbornly, firmly, irreducibly' on Patrick Bowles, of *Merlin*, as translator, and the novel duly appeared under the magazine's imprint in March 1955. Seaver continued to work with Beckett, at Grove Press in New York, for many years to come. And on the appearance of Trocchi's first novel, Beckett wrote to congratulate him: 'My Dear Alex . . .'

*

Unlike the *Paris Review*, *Merlin* did not have a wealthy publisher or a splendid address. It did not have an address at all, or at least not one to call its own. For the first few issues, the editors gave 37 rue de la Bûcherie as *Merlin*'s headquarters – the home of George Whitman's rapidly expanding Librairie Mistral. Between issues four and five, the magazine adopted another address: this time it was the English Bookshop at 42 rue de Seine.

Like the Old Navy, the Mabillon, La Reine Blanche and other cafés, the English-language bookstores served as talking shops for the young literati. Whitman had ambitions far beyond those of the average bookseller. The Mistral doubled as 'The Left Bank Arts Center' and announced 'a program of cultural events' which in the year of *Merlin*'s birth included 'lectures and art exhibitions, the first annual American Writers and Artists Fair, a Seminar in Creative Writing by Peter Matthiessen', a course in Shakespeare, and discussions on the place of art in society.

The Librairie Mistral was housed in an ancient building near St-Michel, facing Notre Dame Cathedral. Before Whitman bought it, using money from an inheritance, it had been an Arab grocery store. Not content with offering lectures, exhibitions and the rest, he set up a lending library with an estimated 10,000 books. Borrowing rates varied from five to ten francs per day, which meant that the voracious reader could carry away an armful of books for the price of a cup of coffee; for those who could not afford even that, there was a reading room on the first floor, looking on to the cathedral. On Sunday afternoons, Whitman held open house: 'You are invited for tea,' he announced in *Merlin*. Richard Wright gave readings, signed books, and took a fatherly interest in the new magazines (though he did not contribute either to *Merlin* or to the *Paris Review*, and was not included in the 'Art of Fiction' series of interviews). Baldwin also read at the Mistral, and in hard times sold books from his own collection, for which Whitman gave him a few hundred francs. The Librairie Mistral stayed open until midnight, every day of the year.

Gaïte Frogé's English Bookshop on rue de Seine was a smaller affair, and necessarily more discriminating in its stock. Whereas the Mistral boasted books 'in English, French, Spanish, Italian, Russian and German', she offered a mix of classics and the latest productions of the avant-garde. Frogé was a cultured woman from Brittany, with a talent for friendship. Once *Merlin* had accepted her offer of the use of an address, it became the natural base of Collection Merlin, too. In an advert placed in *Points*, the English Bookshop offered for sale, in trendy lower case, 'pound, joyce, hemingway, cummings, eliot' – to which could be added, once Trocchi got things under way, 'beckett'.

*

Trocchi's original scheme for Collection Merlin had been to publish something scandalous. He did not fear opprobrium – indeed, he was beginning a career which would thrive on it. He heard word that there was a young American living in Paris who had set himself to work translating the Marquis de Sade, an author rarely before translated into English, and for the most part published clandestinely in France.

The Paris publisher Jean-Jacques Pauvert had begun to publish Sade's terrible works in the late 1940s – *Justine, ou les Malheurs de la vertu*, *Les cent-vingt Journées de Sodome*, etc. – in a series he was editing himself. He proceeded with caution, however, as the law governing obscenity was ill-defined. Since the books had started to appear, Parisian intellectuals, including Simone de Beauvoir and Georges Bataille, had been debating Sade's ideas and probing their relevance to the post-war world.

Sade's distortion of Enlightenment thought was infamous. The problem did not lie in the basic idea – that Nature in general is indifferent to moral human values – but from the consequences which led from it. The order which human beings attempted to impose on the amoral randomness of Nature – civilization – resulted in oppressions and persecutions carried out with the intention of keeping the 'order' intact. These were vain attempts to deny the true 'Nature' of humankind. Turning Voltaire on his head – 'Let us cultivate our garden' – Sade believed in letting the garden run wild, even helping it to do so. In the dedication to one of his books – 'To Libertines' – he wrote:

> Voluptuaries of all ages and every sex, it is to you only I tender this work; nourish yourselves upon its principles; they favour your passions, and these passions, whereof coldly inspired moralists put you in fear, are naught but the means Nature employs to cause man to arrive at the end she prescribes to him; . . . there is no voice but that of the passions that can conduct you to happiness.

In his fictions, long philosophical disquisitions blend with elaborate accounts of sexual orgies. His helpless, hapless heroines, as they are whipped, raped, sodomized and frequently much worse in their course of 'instruction' as to the rightful ways of Nature, are often lectured on the right of the strong to commit any act they so wish against the weak, since Nature sanctions the priority of strength over weakness. This axiom the Marquis put into practice with a fervour derived from his own particular passion, to which he gave his name.

Trocchi must have been delighted to hear about the American Sadean and his project. What could be more assured of heaping disapproval and scandal – and, he hoped, money for the magazine – on to him than the 'monster author', whose characters blasphemed in every breath, oozed corruption and cruelty, swore to do evil whenever the opportunity arose, and, when it did not, 'at least to find the sensation's equivalent in the minor but piquant wickedness of never doing good'. They condemned virtue, charity, fidelity, marriage, love of one's parents; and celebrated incest, paedophilia, sodomy, coprophilia, torture – all things loosely collectible under the name of debauchery. *Merlin* 'will hit out at all clots of rigid categories in criticism and in life', Trocchi had promised. Here was his chance.

The translator's name was Austryn Wainhouse. Trocchi contacted him by way of *pneumatique*, summoning him to the Librairie Mistral within the hour. 'Impertinence showed even in the handwriting,' Wainhouse recollected. 'It was a great lean rascal in a raincoat . . . very winning, and manifestly not to be trusted.'

The prospect supplied by Wainhouse is intriguing: why should this American graduate in his mid-twenties, in Paris on the pretext of continuing his studies, take upon himself, without much chance of publication, the job of translating the Marquis de Sade? Wainhouse was not merely idling away his time; he was fully committed to his task, intellectualizing it so as to conceive of it as being properly fitted to what he called his 'situation'. He did not condone the vilest fantasies of the Marquis; he did not think it necessary to do so in order to proclaim sympathy with what he perceived as the liberating sociopolitical set of beliefs which gave rise to them – favour your passions; abandon suppression; resist oppression.

The actual situation Wainhouse was in was that of a young, unpublished writer living in a foreign city. An ordinary enough existence, with a more than usually pleasant backdrop. But this 'political thinker', as he styled himself, found himself constantly dwelling on another backdrop, invisible, but which, once resident in the mind's eye, blinded one to the beautiful streets and genial cafés. It was the political climate: the lingering stench of the camps, the visual recollection of a mushroom cloud, the fumes from the laboratories dedicated to refining the H-bomb, the sweat dripping over Europe's head from the shadow boxing-match between East and West, the seemingly unstoppable Coca-colonization of the entire world. The American Way of Life did not permit freedom of political choice, at home or abroad. The US Army was in Asia, engaged in what was to seem, as the years passed, an endless, murderous attempt to resist the tide of Communism. For Wainhouse, the 'situation' came down to keeping fine and taut the delicate threads of individual integrity in the morass of 'non-existence'.

The project was to keep the intellect free, and 'Sade's was one of the freest'. Sade decoded the paradox of freedom in an oppressive society, and trumped it in his own suit. 'Where madness defines madness', Wainhouse wrote, 'it is a sign of health and virtue to be "mad".' This is how Wainhouse conceived the incarcerated Marquis's position, which, he wrote, not without the self-importance which characterized him, 'appears to be in its most significant aspects similar to my own'. He opted for a personal resistance. What greater act of identification with the supreme resistor could there be than to translate him?

'None of us can pretend to confusion,' Wainhouse wrote in *Merlin*;

> Unless we are willing to falsify our lives and accept living and participating in a false world. . . . Unless we are willing to identify ourselves with this non-existence, there is nothing else to do but live the important, essential, part of our lives underground . . . we are outlaws.

In order to reduce the risks implicit in having brought into the light that which had been condemned to a deep and dark prison, Wainhouse concocted for himself a pseudonym-à-clef: Pieralessandro Casavini (Casavini meaning 'Winehouse').

Trocchi was impressed by this unusual character and his appointed task. Wainhouse was a self-confident young man, with a touch of dandyism both about his prose style and his dress. He was dark-haired, wore a belted raincoat – 'always very prim and proper, hair properly styled', as one contemporary recalls. He told Trocchi in the course of their meeting that he had almost completed a translation of *La Philosophie dans le boudoir*, never before rendered into English, calling it *The Bedroom Philosophers*. Purporting to portray the education into the true ways of Nature of Eugénie, a fifteen-year-old girl, it exhibits Sade's vice in abundance, in the almost comic form of one acrobatic orgy after another:

> *Dolmancé:* . . . 'Tis unheard of – how this fine lad's superb ass does preoccupy my mind while I talk. All my ideas seem involuntarily to relate themselves to it. . . . Show my eyes that masterpiece, Augustin . . . let me kiss it and caress it, oh! for quarter of an hour. Hither, my love come, that I may, in your lovely ass, render myself worthy of the flames with which Sodom sets me aglow. Ah, he has the most beautiful buttocks . . . the whitest! I'd like to have Eugénie on her knees; she will suck his prick which I advance; in this manner, she will expose her ass to the Chevalier, who'll plunge into it, and Madame de Saint-Ange, astride Augustin's back, will present her buttocks to me: I'll kiss them; armed with a cat-o'nine-tails, she might surely, it should seem to me, by bending a little, be able to flog the Chevalier . . . .

Just the sort of thing Collection Merlin needed to give it a hefty kick-start, thought Trocchi. He proposed to Wainhouse that they publish his translation of *The Bedroom Philosophers*, and Wainhouse, who could have had little expectation of ever finding a sponsor, never mind so quickly, accepted.

Not everything in *The Bedroom Philosophers* is sprightly lust. When the Marquis spoke of doing evil, he had in mind more than the gentle cuffing of a lad or lass's buttocks. Sade's sadism was fully *engagé*. At the end of *The Bedroom Philosophers*, Eugénie – who was innocent at the beginning of it all – having been encouraged to confess her true feelings of hatred for her mother, is given the opportunity to exact revenge on 'the whore'. Taking turns with a 'large needle' and 'heavy waxed thread', Eugénie and her instructor, Dolmancé, sew up Eugénie's mother's vagina and anus:

> *Dolmancé*: ... (He stabs Mme de Mistival's buttocks) Here dear Mummy, take this . . . and again that! . . . (He drives his needle into at least twenty places).
> *Madame de Mistival*: Oh pardon me, Monsieur . . . you are slaying me . . . .
> *Dolmancé*: (wild with pleasure) I should like to . . . 'tis an age since I have had such an erection . . . .
> *Eugénie*: Ah fuck! Look at the bugger bleed!

Eventually, Mme de Mistival, deliberately infected with the pox, is kicked out on to the highway (literally, by Eugénie) and the orgiasts settle down to a slap-up feast.

Wainhouse, his mind on higher things, presumably, completed his English version of these adventures, and then set about doing the same for another work by the Marquis de Sade, *The Story of Juliette*, five volumes of it.

*

Trocchi must have felt that everything was going splendidly. Here he was, on top of everything else now running his own publishing firm, soon to nourish it on a strictly forbidden fruit of erotic literature. *The Bedroom Philosophers* was sure to make enough money to keep *Merlin* – his ego – in business.

There was something else to consider, of which a friend was kind enough to advise him: if he published this scabrous work in English, and what's more without first satisfying French business regulations, he was certain to land in court, and from there to proceed – like the Marquis himself – to prison, or at the very least on to the next boat departing for Dover.

This led Trocchi to pause. Prosecution, a fine he could pay, even prison – these would not have shaken him (all good publicity for *Merlin*) but he had no wish to get himself deported. And so Collection Merlin began to look to other books: *Watt*, then something by the contemporary monster-author, Genet, *The Thief's Journal*, then *Molloy*. To add to these, there were the works of the group itself: Logue's collection of poems, *Wand and Quadrant*, was made ready and put out late in 1953. After that came a novel by the industrious Wainhouse, a long way from absurdity and existentialism, sexual deviance and 'I decided to be what crime made of me', which was Genet's creed. It was called *Hedyphagetica: A Romantic Argument After certain Old Models & Containing an Assortment of Heroes, Scenes of Anthropophagy & of Pathos, an Apology for Epicurism, & Many Objections raised against it, Together with Reflexions upon the Bodies politic & individual, their Affections, Nourishments, &c.*

'*Hedyphagetica*' means, in Greek, 'feastings', and comes from the same root as *hedone*, pleasure. It is a book full of linguistic indulgence and self-regarding pedantry: 'Pricker John Stearnes of Wim, the most celebrated of his age's finders, was one of those persons who appear to metaphysicians as epiphenomena, and, like the discovery of the wheel or gunpowder, as primary material to historians', and so on.

Printing and publishing such books, not to mention paying their authors, required considerable amounts of money. *Merlin* had none. However, a partner was found, a publisher who was willing to underwrite their enterprise – at least to pay the printers – and to act as *gérant*, thereby satisfying the law in respect of that part of their affairs. It must have seemed like a dream: you lot find the books, I'll take care of that dreary business of settling the accounts. Maurice Girodias came along just at the time when the *Merlin* juveniles were preparing *Watt*, and that book, and all Collection Merlin titles thereafter, although they constituted a separate list, were published in co-operation with the Olympia Press.

It was Wainhouse who made the connection. Reluctantly rejected by a sorrowful Trocchi, he still had his translation of *The Bedroom Philosophers* on his hands and was getting down to *The Story of Juliette*, when he met Girodias. 'His avowed aim was to confound puritanism, hypocrisy and censorship,' Wainhouse wrote of him. 'He wished to publish books in

English.' They met in a café. (Wainhouse recalled that it was the Deux Magots, and by appointment; Girodias has it that it was the Select, in Montparnasse, where they just happened to strike up a conversation.) After having established certain things in common, they got on to the subject of Wainhouse's talented friends and their intention to break into book-publishing, a field in which the somewhat older Girodias – he was then in his mid-thirties – was already an experienced player. Wainhouse arranged a meeting at the warehouse in the rue du Sabot. They discussed books, naturally:

> Of the sort he would be specializing in, some already existed in French, and they were to be translated. Others would have to be written. The very scope he meant to give to his activity would, he foresaw, provoke the intervention of the law. There was no precluding trouble. It must not, however, fall upon shoulders unable to bear up under the burden. In this line of business, amateurs were doomed in advance. He exhorted us to devote ourselves to *Merlin*. It had a deficit? He had underwritten other literary reviews in the past. . . . Collection Merlin must not be abandoned. *Au contraire*. He would continue to be frank with us. It and the review as well would serve him as a smoke-screen: his list must include a sprinkling of bona-fide titles, reputable authors, harmless works of art. Risks, nuisances, distractions, he intended to safeguard us against them all. He paused. Something wistful blended with the fatigue in his eyes. Without the Olympia Press, how on earth were we, as writers, to survive in Paris?

Girodias took leave of his crew with some plain speaking: he wanted pornography, and was willing to commission it; and he was willing to pay for translations of certain forbidden works from French into English. They were a team for the era. Girodias was, at bottom, *risqué*: all for baiting 'the hounds of decency' – his name for officious representatives of the bourgeoisie – and exposing hypocrisy and cowardice; he reserved a particular contempt for Britain's 'nanny judges' and 'bowler-hatted policemen' (which impressed Trocchi).

The members of the *Merlin* group, on the other hand, were

high-minded and discriminating; the risks they took were with form and content, aesthetics, everything in the literary arena. But they weren't above a little prostitution on the side, if it helped to pay the bills. Their medium was the written word, Girodias's the four-letter word. The confluence of these separate personalities would create the identity of the Olympia Press.

We will spit on Boris Vian

The question of obscenity, what was and what wasn't, what effect it had on the young and those of 'esprit faible', had vexed the French for centuries and now was up for renewed debate. The appearance of Genet had caused great amounts of hand-wringing, but Genet's originality and mastery of the language had won over most literate folk. He had been championed by Sartre (*Saint Genet, comédien et martyr* was published in 1952) and his *Oeuvres complètes* were now in preparation at Gallimard. The outlaw was in.

When the law did take hold, and proceeded with charges of obscenity, it was against two American writers – or rather, one authentic American, Henry Miller, and the imposter 'Vernon Sullivan'. The Miller book was *Tropic of Capricorn*, which had been available in Paris in English since the 1930s under the imprint of Obelisk Press. It was only when Maurice Girodias put out a French translation from his own Editions du Chêne (*Tropique du Capricorne*) that the sword came down. Girodias lined up a panel of celebrities to defend his right to publish this modern erotic classic by an author who was long since repatriated and living in California. It included Bataille, Paulhan, Queneau – but a ban was slapped on the novel anyway (later reversed). Girodias shrugged his shoulders at what he considered a further demonstration of infantile puritanism, and continued to peddle the English edition.

The Cartel d'Action Sociale et Morale and its chairman, Daniel Parker, who had initiated the offensive against the Miller books (*Tropique du Cancer* was also involved), then turned towards the novel by the 'black writer', Vernon Sullivan. As a result of this, *J'irai cracher sur vos tombes*, published six months earlier and selling slowly, suddenly took off. Until the moralists' crusade, few outside of St-Germain-des-Prés had taken much notice of the *Série noire*-style *policier* by the ghostly '*écrivain noir*', whom many already suspected was the talented young trumpeter and soon-to-be Gallimard author, Boris Vian.

Vian continued to deny any stronger association with Sullivan other than that of translator and spokesman (Sullivan was said to abhor publicity), even to close friends such as Queneau; meanwhile, he seemed to be enjoying the attention it gave to the forthcoming novel to be published under his own name, *L'Ecume des jours*.

The affair took a sinister turning, however, in April 1947, when a Parisian salesman, Edmond Rougé, strangled his mistress, Marie-Anne Masson, in a cheap hotel next to the Gare Montparnasse. Both were married. They had spent the early part of the evening on a regular outing to the cinema. Back at the hotel, the twenty-nine-year-old 'jolie femme' broke it to the lame, middle-aged Edmond that she did not wish to continue seeing him; she had found another lover. So Edmond said in a note left beside the body, adding that he now intended to kill himself, which he duly did, in a wood outside Paris. Also on the bed was a copy of *J'irai cracher sur vos tombes*, in which Lee Anderson kills the Asquith sisters, one of them with his bare hands, as Edmond had throttled Marie-Anne.

The press leapt on it. Here was proof enough that the written word could corrupt the feeble in spirit. 'Haunted by his reading, a man strangles his mistress,' said the headline in *France-Libre*. 'The killer repeated the act of the pitiful hero in the book which had unsettled his mind,' declared *France-Soir*. The report in *Libération* opened with a phrase from the book itself, describing how Lee murdered one of the sisters, illustrating the story with a facsimile of the page 'which inspired the killer'. Having read these words, ran the caption, 'Edmond strangled Marie-Anne'. The paper solemnly declared that the copy of the novel on the bed had been left open at this page.

Questioned about the affair, Vian responded with ironic detachment, which did not always strike the right note. Investigation into his own life and medical history by the press enabled a further grisly twist. On May 4, *France-Dimanche* ran this story:

> When he learned about the crime which he had inspired, of which he was even a kind of author by proxy, the young writer smiled and made the following curious statement:
>
> 'A novel is meant to relieve pressure. This crime therefore suggests that my book was not violent enough. What I write next will be much more virulent.'
>
> But if this drama seems to be having little effect on Boris Vian, there is another drama in the young novelist's life.
>
> He has a serious heart condition (so he says) and at the same time is trumpeter in an orchestra. Playing the trumpet is forbidden him.
>
> 'If I continue, I will be dead in ten years,' says he. 'But I prefer to die and to go on playing the trumpet.'
>
> Thus (if one is to believe him) Boris Vian, murderer by proxy, is condemning himself to death: one wonders whether this, too, is a publicity-stunt?

In another paper, Vian saw his picture printed beside that of Edmond. Clearly, his cover was blown. Vernon Sullivan – his *alter ego* forged in the image of Richard Wright – was exposed for what he was, an invisible man. With a court case in train against Girodias, and similar charges looming against Vian and his publisher, Les Editions du Scorpion, Daniel Parker of the Cartel d'Action Sociale et Morale was triumphant.

But Vernon Sullivan, unmasked, unblacked, refused to disappear. Some people, Sartre among them, felt that 'Sullivan' was better suited to the expression of Vian's dark-edged playfulness than the works the author wrote under his own name (in such a reckoning, 'Boris Vian' would be the pseudonym), and indeed 'Sullivan' had already completed another book. It was called *Les Morts ont tous la même peau* (The Dead All Have the Same Skin), and featured a deeply confused character, whose overriding fear in life is that he may have Negro blood in his veins. Blackmailed by a man who claims to be his brother, and who threatens to denounce him in his prim white community, he kills him, which leads to perdition. Up till then, Vian had been unable to settle on a name for his pathetic hero. Now he had it: Daniel Parker.

When the case finally came to trial, in May 1950, Vian and his publisher were found guilty of committing an outrage against good morals, and each fined 100,000 francs (about $200 or £70). Three days after the verdict, Vian wrote an article for *Combat*, called 'I Am a Sex Maniac'. In it he marvelled at the fact that his eight-year-old son, forced to live with a sex criminal in a house containing the works of Miller, Sade and Vernon Sullivan, 'nevertheless prefers *The Adventures of Tintin*'.

THREE

Normal Life Is Absurd

I

'The café is a fullness of being,' apostrophized Sartre, in *Being and Nothingness*. Vian, the existentialists' court jester, added a refinement, parodying Pascal along the way: all the misfortunes of man, he wrote, 'derive from his being unable to sit still at a table in a café'. Each was seated in a café at the time of writing, probably. The picture of the writer in the café is an icon of the era; Sartre in the Flore, pipe jutting from his mouth, coffee cup and ashtray on the table in front of him, is the very image of the writer in Paris. At the beginning of the 1950s, the Flore advertised itself in magazines as 'Le rendez-vous des existentialistes', while the Deux Magots promised new clients an initiation into 'Rendez-vous de l'élite intellectuelle'.

By the time the image had taken hold, 'le pape d'existentialisme', tired of being an exhibit, had decamped: first to quieter café tables, and eventually to the peace of his apartment on rue Bonaparte, round the corner from the Flore, overlooking the Place St-Germain. Here the scourge of the bourgeoisie lived in contentment with his elderly mother.

Les journaux du scandale would not leave him alone, however. 'Revolutionary Thinker Plays Piano Duets Nightly with Mama' was, in its own way, a scandal. At the time of some new Sartrean outrage, a photographer from *France-Dimanche*

95

banged on the door of the apartment late at night and, when an old woman opened it, snapped her. After the picture was published the following day, with accompanying story – 'What can she be like, the mother of Sartre?' – Sartre dropped a line to the editor of the weekly journal, suggesting a correction in the next week's issue: 'The photograph you published was of old Eugénie, our maid.'

The practice of café-writing did not begin and end with Sartre, though, and less conspicuous writers continued to make an office out of a quiet table in a corner. It was a pleasant way of being both outdoors – at play – and indoors – working – at once. In the café, the solitary writer could be writing and yet socializing at the same time. A good café was like a ship at sea: a closed society, of varied parts and activities. Friends, acquaintances, enemies were all within shouting distance, but there was no obligation to talk to them. For a New Yorker or a Glaswegian, the nearest thing to a café at home was the coffee bar or the pub. But in place of the icon of the writer with pen or book in hand, the coffee bar offered the image of the teenager poring over a jukebox; and while Glasgow pubs were never lacking in philosophers, they were not the type to discuss the duties of 'l'homme révolté' in an era of 'non-existence' (or maybe just not in those terms).

'As if to bring the conversation down to earth,' Wainhouse wrote in his essay on Sade, '. . . to this booth in the depths of a rue de Tournon café where I work . . . the person who has been listening to me asks me honestly: "Why are you interested in Sade?"' There follows an account of a conversation between the writer, looking up from his notepad, and his interlocutor, taking in madness, freedom, the death of civilization, the duty of 'our generation' to live underground . . . ending with the prescription: 'in order to preserve the *yes* in you, continue to say *no*'.

This was a cast of outlaws: some serious and dedicated, like Wainhouse; others merely playing, until the family allowance ran out; yet others seriously dedicated to the vocation of play, like Trocchi. The setting for the conversation about Sade is the Café de Tournon, where Wainhouse rendered the Parisian monster into an Augustan English that some mistook for a contemporary eighteenth-century version. The interlocutor is nameless, but he was probably Trocchi, since Wainhouse says of him: 'He understood [my] situation better than anyone.' For Trocchi, too, the café was a fullness of being of a sort not known in Glasgow or London. The café and its modern accoutrements lit up his self-modernizing mind:

> In the pinball machine an absolute and peculiar order reigns. No scepticism is possible for the man who by a series of sharp and slight dunts tries to control the machine. It became for me a ritual act, symbolizing a cosmic event. Man is serious at play. Tension, elation, frivolity, ecstasy, confirming the supra-logical nature of the human situation. Apart from jazz – probably the most vigorous and yea-saying protest of *homo ludens* in the modern world – the pinball machine seemed to me to be America's greatest contribution to culture; it rang with contemporaneity. It symbolized the rigid structural 'soul' that threatened to crystallize in history, reducing man to historicity, the great mechanic monolith imposed by mass mind. The slick electric shiftings of the pinball machine, the electronic brain, the symbolical transposition of the modern Fact into the realm of play. (The distinction between the French and American attitude towards the 'tilt' ['teelt']; in America and England, I have been upbraided for trying to beat the mechanism by skilful tilting; in Paris, that is the whole point.)

'Man is serious at play' – the motto could be posted above the entrance to every good Paris café (but hardly above the door of a Glasgow pub). Though invisible to the naked eye, it was written over the entrance to the Café de Tournon.

The rue de Tournon runs between St-Germain-des-Prés and the Jardin du Luxembourg, and the café sits at the top end of the street, near the gates to the gardens, far enough away from the boulevard to keep its tables generally free of tourists. Modest in style compared to the fashionable spots of the Left Bank, its fare was correspondingly cheaper. There were other hang-outs: Trocchi and the *Merlin* juveniles liked the Old

97

Navy, a small place on Boulevard St-Germain; Richard Wright and his friends often preferred the Monaco, near Wright's rue Monsieur le Prince apartment. But the Tournon was where black and white came together.

It was run by a French couple, Monsieur and Madame Alazar. Inside, the café was rather seedy and rundown – 'not immaculately clean', as one regular put it – and painted in red and garish greens, with hideous illustrations of the neighbouring gardens and their statues on the walls. Although it was patronized during the day by tradesmen and bookdealers from local shops, the Tournon gained a reputation as a café for foreigners rather than the French. In the early and mid-1950s its terrace served as the stage for a scene comprising mainly American writers and journalists, some of whom worked on one or other of Paris's two English-language dailies, the *Herald-Tribune* and the *Continental Daily Mail*, or for one of the news-gathering agencies; and for jazz musicians, artists, magazine editors and their secretaries, together with the usual assortment of camp-followers and ordinary hustlers.

The rue Garancière, where the *Paris Review* had its office, contained within the larger office of La Table Ronde, was just around the corner from the Tournon, and the magazine's editorial team settled into the café and made it their local. Plimpton recalled that the French publishers 'worked with the kind of silence one associates with clerking in nineteenth-century banking institutions', and the *Paris* team preferred instead to read galleys and new submissions snugly enveloped in the congenial smoke of the Tournon.

Besides writers writing, and people playing chess or draughts, the café hosted a discreet little drugs scene. 'We used to turn on in the toilet of the Tournon,' says Danny Halperin, a Canadian working on the *Continental Daily Mail* who was the intimate of several of the city's resident American jazz musicians. 'You could get drugs quite easily then. Big bags of ganja – lots of sticks and stones but a lot of leaves in there too. There were hard drugs around for those who wanted them

– Kenny Clarke, the drummer, he always had horse – but most people were only into grass.'

Drugs were not – yet – an integral part of the fully up-to-date writer's imagery. Black jazz musicians had a close relationship with heroin, but black writers preferred beer and whisky. Baldwin explained it in social/anti-social terms: drugs, soft and hard, turned the mind in on itself, whereas alcohol provided an excuse for sociable relaxation after a day's solitary writing. 'We put hash-hish on the table beside his bed,' wrote one of Baldwin's Verneuil friends to another, waiting expectantly for him to visit a holiday house on the Côte d'Azur. 'And still he doesn't come.' A bottle of Johnnie Walker might have drawn him, but not 'hash-hish'.

The literary identification with the opium-eaters of the past was just beginning in New York as hipsters began to fit the black man's code to the facts of Baudelaire and Rimbaud, but it would not float across to Paris for another few years. Logue sampled marijuana for the first time at the Tournon, but his only serious drug was poetry. Alone among the Tournon writers, it was Trocchi – ever on the watch for new identities in which to cloak his ego – who saw a future in narcotics.

If they knew about Halperin and his friends turning on in the toilet, the café's *patronne* and her husband tolerated it without fuss, together with occasional fights and customers asking for credit. Mme Alazar – 'a big, imposing person', according to Halperin – would lend small sums of money to hard-up writers. A clue as to why the Tournon came to be patronized more by foreigners than by locals might lie in the fact that the Alazars were stigmatized as having been 'collabos' during the War. Accusations were still flying freely. Café-owners and waitresses probably came into contact with German soldiers as much as any other group of Parisian civilians, and sometimes the outcome of a situation which had started cool, then developed into civility and then more, could be dismal. There were few Jews among the Tournon's bohemian crowd, but Halperin was one, and Mme Alazar gained his admiration for her *chutzpah*: 'Behind the counter, for all to see, was a large photograph of her walking down the street in Paris, followed by a jeering crowd, with not a hair on her head. She had had a Gestapo lover, but she didn't try to hide it, unlike a lot of people who had collaborated and then became *résistants* overnight.'

*

The Café de Tournon was expatriate bohemian Paris in black and white. It hosted two literary scenes, occasionally overlapping, but at other times separated by resentment or indifference. Austryn Wainhouse described the black novelist William Gardner Smith as 'my chess partner and closest of friends', while another black writer, Chester Himes, bristled continually at the sight of innocent grins on white faces scrubbed clean with privilege. Plimpton claims not to recall the presence of a black congregation at the Tournon at all, but Christopher Logue says, 'When I think now about the Paris of those days, it is the black voices that rise up and speak to me.'

There were very few black faces in post-war London, where Logue had come from, but here he got to know people like Wright, Smith, the mathematician Joshua Leslie, the pianist Art Simmons, the cartoonist Ollie Harrington – practically the first blacks he had ever met. Logue's primary objective in coming to Paris had been to follow the traces left by his mentor, Pound, but he gained a different type of education, in day-to-day strategy, from his black neighbours at the Tournon. Logue might try to sympathize with his *Merlin* colleague Wainhouse when the latter theorized about his 'situation' in high-minded terms; but he could understand immediately the situation of Wright or Smith. On learning of Logue's socialist leanings, Richard Wright, ejected from the Communist Party and inclined to be impatient nowadays on the subject of left-wing politics, stabbed a finger into Logue's chest and told him: 'None of your en-ga-jay, *please*. You've got nothing to fight for, boy – you're just *looking* for a fight. If you were a black boy, you're so cheeky, you'd be dead.' When the friendly and much-liked William Gardner Smith asked Logue why he was in Paris, Logue mentioned Pound, poetry, the beauty of the architecture . . . . When Logue asked Smith the same question, the answer was framed in words like 'refuge' and 'safety'.

A whiff of petty prejudice was often in the air amid the pleasant fug of tobacco and marijuana smoke at the Café de Tournon. It wasn't only racial, but sexual too. Baldwin, for example, was apt to give the Tournon a miss, preferring the company of his own mixed bag of friends – black and white (mostly white), 'ambiguous', to use his own terminology of the time, and unambiguous, male and female, and a general assembly of nationalities. Richard Gibson, another black intellectual who came to Paris in search of safety and a refuge, says, 'Jimmy Baldwin did not often come to the Tournon. He didn't feel comfortable there. Not only did he feel out of place in the leftist atmosphere of the café, but many of the Tournon habitués had little sympathy for homosexuality. Sex of a very crude macho variety was the tenor of the discussion among the black writers at the Tournon. The painter Beauford Delaney, a friend of mine and Jimmy's, also rarely went to the Tournon, for the same reasons.'

In addition, the political weather in the expatriate colony was starting to turn. Cold War chill was setting in here too, numbing the perception, sometimes of even the most intelligent person, leaving the senses exposed to suspicion. Liberals in the United States had seen lives and careers wrecked by the McCarthyite storm, and news of 'blacklists' and 'redlists', of writers being put out of work for their political views, wafted under the café tables on a persistent draught of paranoia. 'Everybody thought everybody else was informing on someone or other for somebody,' says Logue. 'Austryn Wainhouse, for example, was very much in the grip of spy paranoia – you know, "They're watching us."' And everybody was saying that the *Paris Review* was funded by CIA money.

Both Smith and Gibson had grown up in Philadelphia,

where they had been friends before coming to Paris, and both aspired to a career in literature. Smith was a talented and gregarious man – Gibson describes him as 'the presiding genius of the Tournon' – who had already had a touch of success with an end-of-war novel, *The Last of the Conquerors*, published in 1948 when he was only twenty-one. He wrote a quick follow-up, *Stone Face*, but by the mid-1950s his career had taken a dive. There was a rather ignoble attempt at earning money with a pot-boiler, *South Street* – which contains such characters as Slim the numbers-runner and his girlfriend Lil, a waitress – but the publishers turned down his next two novels, and, disheartened and disillusioned, Smith concentrated on his job at Agence France Presse, where the next desk was occupied by Gibson.

Like others, Smith had left the US to evade the 'corpse' on the back. Like others, he had heard stories about the different attitudes which existed towards American blacks in Europe, Paris in particular, but he had no reason to believe in them until he stumbled on his job at AFP:

> I applied for [the job] by phone and I said to myself, 'When they see me, that's the end.' Back in the States I took civil service typing tests. I was fast and I was accurate, but I was never called.
>
> I went down to the office and took a test. They gave me a story in French and asked me to make an American story out of it in English. I finished it and the Frenchman said, 'There's nothing right now, but come in on Friday.' I didn't. The man called me and wanted to know what happened. He had a job. I started on Monday.

The official American presence in Paris was on the increase all the time, just like the unofficial one, and the spectre of the American Embassy on the Avenue Gabriel loomed ominously in the lives of some expatriates; especially black expatriates, and more especially blacks on the left. There was a general insecurity abroad about the validity, or sudden lack of it, of one's passport. Fear of McCarthy was spreading like a virus, contaminating people even in far-flung places. 'McCarthyism, Forerunner of Fascism in the USA' was a typical French newspaper headline in the spring of 1953. Inside, the editorialist expressed the view that 'In his best days, Goebbels did not do it better.' *Le Monde* ran a story in May under the banner 'The Mania of the Witch Hunt: Every day McCarthy weighs more heavily on the lives of Americans' – which included Americans abroad.

The CIA was forever on the lookout for friendly Americans to keep it informed about unfriendly opinion in American expatriate circles. Such a person might just be a student, a nurse at the American Hospital, or an artist over on an official visit. A spy might not even think of him or herself as a spy – might be horrified at the very sound of the word. All it would take would be a lunch from time to time, at which the conversation could roam freely over certain topics and individuals and groups. The only reward might be a life free of passport problems and maddening French bureaucracy.

A number of people among the Tournon set became the subject of murmured suspicion. Smith was one. 'He was working for the CIA, I know it,' says Lesley Himes, the English-born widow of Chester Himes, and herself a journalist on the *New York Herald-Tribune*. Did her husband feel the same way? 'Definitely.'

As head of the American desk at AFP, and a full-time member of the Tournon set, Smith would be an obvious person for them to approach. But there is no proof that they did, or, if they did, that he complied. Paranoia is a state of mind which shoots first and asks questions later. Suspicion in a small community spreads easily: the *Paris Review* is funded by dubious sources; *Merlin* is under investigation; William Gardner Smith is in the pay of the CIA . . . . Repeat these things often enough and they become 'true'. Eventually, even Richard Wright was the subject of rumours.

But then, there exists something, on record, to substantiate these rumours; a little, but something. As for Gibson, he became, in time, the focus of the most intense suspicion of all.

This was the worm in the Tournon woodwork.

*

> Read Dick W's book . . . Wright's boy is always
> trying to redeem the world by just one more
> murder.

James Baldwin to William Cole, April 1953

Richard Wright's star still shone in the Paris sky, but no longer as brightly. *Les Enfants de l'Oncle Tom*, *Un Enfant du pays* and *Black Boy* had come and gone, and with a certain success, but it was eight years since Wright had published a book in the States. Ralph Ellison's novel *Invisible Man*, winner of the National Book Award, had made him – however egregious the epithet might have been – 'the next Negro novelist'. Wright, in voluntary exile, was scarcely visible at all nowadays in the eyes of a fashion-led American public.

A large amount of his energy in the past few years had gone into the making of a film based on *Native Son*. The part of Bigger Thomas had been offered to Canada Lee – who had played the leading role in Orson Welles's production of an all-black *Macbeth* – but he had turned it down. Who else to approach? Wright and his French director, Pierre Chenal, cast around for ideas, before coming up with the answer – why, Richard Wright, of course. 'Richard returned from wherever he had been to film *Native Son*,' Baldwin recollected afterwards, 'in which, to our horror, later abundantly justified, he himself played Bigger Thomas.' He had been to Argentina, where the low-budget filming took place in a specially fabricated Chicago slum. Wright had slimmed down from 185 to 145 pounds in order to try and squeeze himself into the role of the fictional avenger he had created and with whom he identified so closely. But Bigger was in his teens, and Richard Wright now into his forties. To add to that, he had never acted before, a disadvantage shared by several other members of the cast.

The film failed to gain widespread distribution and Wright, who had invested in its production, returned to Paris a poorer man.

That had happened in 1951. In the following year, he was interviewed for the *Pittsburgh Courier* by William Gardner Smith, whom he might have seen as a presumed rival, like Ellison and Baldwin. The piece appeared in January 1952, in Smith's regular column, entitled 'European Backdrop':

> Wright himself still writes, though lately he's been tearing up a lot of what he's done. He's still vigorous; his energy rushes out to greet you. You tell yourself: 'With all that energy, he's BOUND to produce something else!'

This back-handed compliment could not have gone down well at rue Monsieur le Prince. Wright was only forty-three ('He's still vigorous'!) and Smith was wrapping him up as a has-been.

He was still writing, but when his new novel, *The Outsider*, was published in the spring of 1953, it was an abysmal flop. In the book's anti-hero, Cross Damon, he had invented a figure to embody the rotten soul of America. The creation of dramatic situations, not the manipulation of ideas, was where Wright's strength as a novelist lay. But Wright *liked* ideas, wanted to work with ideas. The author of *Native Son* had been a Communist, while the author of *The Outsider* was an existentialist, and in each case the system of thought can be seen directing the action. But, no matter which system the author chose, the 'choice' offered to the protagonist led to the same end, the end to which virtually all Wright's fiction had led: bloody murder.

In a letter to his agent, Wright claimed that he had written a study of 'character and destiny'; there are 'four murders, a suicide murder, an ambush murder', which, he says – and is he only joking? – ought to be 'enough blood'. It was more than enough for most critics, who complained variously of its 'ghastliness', its 'moral weakness', its 'incoherence'. An anonymous reviewer in the *New Yorker* called it 'intense, garrulous, rowdy and often flowery'; he (or she) also objected to the philosophical debates getting in the way of the (too grisly) action. This is what he meant:

To slay Gil and Herndon and Hilton in a fit of cold rage because they had outraged his sense of existence was one thing; but only if he were *outside* of life, beyond existence, could he make such a judgement about Eva whom he loved. How would he ever be able to tell, after killing Eva, that his judgement had been a correct one? Hate yearned to destroy and sought to forget, but love could not. Love strove creatively toward days yet to come. If he killed himself, his processes of thought stopped. Or did they? How could he ever tell after having killed himself that his judgement-act had been the right one?

It was a mix of existentialism old style, of which Wright had had an instinctive grasp in the writing of *Native Son*, and existentialism new style, which he had picked up from reading Sartre. Wright seemed befuddled by his 'sense of existence' and his 'correct' judgement. The novel worked neither in artistic nor in commercial terms. His previous two books had sold by the hundred thousand – over half a million of *Black Boy* in the United States alone in the first six months of publication – but sales of the new one started slowly and never picked up.

Wright had feared this, as had his agent, Paul Reynolds. 'I am sort of worried about a man living in Paris', Reynolds admitted to his client, 'writing novels laid in this country' – by which he meant the United States. Wright had no intention of going back to live in the States. He had returned briefly during the making of the film, but he would never go home again. Reynolds's well-meaning message was sent on April 6, 1953. The date suggests that it was prompted by a less well-meaning article about Wright which had appeared in *Time* magazine a week earlier. *Time* was the sort of high-profile publication that mattered to Wright, and his displeasure at the piece would have been doubled by the inclusion of a barb from the 'next' Negro novelist, who, it happened, had been a friend of his – or so he thought – since the 1930s:

While Wright sits out the threat of totalitarianism in Paris, an abler US Negro novelist sees the problem of his race differently.

> Says Ralph (*Invisible Man*) Ellison: 'After all, my people have been here for a long time. . . . It is a big, wonderful country, and you can't just turn away from it because some people decide it isn't your country.'

What *Time* was suggesting – and neither Reynolds nor Ellison appeared to be of a mind to disagree – was that it was Richard Wright who had become the outsider.

*

There was a knot in Wright's head, a hard ball of wrongs, some buried so deep in memory that they were forgotten, their only record a tension in the sufferer's eyes, or an unpredictability of manner, the sort that causes others to ask: 'What's bugging *him*?' As 'all his friends knew,' Chester Himes remarked, 'Dick had an excitable temperament and was given to such self-indulgent exaggeration that the buzzing of a blowfly could rage like a typhoon in his imagination.' Baldwin noticed how he had managed to 'estrange himself from almost all of the younger American Negro writers in Paris'. In a rare visit to the Tournon, Baldwin saw Wright 'compulsively playing the pinball machine, while they, spitefully and deliberately, refused to acknowledge his presence'. The romance of life in the City of Light had turned into a chilly exile. It brought 'a strange perturbation of heart'. It also brought a new inventory of problems concerning his role as a political activist, and even his continuing residency in France.

On political and racial issues about which he felt strongly, Wright could not keep silent. To do so would be to go against the grain, against the cause, which was the achievement of the greatest possible freedom for the individual, regardless of race or creed. Yet political outspokenness was ever more likely to be regarded with displeasure by the American government and an unsympathetic American press ('While Wright sits out the threat of totalitarianism in Paris . . .'). Fleeting celebrity in France would not protect him should he be judged to have overstepped the line of plain speaking into the arena of political subversion. It was not unknown for Americans in Europe to have their passports confiscated when attempting to renew them, if they had been openly critical of US policy.

Wright lived in fear of this. Yet he refused to shut up. He was opposed to the Marshall Plan – in which he perceived the germ of American imperialism – and not shy of saying so. He had become associated with a French left-wing coalition – the Rassemblement Démocratique et Révolutionnaire, headed by Sartre and the French socialist David Rousset. And he continued to grant interviews to French journalists on subjects related to racism in America, leaving himself open to the almost automatic charge of being a Communist, or, in the new terminology, un-American. Were he to be expelled from France on any pretext, he would find himself standing before the House unAmerican Activities Committee. The result was that he was constantly watching his back.

To Wright, of course, the McCarthyite view of what was un-American was wilfully and maliciously short-sighted. In an article written for the magazine *Ebony*, Wright declared his faith in a different set of ideals:

> I'll define my idea of freedom, though I'm certain I run the risk of being branded as Un-American. If I am, then I readily plead guilty; but I insist I am *not* Anti-American, which, to me, is the important thing.
>
> My Un-Americanism, then, consists of the fact that I want the right to hold, without fear of punitive measures, an opinion with which my neighbour does not agree; the right to travel wherever and whenever I please even though my ideas might not coincide with those of whatever Federal Administration might be in power in Washington; the right to express publicly my distrust of the 'collective wisdom' of the people; the right to exercise my conscience and intelligence to the extent of refusing to 'inform' and 'spy' on my neighbour because he holds political convictions differing from mine; the right to express, without fear of reprisal, my rejection of religion.

Ebony declined to publish his article, however, which only fuelled his paranoia and hardened the knot.

*

FBI interest in Wright, which had begun during the term of his affiliation with the Communists, had dwindled when he first came to live in France, then been revived in the early 1950s. The Bureau took note, for example, when, in 1951, together with some prominent French intellectuals, Wright founded the Franco-American Fellowship (FAF) with the specific purpose of highlighting examples of American racism on French soil (he was quick to add, in the article he wrote setting out the aims of the FAF, that the organization would keep 'scrupulously clear of French domestic politics'). With the Marshall Plan fully operational, and American firms flocking to the city, jobs for Americans in Paris were more plentiful than ever before; but, Wright complained in the black American magazine *Crisis*, 'not a single American commercial firm in all France employs a single American Negro. . . . Until a year ago, US Government agencies in Europe rarely employed Negroes. . . . The American Hospital in Paris, in 25 years of existence, has never employed an American Negro'. Wright also reported that he had heard of white American tourists, 'laden with dollars', making French hotels 'enforce racial practices for the first time in recent French history' (that's to say, 'If *they* stay here, *we* don't'), and of the harassment of black civilians in Paris streets by white GIs looking for a fight. The aim of the FAF was to keep alive 'the concepts of freedom, generosity, the dignity and sanctity of the individual'.

The organization's accomplishments were limited. Wright was being naïve in claiming among other things that hoteliers had been forced to adopt racial practices 'for the first time in recent French history'. A society that can be bullied into racism by tourists wielding dollars would not have to be pushed very hard. Wright surely knew about French attitudes towards North African Arabs, and about the treachery which had led to French Jews being liquidated during the War. But the FAF had its point. It was simply the latest of Wright's energetic efforts to raise the consciousness of his compatriots and French hosts alike. It was also precisely the sort of awkward squad which raised hackles at the American Embassy. The FAF was quickly branded a Communist front, and infiltrated by informers from within the black community itself.

Baldwin, not yet entirely estranged from Wright, was, though somewhat wearily, enlisted in the service of the FAF. He was allotted the task of monitoring the employment of Negroes at the Economic Cooperation Administration, a Marshall Plan body staffed by Americans. Wright's plan was to put pressure on American firms, and, most especially, American government offices, to make them hire blacks on a proportional basis. Baldwin was sceptical:

> How, I asked him, in the first place, could one find out how many American Negroes there were in Paris? Richard quoted an approximate, semi-official figure . . . but I was still not satisfied. Of this number, how many were looking for jobs? Richard seemed to feel that they spent most of their time being turned down by American bigots, but this was not really my impression. . . . Most of the Negroes I knew had *not* come to Paris to look for work. They were writers or dancers or composers, they were on the GI Bill, or fellowships, or more mysterious shoestrings. . . . Unlike Richard, I had no reason to suppose that any of them even *wanted* to work for Americans – my evidence, in fact, suggested that this was just about the last thing they wanted to do.

However, Baldwin did his research, reached some vague conclusions, and turned up for the first meeting of the FAF, at a venue situated 'in some extremely inconvenient part of town'. According to Wright's instructions, the forty or so people who attended made their way there separately or by twos. There was some vague notion, Baldwin wrote sardonically, 'of defeating the ever-present agents of the CIA, who certainly ought to have had better things to do, but who, quite probably, on the other hand, didn't'.

He was correct, as it turned out. Spies were indeed present at FAF meetings, not of the CIA but of the US Army, one of several intelligence-gathering organizations which reported on the activities of Wright in Paris. (The US Information Agency, the Foreign Liaison Service, and the intelligence units of the Army and the Navy, all filed reports on Wright, which then made their way into his FBI dossier.) It might not have surprised Baldwin to find that out, but it surely would have shocked him to discover that *he* was being used in the case against Wright. The main opposition to the older writer, stated the informer who attended a meeting of the FAF at the end of November and reported to his agent on December 16, 1951, comes from 'one James Baldwin', who 'attacks the hatred themes of Wright's writings'. Thereafter, 'one James Baldwin' is a recurring figure in Wright's FBI file, unwittingly drafted in to support the claim that Wright was stirring up anti-American feeling in Paris, consequently justifying the watch being kept on his movements.

The information concerning the FAF was passed on to the Army intelligence unit by a Negro musician from Philadelphia. The file reveals that he already had the reputation of being an informer, following some dealings with Paul Robeson. The Special Agent controlling him made a note to the effect that 'SOURCE volunteered the information [about Wright], explaining that he was not seeking money or any remuneration but wanted to do his patriotic duty'. The agent appears to have been troubled momentarily by his source's 'anti-Semitic tone', and also makes reference to a possible 'mental quirk', but he nevertheless saw fit to devote several closely typed pages to his source's statements. These included the opinion that 'even though Wright had publicly renounced Communism, he was as much a Communist as he had ever been'.

The Army also received separate information from 'an American citizen', who 'advised that her niece, who was a student, had been invited to join the Franco-American

111

Fellowship Group by Richard Wright. . . . The niece attended one meeting of the organization and came to the conclusion that despite its denials of Communism, the group espoused the Communist Party line as the girl had known it in the United States.'

On December 18, either the musician or another source made a statement in which he professed that 'WRIGHT is active in the Communist Party in France and has been engaged in spreading the Communist Doctrine through the Franco-American Fellowship Group. Mrs Richard WRIGHT is the active Communist member of the family and has made a point of insulting Negro personnel who hold views other than Communist. . . . SOURCE stated that WRIGHT has boasted that he had "the State Department in my pocket – they call me in for conferences the fools".'

Sometime in January 1952, yet another informant, 'an American Negro male student attending the University of Paris', let it be known that Wright had asked him 'to join a "protest" group aimed at "forcing the employment of more of the Americans of African ancestry" in US government jobs in Paris. Source told WRIGHT that it would be better to be certain of facts before "going off half-cocked". WRIGHT then accused Source of having "an Uncle Tom attitude".'

These reports were summarized and incorporated into the main FBI file on Wright. Even if it was not routinely accepted as a fact – on the basis of information supplied by a source with a 'mental quirk' – that Wright was as much a Communist now as ever, there could be no denying that he had been one once. He could be useful, therefore, in supplying information on others.

One afternoon in the spring of 1953, Wright was in his apartment on rue Monsieur le Prince, entertaining Chester Himes, when there was a knock at the door and Senator McCarthy's special investigator David Schine was ushered in. Schine and his partner Roy Cohn had been sent to Europe to investigate the loyalty of employees of American government offices in Europe, and to persuade American libraries in foreign capitals to ban 'un-American' books. In April, Cohn and Schine – the Katzenjammer Kids, as they were known by some of their countrymen – had caused amusement in the French press by claiming to have investigated the loyalty of more than a thousand workers at Radio Free Europe in Munich in half an hour.

On this particular day, Schine was seeking information about a recent appointee of the State Department, and wished to question Wright about the man. Wright told Schine that he had no knowledge of him, but Schine persisted, and suggested that they had been members of the same John Reed Club in Chicago. Wright denied that he had ever been a member of the club Schine mentioned, and repeated that he had no memory of meeting the man in question. Schine then reminded Wright that he had got Langston Hughes before HUAC, forcing the poet to recant some of his political opinions and to disown certain of his own writings. If he wished to avoid similar humiliation, Wright had better try and refresh his memory. Himes recalled that after Schine left, Wright exploded: 'That stupid son of a bitch thinks he can threaten me; I'll never testify.'

Wright's situation remained as full of paradoxes and contradictions as it ever had been. Having left the United States to avoid persecution, he looked behind him on a Paris street and could swear he saw the shadow of that persecution taking cover in a doorway. Paris handed him one variety of freedom, while depriving him of another. Worst of all for the writer, it was beginning to seem as if he had left his story at home. Free as a man was what he had wanted to become; but if he believed the critics, if he read between the lines of the letters from his agent, if he perceived a gleam of truth in the attacks made on him by the younger generation, he could see that as a writer he was becoming free of a subject.

*

Wright's problems with the authorities came to a head in the summer of 1954. Planning a visit to Spain with a view to writing a book about the country (a project suggested to him long before by Gertrude Stein), he had applied to the American Embassy in February for a renewal of his passport. This was necessary even though it had last been renewed only two years earlier. Wright got his passport and made a reconnaissance trip. On his return to Paris, he wrote to his agent encouraging him to seek a contract for the book about Spain. He had first thought of writing about the Far East, and his letter reveals the anxieties that assailed him these days even before he picked up his pen:

> Going into the Far East would be interesting, but I'd have so many strikes against me in such areas that I doubt if I'd be able to get the information I wanted. The Reds would be hostile; the French would be suspicious; and the local reactionary natives would be hostile, that is, those on the Right. And the Leftish Nationalists are so far to the Left, that is, so far sold on Moscow, that I fear that I'd really be on the outside.

All things considered, then, Spain, 'its religion and everything else', seemed a safer bet. The contract from Harper's duly came through, and Wright departed for Spain on November 8. Before leaving, however, he had an obligation to fulfil at the American Embassy, which was, in fact, related to the latest successful passport renewal.

The American Consul was a woman named Agnes Schneider, little liked among sections of the expatriate community. With the power of granting or withholding passports at her disposal, together with information on Wright's 'Communist front' organization, she apparently felt she had sufficient ammunition to force a deal.

On September 16, 1954, RICHARD WRIGHT appeared before AGNES SCHNEIDER, Consul of the United States of America

114

at Paris, France, being duly sworn, furnished a statement consisting of answers to questions annexed to his statement.

Subject stated that he disaffiliated with the Communist Party of the United States sometime during the year 1942, and that his disaffiliation came about because of a series of ideological disputes he had with the following Communist officials: [names blanked out] and others . . . .

Subject was asked if he was acquainted with [blank] in the Office of War Information . . . as he recalls he was introduced to [blank] and that this introduction took place in the presence of [blank]. Subject stated that [blank] was known to him as a member of the Communist Party, and he described [blank] . . . .

Subject stated that [blank], one of the leading Communists of the United States, approached him shortly after his introduction to [blank] and asked him to make a formal application to work for the Office of War Information. Subject stated that this would be rather difficult since he was a publicly known Communist writer and had been Chief of the Harlem Bureau of the 'Daily Worker' . . . .

Subject stated that [blank] informed him that the Communist Party knew exactly what it was doing in asking him to make this move . . . .

In the end, though Wright told Agnes Schneider that he never learned the precise outcome, it appears that the Communist Party chose someone less prominent to infiltrate the office of War Information.

It is possible that the people whose names Wright gave, or merely affirmed, were already known to the agents who recorded his statement. But his evidence could scarcely help their cause, should any of them be called before McCarthy's committee to answer questions about the past.

II

While anti-Americanism in general increased in France during the early years of the decade, the American black man or

115

woman could still feel more at home in Paris than when actually at home. The reception here was often a mixture of curiosity and friendliness. Jazz was still popular, and the American Negro, to French eyes, *was* jazz. 'Jouez-vous la trompette?' was a typical way of starting a conversation. Charming, but rather limiting. Baldwin joked that if he ever came to write an account of his Paris years, he would call it 'Non, nous ne jouons pas la trompette'.

In the autumn of 1952, the weekly *Paris-Match*, which had begun publication three years earlier, made a polite list of the main grievances behind French anti-Americanism. The article made the following points:

Seven years after the end of the War, French patience with the American 'occupation' was exhausted, and most people thought that the Marshall Plan had reached a limit.

American anti-Communism, at first laughable, had now passed beyond a joke. The Americans, having helped to liberate France from the Nazis, seemed likely to career her into another war, with the Russians. Furthermore, the ordinary French citizen foresaw this war taking place not over America or Russia, but over France.

As a result of McCarthyism, American immigration restrictions were severe, even paranoid. The case had recently been publicized of a French student, who, wishing to study for a year in America, had had to submit to embarrassing medical examinations and personal (i.e. political) interviews. By comparison, Americans entering France floated through French Customs with ease. America was too quick to criticize French treatment of its colonial subjects, while slow to do anything to improve the lot of its own, imported 'colonial' population, the blacks. In the South, official segregation was still in place, and the vote continued to be withheld from Negroes.

The *Match* article concluded: 'No country was worse prepared than America for the worldwide role that she suddenly had to play, and on so immense a scale.'

Such a striking of attitudes cut deep into American *amour-*

propre. But, as the article suggested, the expanding black colony need not feel that the hostile slogan 'US Go Home', which decorated walls all over Paris, was aimed at them.

It was estimated that there were about 500 American Negroes in France, and that about half of them were living in the capital. In spite of Richard Wright's findings that American firms employed blacks only reluctantly, or not at all, they included doctors, nurses, scientists, military personnel, journalists, actors, dancers, writers, and of course *trompettistes*. Passion for *le jazz hot* modulated, in keeping with developments in New York, to a fad for 'jazz cool', whose principal exponent was Miles Davis. New clubs opened up: the Club St-Germain, where Boris Vian was in charge of proceedings; the Ringside, near the Champs-Elysées, and the slightly larger Mars Club, off the same avenue, where Annie Ross sang, sometimes accompanied on drums by her lover, Kenny Clarke; Chez Inez was named after the black American singer Inez Cavanaugh, who – like Kenny Clarke – had come to Paris for a season and decided to stay; and there was the Club Galerie in Montparnasse, run by the black painter Herbert Gentry, where his wife, Holly Johnson, sang, and Art Simmons, habitué of the Café de Tournon, played piano. Paris became a haven for musicians banned from working in their own country for want of a 'cabaret card', often as a result of trouble with the police.

In spite of all this, though, France did not develop a jazz scene of its own. There was no 'Paris school' of trumpeters, saxophonists, pianists. Growth in the music was taking place somewhere else – in New York – and those in Europe couldn't hear the changes. To be far away from New York might reduce the amount of tension in one's daily life, but what if the music was also drained as a result? The dynamic of jazz, after all, derived from its oblique and ironic relation to the dominant culture. Jazz was born by being conceived in opposition to a threat, had grown up by forging a vocabulary through which the threat could be confronted and transformed. That was the source of the 'blue note'. Miles Davis came to Paris more than once around the turn of the decade, had a celebrated affair with Juliette Gréco, and met Vian and Sartre. In 1957 he composed the music for the first film directed by Louis Malle, *Ascenseur pour l'échafaud* (*Lift to the Scaffold*). He thought of staying, but decided against. 'The musicians who moved over there', Davis reflected later, 'seemed to lose something . . . . an edge, that living in the States gave them.'

The same was being said of Richard Wright ('The brightest faces were now turned from him,' Baldwin wrote), and of some other expatriate artists. But the process was not inexorable. At least one writer found his 'edge' – or recognized the sharper edge of his talent – only after arriving in Paris.

*

Anyway, I never really got settled. I didn't particularly like the bistros; I've seen them all somewhere before. The good restaurants were too expensive (four to ten dollars a meal) and the inexpensive ones were bad. I found the sexuality (I'm sorry to say) dull and unimpressive. The naked women in Place Pigalle were just naked women; the titillating shows up on Montmartre were just tourist traps. Maybe the trouble is with me.

I loved the Seine, Notre Dame, the Louvre, the sidewalk cafes (Aux du maggots [*sic*] was my favourite). I didn't find the traffic as senseless as Detroit or as violent as Los Angeles. The drivers of the taxis I rode (and I rode many) drove much tamer than a New York taxi driver, much tamer than I would drive. I found too many Cadillacs and hard hurried American women along the Champs Elysees. I saw too many chalk scribblings on the walls of the narrow streets of the Latin Quarter, 'US GO HOME', and although the French whom I met swore it was the 'other Americans' they hated because I wasn't 'really an American' I didn't particularly like the connotation or the exclusion. If I'm not an American, what am I? I was always overcharged. I didn't find any great welcome by the French girls. Most French girls shun Americans, Negroes included. The American Negroes who hang around the Monaco (Dick Wright's hang out) sleep with the Swedish, Norwegian and American girls.

118

Chester Himes arrived in France by ocean liner at the beginning of April 1953. He was hard, but when the hardness cracked it revealed wit, and showed itself to be the carapace of a bitter integrity. Occasionally the qualities combined in his fiction, to create what one of his editors called 'lovely lunacy'. The disenchantment he described in his letter to Carl Van Vechten led him to quit Paris after only a month and embark on a tour of Europe, making a succession of halts – Mallorca, London, the Riviera – before returning first to New York, and then again to Paris at the end of 1955.

Himes was in his mid-forties. He had lived a life of constant agitation, settling only once: to serve seven years of a twenty to twenty-five-year prison sentence in the Ohio State Penitentiary, the outcome of an armed robbery he had staged single-handed at the home of a prosperous white couple in Cleveland, Ohio. Himes was nineteen years old when he entered prison. He had already been a thief, a pimp and a bootlegger. In prison, he began writing, and his first short stories were published in *Esquire*.

Himes wrote over twenty books, including two volumes of autobiography. His novels have come out at different times under different titles: many were published first in French. His writings, especially the early and late work, are full of brutality, hatred and self-hatred. This turbulence grew out of what Himes called a 'life of absurdity', though it was not absurdity in the sense that either Camus or Beckett would have recognized. 'Given my disposition, my attitude towards authority, my sensitivity towards race, along with my appetites and physical reactions and sex stimulations, my normal life was absurd.' In describing his own reactions – typically to someone he suspects of having put him down for being black – he uses phrases such as, 'My head was throbbing like a mashed thumb . . .'; or 'I'd feel my brain lurch. . . .' When a friend wrote to him about 'the most popular of the colored writers', Himes noted his private reaction as '*What motherfucking color are writers supposed to be?*' His two-volume autobiography, *The Quality of Hurt* and *My Life of Absurdity*, is at times a catalogue of misogyny, grievance and self-aggrandizement:

> Her eyes filled with conflicting emotions as she watched me go. Black pimps had taken thousands of white girls like her from the coal-mine towns of West Virginia and the little steel-mill towns of Ohio and put them to work as prostitutes in the ghettos. They liked it; they made the best whores.

> I called the night bellman and told him I wanted a mulatto whore and afterwards a white whore, and after I had finished with these two I decided I wanted the very best and most elegant black whore available to spend the night with me.

> When Judge MacMahon sentenced me . . . I was shocked. At that instant I suddenly knew that this motherfucking bastard had hurt me as much as I ever could be hurt.

These examples are drawn from just a few pages of the first volume; the second part is even richer in similar expressions, particularly of dislike of women who have crossed him. Of one girl, he writes that she was 'beat up by her Spanish lover, but she deserved it for she was a nymphomaniac from the first'. Of a girlfriend, he says: 'I hit her hard in the stomach with my left and crossed a right to her mouth.' Earlier, he had described the same woman as having 'vomit-colored hair'.

Himes's family background was different, in just about every respect, from Wright's. His father was a professor in various colleges across the United States, usually as head of the Mechanical Department, teaching such skills as blacksmithing and wheel-wrighting. Himes himself attended Ohio State University, before swapping enrolment there for a prison sentence. His mother claimed that his grandfather's father 'was a descendant from an English noble family', and was proud of it. Her relatives were 'very fair, and some had moved into the white race'.

Himes himself was a light-skinned man, often taken for Spanish. He was liked in the Café de Tournon. 'He was a fabulous raconteur,' Gibson says. 'He looked like a spiv,' says Logue, 'but he was attractive with it.' By the time he reached Paris,

Himes had published four novels: *If He Hollers Let Him Go*, *Lonely Crusade*, *Cast the First Stone*, and *The Third Generation*. But each was less successful than the one before. He had left a fifth book with his New York publisher, William Targ. No sooner had he set foot in Europe than he received a response.

> This is to me a kind of walpurgisnacht, a nightmare of alcoholism, homo- and heterosexuality, scatology, nymphomania – and a good deal besides. And I'm not concerned only with the four-letter words, necessarily, when I say that if published, it would bring down the roof on all of us. For purposes of personal catharsis, I can understand why you wrote it. . . . But it is simply not publishable in my opinion.

The shell-shocked Targ had one last-ditch idea to offer: 'Obelisk Press, publishers of Henry Miller', which was now run by Maurice Girodias as part of the Olympia set-up. Himes ignored the suggestion.

Himes felt he had exhausted what luck was likely to come to him in his own country. Ahead, he faced a strange land, a foreign people, a language he did not understand, and a career on the downward slope. It was as much to his own surprise as anyone else's, then, that he became the most popular among the French reading public of all the black writers who emigrated to Paris in the 1950s.

*

This success he owed to the creation of a pair of Harlem detectives called Coffin Ed Smith and Gravedigger Jones, who featured in a series of books, including *Cotton Comes to Harlem*, *A Rage in Harlem*, and *Blind Man with a Pistol*. After years of corresponding with American publishers over his manuscripts, trying to get his hands on royalties he claimed were due to him, accusing publishers of swindling him (and 'all the black writers'), Himes was invited by Marcel Duhamel of Gallimard to write a book for the list he directed called *Série noire*. The books were crime novels, in many cases translated 'de l'américain', in others drawn from American models. Duhamel gave Himes the equivalent of $1,000, the largest advance he had ever had, and a hint about the kind of books he wanted: 'Make pictures. We don't give a damn who's thinking about what – only what they're doing.'

This turned out to be first-rate advice, for when Himes started thinking, or started one of his characters thinking, his thoughts inevitably turned to grievance and grudge, and then to anger. The novel Targ had described as 'a nightmare', *The End of a Primitive* (originally published as *The Primitive*), is one of the angriest novels ever written by an American. In his detective novels, however, Himes concentrated on the 'pictures'. He was not greatly familiar with the real Harlem, but then he hardly cared to make Harlem real in his novels. Everything is highly imaginary, from the settings to the characters and their actions:

> One joker slashed the other's arm. A big-lipped wound opened in the tight leather jacket, but nothing came out but old clothes – two sweaters, three shirts, a pair of winter underwear. The second joker slashed back, opened a wound in the front of his foe's canvas jacket. But all that come out of the wound was dried printer's ink from the layers of old newspapers the joker had wrapped around him to keep warm. They kept slashing away in buck-dancing fury, spilling old clothes and last week's newsprint instead of blood.

'I thought I was writing realism,' Himes declared. 'It never occurred to me that I was writing absurdity. Realism and absurdity are so similar in the lives of American blacks that one cannot tell the difference.'

Himes was on guard all the time against injury ('I was always overcharged'), both physical and emotional, even in the presence of friends and lovers. A good illustration of his small-boy, chip-on-the-shoulder vulnerability is provided by his English widow, Lesley. When she met Himes in 1958, by which time he had been in France for five years, he still could speak no French. He had been attending the Alliance

Française in an attempt to improve his grasp of the language, but without making progress. One day, Lesley met him after his class and Chester asked her to go to the local kiosk to buy his cigarettes, as he was embarrassed even to hear himself mispronounce the words 'Gitanes filtres, s'il vous plaît'. Lesley encouraged him to go by himself, however, and spoke the words to him slowly, getting him to repeat them. But the woman at the kiosk, seeing an American and failing to take in what he had said, handed him a packet of Chesterfields – as she had the last time, and the time before. 'He said: "Right, that's it. If they won't let me speak their language, I'm not going to try and learn."'

*

From the moment he arrived in the city, Himes took up a defensive position vis à vis Wright, who, he believed, resented his presence – or any form of competition – in Paris.

After a series of farcical errors, which saw him miss Wright at the station, then be chased from the Wrights' house on rue Monsieur le Prince by a belligerent concierge ('Allez! Allez! Vite! Vite! Vite!'), then check in by himself to the very hotel in which Wright had reserved a room for him anyway, Himes finally got together with Wright at breakfast in the Monaco the next day:

> Dick had expected a gathering of our soul brother compatriots, all of whom knew I was to arrive the night before, but not one of them appeared, an eccentricity which I was later to learn was the natural reaction of envious and jealous blacks who lived in Paris. . . . They did not want any arriving brother to get the idea they thought he was important.

In a letter written to Carl Van Vechten after he had decamped to the Gironde region, where his translator had a house, Himes described his reactions to the 'brothers' when at last he did see them:

> I didn't get to meet many Negroes in Paris. But I met William

123

Gardner Smith, I saw Ollie Harrington, and a few others. They all hang around the Monaco in the shadow of Dick Wright. The real French don't have anything to do with them but take their money. . . . To me they seem a lost and unhappy lot. But they swear they love Paris.

Packed in Himes's luggage, as if he were a messenger bearing tidings of the woe to follow, was a batch of copies of Wright's novel *The Outsider*. Himes remarked Wright's impatience to get at the books, how he personally delivered copies to the English Bookshop in rue de Seine, and pestered its owner, Gaïte Frogé, until she displayed them in just the arrangement he wanted. In Himes's eyes, these actions seemed to stress the division between them: Wright was more concerned about the book, a symbol of his success, than about the welfare of the friend who delivered it.

But it turned out to be an ironic symbol, for Himes's fortunes rose as Wright's fell. Paris did for him the opposite of what it now seemed to be doing for Wright, as Wright found that, together with the corpse on his back, he had shaken off his style and content, too. Himes, on the other hand, gradually found that exile was good for his style, paring the hatred away, without sacrificing its violent energy. The nervy, potentially explosive bitterness of *The End of a Primitive*, with its male and female lusts locked like intertwining snakes together, its alcoholic blackouts, its final crowning horror, becomes something closer to exuberance in the books he began to write after receiving his first commission from *Série noire*. France did not make him a free man – it was too late for that – but it did free him from the threat of madness, guiding him to lovely lunacy instead.

*

Himes scarcely saw Baldwin during his first few weeks in Paris. The two did not know each other from New York, except by name, and anyway had little in common besides their profession and their race. There was dislike, on Himes's side, of homosexuality, and wariness, on Baldwin's, of machismo and left-wing politics, both of which Himes subscribed to. Baldwin had written an unfavourable review of Himes's novel *Lonely Crusade* six years earlier in the *New Leader* magazine, and Himes, sensitive to all slights, remembered it. Moreover, Himes was of a different generation, being now aged forty-four, while Baldwin was not yet thirty. All of these things kept them apart.

However, there was a confrontation one evening in St-Germain, involving Baldwin, Himes and Wright, and an account of it exists which freezes the Baldwin–Wright quarrel for a moment in the heat of battle.

Or does it? For the odd thing about this incident is that all three participants left behind a record of it, each one differing substantially from the others. To collate them is to discover at least as much about the frailty of memory – all were written from a distance of seven years or more – as about the passionate, furious, father-and-son relationship of Wright and Baldwin.

The date can be narrowed down to mid April, early May 1953, as Himes arrived in Paris in the second week of April and stayed only one month before departing for the Gironde. Take Wright's version first: he recalled that he was sitting on the terrace of the Deux Magots, enjoying a beer with Himes, when Baldwin 'heaved into view', accompanied by a white American woman, 'a Mrs Putman'. The other two welcomed him 'with friendly greetings', which were not returned. Baldwin (Wright spells his name 'Balwin' throughout his account, even though the two men had known each other for fifteen years) threw down the gauntlet. He told Wright he wanted to talk to him. 'Sure,' Wright replied. 'Why not? I'm here.' Baldwin challengingly asked what Wright had thought about 'that article' he had written about him, meaning probably the essay 'Many Thousands Gone' which had appeared in *Partisan Review* a year and a half before. Wright was condescending.

> 'Balwin, I didn't know what you were talking about in that article,' I said softly, trying to smile to cushion the shock of my statement.
> Balwin glared at me.

125

'Don't take me for a child,' he warned.

'What are you talking about?' I asked, laughing a bit. That did it. My laughter spurred him to rage.

He leaped to his feet, pointing his finger in my face and screamed:

'I'm going to destroy you! I'm going to destroy your reputation! You'll see!'

'What are you saying? What are you talking about?'

'I said that I am going to destroy you!' Balwin screamed.

'Tell 'im, Jimmy; tell 'im!' the woman, Balwin's friend, egged him on.

'Why don't *you* tell me?' I challenged her.

'He's telling *you* for *me*,' the white lady said, her face excited with a kind of sensual hate.

'Jesus Christ,' Himes exclaimed, rising. He wiped sweat from his forehead and said: 'Excuse me. I'm going to take a walk around the block. I can't take this.'

He left. Since I was the object of attack, I could not leave. I sat on, looking pityingly at Balwin.

'Look, guy, forget me,' I begged him.

'I'm going to destroy you,' he vowed hysterically, over and over again.

I said nothing. I let him empty himself of his abuse of me in public. Finally, Balwin and his white lady friend rose and left. Himes rejoined me.

'That was horrible,' Himes sighed.

'Well, I guess it's better for it to be said openly than just thought of in private,' I said.

'But he said that in front of that white woman,' Chester Himes voiced the heart of his and my objection.

'That was the point,' I said.

This is unforgiving. But the Baldwin it presents is not immediately recognizable. While he was known to flare up in the heat of argument, Baldwin was seldom reduced to venomous incoherence. What's more, there is no contemporary evidence to suggest that he felt that way about Wright at the time. On the contrary, in a letter written a few months earlier to his publicist at Knopf, William Cole, Baldwin recommends sending an advance copy of his own forthcoming novel to Wright: 'Why the hell not? We're perfectly pleasant to each other.' When *The Outsider* was published, Baldwin wrote to Cole – only a few days before the three writers came together at the Deux Magots – expressing resigned indifference over Wright and his novel. The problem with this book, he wrote with cool intelligence, was the problem 'of the impossible brutality of the pure idea . . . when it is introduced into life, which is not an idea'. When he laid the novel down, he did not feel, as he believed Wright intended one should feel, 'that one has read a novel of ideas', but instead a novel filled with gratuitous violence, in which ideas were endlessly talked about.

This does not sound like a man liable to fly into hysterical anger at the drop of a patronizing smile, but rather like someone who knows where he stands and what he thinks. So perhaps Himes can shed some light on the puzzle, in the account of the meeting he left behind. In this version, the woman is called not 'Putman' but 'Putnam', and she is not Baldwin's 'white lady friend', but the wife of James Putnam, one-time secretary of the US Chapter of the PEN Club. In place of the picture of the two mature black writers being rudely surprised by the juvenile interloper on the Boulevard St-Germain, we are informed that Wright and Himes went to the Deux Magots specifically to meet Baldwin, who had telephoned earlier in the day to ask Wright for a loan of ten dollars. This meant postponing their arrival at a cocktail party to which Wright had been invited – by none other than Mrs Putnam.

> We hurried to the Deux Magots and found Baldwin waiting for us at a table on the terrace across from the Eglise Saint-Germain. I was somewhat surprised to find Baldwin a small, intense young man of great excitability. Dick sat down in lordly fashion and started right off needling Baldwin, who defended himself with such intensity that he stammered, his body trembled and his face quivered. I sat and looked from one to the other, Dick playing the fat cat and forcing Baldwin into the role of the quivering mouse. It wasn't particularly funny, but then Dick wasn't a funny man. I

never found it easy to laugh with Dick; it was far easier to laugh at him on occasion. Dick accused Baldwin of showing his gratitude for all he had done for him by his scurrilous attacks. Baldwin defended himself by saying that Dick had written his story and hadn't left him, or any other American black writer, anything to write about. I confess at this point they lost me.

At that moment, 'a large group of people' approached them. Himes looked up and found himself staring into the face of Mrs Putnam. 'Dick and Baldwin kept on going at one another,' Himes writes, and before long:

> Mrs Putnam and all of her friends had gotten to the heart of the argument and taken sides. All of the women and the majority of the men . . . took Baldwin's side – chiefly, I think, because he looked so small and intense and vulnerable and Dick appeared so secure and condescending and cruel. But in the course of time they left us to go to dinner, and still Baldwin and Dick carried on while I sat down and watched the people come and go. Later we went down the boulevard to a Martiniquan café. . . . It seemed that Baldwin was wearing Dick down and I was getting quite drunk.

A different scenario from 'I'm going to destroy you'. It is here and here only that Himes's account chimes with Baldwin's own – in the picture of the three black writers drinking together on the Boulevard St-Germain – though there is no doubt that the meeting being described is the same one.

> Once, one evening . . . Richard, Chester Himes, and myself went out and got drunk. It was a good night, perhaps the best I remember in all the time I knew Richard. For he and Chester were friends, they brought out the best in each other, and the atmosphere they created brought out the best in me.

III

Your obsession with people half queer, half man, is very interesting indeed . . .

Leslie Schenk to Baldwin, March 5, 1957

Go Tell It on the Mountain appeared in the bookshops in May 1953. The attractive, colourful jacket depicted a Harlem storefront church and a brown-skinned family, kitted out in Sunday best, standing before it. The picture represents the family featured in the novel: Gabriel Grimes, his wife and sister, and the two boys, Roy and John. One of the boys is dressed in white and is proudly facing the viewer; the other is turned away, seems to be more shabbily dressed, and is set slightly back from the others, as if about to leave them. This is John Grimes, the fourteen-year-old protagonist of the book. Roy is Gabriel's natural son, but John is the stepson, and while it is foolhardy to identify authors too readily with their fictional creations, there are few dangers in this case: the story of John Grimes, turning his back on the church in which he had wanted to preach, and on his miserable Harlem life, slowly accepting a stirring homosexuality, is the story of James Baldwin.

Baldwin kept his distance from the coteries. Plimpton, for example, for whom life was a literary party, scarcely saw him at all. Compared to the *Paris Review* set, Baldwin was a streetboy, perpetually broke and apt to spend what little money he earned from magazines as quickly as he could before his creditors caught up with him. ('Now Baldwin has the nerve to call me to borrow five thousand francs' – Wright to Himes. 'I am rather despairingly considering what are the possibilities of a loan' – Baldwin to Cole. 'At one stage, he went to Spain, reputedly to escape creditors' – David Ross, an English friend, to Mary Keen, another. 'I'd like to raise my debt to you by two hundred dollars' – Baldwin to Cole. 'I would like to borrow from you ten thousand francs' – Baldwin to Jennie Bradley, et cetera.) Yet this street-boy was regarded by many as the brightest young man in the expatriate colony. One of the few occasions on which he and Plimpton did meet was at a gathering in Peter Matthiessen's Montparnasse studio to hear William Styron read from the manuscript of his novella *The Long March*. It concerns a lieutenant, weary of war, who is called back from the reserves to fight again in Korea – scarcely Baldwin territory. When the reading was over, however, Plimpton recalled:

> Jimmy Baldwin leaned out of his chair in the darkness, and he said, 'Well . . . Mister Styron', in such a way that you knew – by how he said it – that it was an accolade, a benediction. It must have been one of the first honors of [Styron's] career and perhaps the most cherished.

The publication of his own novel finally liberated Baldwin from the slum. It also released him from the church. Unfettered of the claims of those two institutions, he felt less reliant on the refuge of Paris. After *Go Tell It on the Mountain* appeared, Baldwin was seen in the city less often, even though he kept a base there. He had completed the novel in Switzerland, in a mountain-village chalet belonging to the parents of his friend Lucien Happersberger. Before publication, he left for New York, in order to settle some minor differences with his publishers, Knopf. Back in Europe, he went to Switzerland once more, then made a series of sorties into the country, then it was back to New York, this time for a longer stay, before crossing the ocean to Europe again and setting off for Ibiza, the Côte d'Azur, Corsica . . . .

In the pauses, Baldwin somehow managed to complete another novel, a play, and enough material for a collection of essays, confirming his talent, his success, his identity. The play was *The Amen Corner*; like *Go Tell It on the Mountain*, it described life in and around a Harlem church, and, like that novel, it contained no white characters. The essays, published in 1955 in a collection entitled *Notes of a Native Son*, were also, in the main, analyses of black life. The book had one foot planted in America and the other in Europe; its centrepiece was a long essay about the author's relationship with his stepfather, the preacher who had been so cruel to him, beating him and mocking him for being 'ugly'. He had died before Baldwin could unpick the screen of mutually uncomprehending hatred and love which had separated them. The title essay, and the

1. Richard Wright in front of the English Bookshop in rue de Seine

2. Wright arriving in Paris for the first time, May 1946, at the Gare St-Lazare. Greeting him is Maurice Nadeau of *Combat*

3. James Baldwin in Paris, 1955

NATIVE SON   WRIGHT

INSTALLMENT 1

"HIT 'IM, BIGGER!" BUDDY SHOUTED

(Continued Next Week)

4. An excerpt from Wright's novel *Native Son*, in the black New York paper the *People's Voice*, with an illustration by Ollie Harrington

5. Ollie Harrington

6. Jean-Paul Sartre,
Boris Vian, Michelle Vian
and Simone de Beauvoir,
c. 1949

7. Boris Vian,
trompettiste

8. Writers and editors from the *Paris Review* and *Merlin*, outside the Café de Tournon, 1953. Front row, from left: Wilma Howard, Jane Lougee, Muffie Wainhouse, Jean Garrigue. Second row: Christopher Logue, Niccolo Tucci (in the white raincoat), unknown woman, Peter Huyn, Alfred Chester, Austryn Wainhouse. Third row: Richard Seaver (over Logue's shoulder), Evan S. Connell, Michel van der Plats, James Broughton, William Gardner Smith, Harold Witt. In the back row are Eugene Walter, George Plimpton (in hat) and William Pène du Bois

9. Alexander
Trocchi and
Richard Seaver

10. Trocchi and
Eugene Ionesco;
the playwright is
holding a copy of
Merlin

11. A handbill advertising the birth of *Merlin*

12. A drawing of Austryn Wainhouse, dated 1955, by Pierre Klossowski

13. Patrick Bowles (left), Jane Lougee and Christopher Logue, outside the English Bookshop, 1953

14. Wright with Peter Matthiessen and Max Steele of the *Paris Review*, *c.* 1954

book as a whole, revealed Baldwin as a master prose stylist, a writer with a natural elegance, a kind of literary Duke Ellington, precociously at ease in his medium.

One of the essays, 'Equal in Paris', described the brief period at the end of 1949 that Baldwin spent in a French prison, charged as a receiver of stolen goods – namely, a hotel bedsheet, which he had accepted from an American acquaintance. The bedsheet turned out to have been pinched from another hotel, a fact of which Baldwin was unaware until the moment the police turned up to arrest him and lead him off to prison. There he remained over Christmas, until being acquitted by the judge. In the course of relating this little tragicomedy, Baldwin sketches a quick self-portrait of the artist down and out in Paris:

> On the evening of the 19th I was sitting thinking melancholy thoughts about Christmas and staring at the walls of my room. I imagine that I had sold something or that someone had sent me a Christmas present, for I remember that I had a little money. In those days in Paris, though I floated, so to speak, on a sea of acquaintances, I knew almost no one. Many people were eliminated from my orbit by virtue of the fact that they had more money than I did, which placed me, in my own eyes, in the humiliating role of a free-loader; and other people were eliminated by virtue of the fact that they enjoyed their poverty, shrilly insisting that this wretched round of hotel rooms, bad food, humiliating concierges, and unpaid bills was the Great Adventure. It couldn't, however, for me, end soon enough, this Great Adventure; there was a real question in my mind as to which would end soonest, the Great Adventure or me.

In the autumn of 1955, he finished his second novel. To those who had been following his development closely – his agent, his publisher, a few interested friends and fellow writers – it came as a surprise. He mentioned it in a letter to William Cole at Knopf in January 1954, describing it as a 'departure', which made him 'rather nervous'. What he meant was, first, that there were no blacks in the story, and, second, that the love-affair at the heart of it was between two men.

Baldwin set *Giovanni's Room* in Paris partly because he just happened to be there, but also because the mythical freedoms the city grants its temporary residents are central to the behaviour of the book's narrator, David. He is enabled to follow, for a short season, his natural desire – which, if he permits it, could lead him to the grail of all Baldwin's stories: love.

There is nothing racy about the homosexuality in *Giovanni's Room*. The touch is as different from Genet's as it is possible to be. There is little here, apart from the course the love-affair itself takes, that would shame a member of the church-going family depicted on the cover of Baldwin's previous book. The English equivalents of *foutre*, *bander*, *putain*, *bite* – words spattered all over Genet's texts – have no place in it. (Perhaps to emphasize the point, Baldwin included a reference to a man 'who was celebrated because he had spent half his life in prison. He had written a book about it which displeased the prison authorities and won a literary prize. But this man's life was over.') Baldwin has scant interest in serving up a picture of the gay scene in St-Germain. Although there are one or two vignettes featuring screeching queens – *les folles* – their appearance provokes disgust rather than desire.

> Occasionally one would swoop in, quite late in the evening, to convey the news that he – but they always called each other 'she' – had just spent time with a celebrated movie star, or boxer. Then all of the others closed in on this newcomer and they looked like a peacock garden and sounded like a barnyard. I always found it difficult to believe that they ever went to bed with anybody for a man who wanted a woman would certainly have rather had a real one and a man who wanted a man would certainly not have wanted one of *them*.

Such descriptions are there in order to set in relief the purity of purpose of Giovanni and, until he collapses under the weight of it, of David, too. For the motive power directing *Giovanni's Room* is puritanical. The blueprint for the novel was the second part of Baldwin's 'Studies for a New Morality', the essay 'Preservation of Innocence', published in *Zero* in 1949. There Baldwin lamented the 'brutality which rages unchecked in our literature', quite like any moral watchdog, except that this one saw in the violence not a link to a riotous sexuality but to a fear of sex itself. It was this theme – in American literature and therefore in American life – that the young black ex-minister chose to address. David – white, Protestant, with a background closer to Ivy League than to Harlem – has a fiancée, and a father who expects him to marry her and to follow a career much like his own. When Baldwin placed this protagonist next to the novel's other chief character, the Italian Giovanni, a fiery lover of life, it was with the aim of showing how David had cut himself off from experience – his experience of his own desires – and hence from love, for the acceptance of the love of another requires the courage to face the truth about oneself.

Baldwin's book is trim and neat; in a way, it resembles the kind of antiquated morality tale in which the heroine is tempted away from the path of virtue, risking doom. In this case, the heroine is called David, and the virtue he/she is blind to is the life-affirming honesty of Giovanni. Virtue in this modern moralizing fable involves the acceptance of physical love between two men. Denial of it is a sin. The realm of damnation is all around, in unhappy social conformity, which is indeed the path David takes.

Others, such as Trocchi, grasped the freedoms Paris offered in order to indulge in licentiousness; but the freedom Baldwin sought was the freedom to fulfil oneself, to be whole. Where, formerly, in his pulpit days, he had preached that fulfilment was inseparable from the love of God, now he preached that it was inseparable from love, full stop.

They're watching us

'Everybody thought that everybody else was spying on someone or other for somebody,' Logue says. Both Austryn
Wainhouse and Jane Lougee were convinced that a close eye
was being kept on *Merlin*. Chester Himes was suspicious of
one member, in particular, of the black community at the Café
de Tournon. William Gardner Smith pointed an accusing finger at Richard Wright – who pointed one back at Smith,
among others.

The foundation of this suspicion is flaky in certain places,
though quite firm in others. Richard Wright had his tussles
with the authorities and accumulated an FBI file running to
just over 250 pages, but Wright was a prominent and influen-
tial figure, and it is not surprising that the security services
should take notes on him, given their attitude towards
Communism, even while he lived outside the United States.

As for the others . . . The FBI amassed a Chester Himes
file, of about 100 pages, but almost all of it concerns articles of
left-wing sympathies written by Himes in the 1940s, in particular a piece entitled 'Negro Martyrs Are Needed', which
appeared in *Crisis* in May 1944. The rest consists of recapitu-
lations of 'subject's' background, date of birth, education, and
possible present whereabouts (mostly a matter of guessing).
The later material is trivial. There are two pages from 1962,
concerning an article in the Black Muslim newspaper

Muhammad Speaks, in which it was stated that a French film-maker planned to turn a story by Himes into a film. Only one page relates directly to the Paris years: it is dated February 11, 1960, and focuses on Ollie Harrington, who, the memorandum says, 'belongs to a group of Negro residents in Paris who are disciples of RICHARD WRIGHT. Other members of this group, according to [blank], are JOSHUA ALLENSWORTH LESLIE, born 2/18/33 at Kingston, Jamaica, a British national, and CHESTER BONAR HIMES.' Once stamped 'Confidential', this fascinating information has since been declassified.

William Gardner Smith's file is fatter than Himes's and, surprisingly, than Wright's. As released under the Freedom of Information Act, it is heavily censored, but there is next to nothing about his term in Paris in the 1950s, as is possible to discern from the file information at the head of each doctored memorandum. The FBI was more interested in Smith's movements during the Civil Rights years, in the following decade, than in his café-crawling in Paris. The CIA noted the departure 'for Europe in October 1951' of Smith, 'alleged to have been a member of the Communist Party in 1948', and then noted nothing else until 1964, by which time Smith was in Africa, working for Ghanaian television. Much the same goes for Baldwin, whose file – though the longest of all, at 1,750 pages – contains nothing about his life in Paris, except a cross-reference from Wright's file concerning the activities of the FAF. The file on Baldwin was not actually opened until three years after he had left Paris for good.

It was with some difficulty, including a wait of more than a year, that the file on the editor of *Merlin* was obtained from the US Department of Justice in Washington. The Freedom of Information Act makes no provision for expeditiousness. Eventually, though, the Trocchi papers arrived. For once, the entire file of a subject was released. It consisted of two pages. One was dated April 27, 1962, and was completely blanked out. The other page, dated June 8 the same year, was uncen-

sored. It contained his name – Alexander Whitelaw Robertson
Trocchi – and that's all.

FOUR

The Hounds of Decency

I

Un pornographe de langue
anglaise, c'était du jamais vu,
c'était moderne ...

Maurice Girodias

Maurice Girodias merits two entries in the great Dictionary of Literary Biography of the future. The first will read in part like this:

> He was a pornographer, trading in books that are at best camply amusing, at worst bad beyond bad taste. Although he published several twentieth-century literary classics, his achievement is tarnished by his unfair dealings with their authors. Beckett, Nabokov, Donleavy, to name only three, all looked back on their association with him with regret.

The other entry, which ought to be printed next to the above, will equally state the truth should it contain the following:

> Girodias was a persistent, courageous battler for the freedom to publish and the freedom to read, in an era when it was forbidden to print the word 'bugger' in a book or magazine, or to say 'buttocks' on the English stage, or to publish, in Britain and America, books such as *Tropic of Cancer*, *Our Lady of the Flowers*, *The 120 Days of Sodom*, *The Story of O*, *Lolita*, *The Ginger Man*, and

137

Naked Lunch. All of the above titles were published originally in English by Girodias, with the exception of *Tropic of Cancer*, which was first published by his father.

Girodias established the Olympia Press in the middle of 1953, though he had been nursing the idea for many years before. His business instinct had been aroused by the arrival of American GIs in Paris at the Liberation, followed, in subsequent years, by boatloads of free-spending tourists. As the most recent publisher of Henry Miller's outrageous, lascivious (and therefore much read) *Tropic* books, Girodias was already known to resident English and American journalists. The *New York Herald-Tribune* frequently carried items about the 'lurid' books which were only available in English in Paris. One which appeared in the paper's 'People' column in the late 1940s related the experience of a schoolteacher who was returning by ship from a summer in Europe:

> Our friend noticed a boy and girl reading a copy of *Jane Eyre*. The next morning she saw half a dozen other young people engrossed, oddly enough, in the same work. As a teacher, our friend was highly pleased. But on the last day of the crossing, she happened to find a copy of *Jane Eyre* on a deck chair and picked it up. . . . Inside were Henry Miller's twin volumes, *Tropic of Cancer* and *Tropic of Capricorn*, neatly packaged by a Paris publisher . . .

– who was, of course, Girodias.

In 1950, the paper ran another story on the publisher. It quoted him as saying he was on the lookout for 'a new Henry Miller'. The author he wanted to find, Girodias said, 'must be an English or American exile, and he must have something to say'. Each of the *Tropics*, he claimed, had sold about 40,000 copies since the end of the War. Now he was looking for a new genius; furthermore, 'I would like to print translations of the great classical erotic works – by Marquis de Sade, Restif de la Bretonne and others. There is much great literature that has never been put before an English-speaking public'. And the reason why no one had read it was exactly the same as the reason why everyone should *wish* to read it: it was full of sex.

He may have hoped to discover the next Henry Miller among the literary apprentices who compiled, wrote and produced *Merlin*. Trocchi, for one, struck Girodias forcefully ('a disembodied intelligence' was how the Scotsman now styled himself). And his luck was definitely in with Wainhouse and Seaver, both literate in the French classics, and capable of translating them.

A bookseller who operated from the courtyard at 13 rue Jacob offered Girodias the use of a small room at the back of the shop, and Olympia was up and running:

> My staff included an ex-sailor with . . . a gift for picturesque swearwords, and a very small secretary who had for a chair the back seat of a Delahaye automobile. We used the same rickety table, behind which I sat on a couch which my friend the bookseller also used as a bed . . . .

None of the four titles which launched Olympia would today be regarded as a 'dirty book'. Dubious though their authors were in the eyes of the law, they were villains of the high-class sort. The first Olympia Press title was by Henry Miller, who had signed up Book Two of his Rosy Crucifixion Trilogy, *Plexus*. It came out in two volumes in May 1953. (Owing to a fault in the production, some purchasers found beneath the separate covers identical contents.) Following *Plexus*, Girodias published Seaver's rendering of *Les Exploits d'un jeune Don Juan* by Apollinaire, an investigation into adolescent sex life, translated as *Amorous Exploits of a Young Rakehell*. Then came Wainhouse's versions of the 1920s erotic tale *L'Histoire de l'oeil* by 'Pierre Angélique' (Georges Bataille), translated as *Tale of Satisfied Desire*; and, at the same time, the Marquis de Sade's *Bedroom Philosophers*.

The list embodies, in effect, the first four statements of a radical decree, according to which Girodias instigated and, for the rest of the decade, fomented a revolution in definitions of 'decency' and 'obscenity'. Many others played their parts, and often Girodias's motives were anything but noble; but half a dozen years of Olympia publishing did more to challenge and destroy the fortress of literary censorship in the Western world than any other post-war enterprise or event. (The 'Lady Chatterley' trial, often cited as a turning-point in Britain, took place in 1960, several years after Olympia had cleared the ground. Liberalization in the United States was slower to follow; when it came, the test cases were frequently Olympia books: *Tropic of Cancer*, *Lolita*, *Naked Lunch*.)

Girodias did not tread carefully in his dealings with the law; he simply published what he wished, and then faced the consequences. Wherever possible, he turned his adversaries' spleen to his own advantage. His eagerness to outrage the 'Establishment' and the 'bourgeoisie' brought a notoriety which eventually eclipsed his brighter aspect – 'It is my job to deprave and corrupt,' he liked to say, which was not calculated to please his more serious-minded supporters – but as his launch list shows, he was more than just a purveyor of pornography. *Risqué* – that he wished to be; but discriminating, too.

*

'Very nice,' Henry Miller wrote to Lawrence Durrell about Girodias in 1947, 'but sadly like his father, tight, wolfish and queer.' The father, Jack Kahane, had published both Miller and Durrell, and Miller's back-handed compliment was a way of recommending that Durrell accept an offer from Girodias as well. Girodias was like his father in other ways. He was expansive in his business gestures, unpredictably generous, equally vengeful, and possessed of a certain taste, even vision, which was yet besmirched by *bad* taste. He enjoyed good food, and, perhaps above all else, good wine. He dressed well, charmed women, and liked to drive expensive-looking cars. Even when funds were low, as they often were, he invested in the keeping-up of appearances. There was not much of the bohemian about Girodias. Shortly after the day on which he rolled up at *Merlin*'s headquarters on rue du Sabot, offering to underwrite the enterprise, Richard Seaver discovered that 'the shiny black Citroën which had so impressed us had not been paid for, and his financial fortunes were at an even lower ebb – if such were possible – than ours'.

Girodias was also capable of a nice line in self-deprecating wit. 'It is true', he once said, 'that I have from time to time compromised for the sake of making a little money. But my excuse is that I've always lost it very quickly.' Where he resembled his father most, however, was in his devotion to books, the fun to be had and the profits to be made from publishing and selling them. Jack Kahane's industry during the 1930s had made him the best-known English-language publisher in Paris. Twenty years later, his son occupied an identical position.

Born in Manchester, Kahane had come to France to fight in the First World War, from which he emerged not only with his life but with a young French bride, Marcelle Girodias. In the late 1920s, he wrote a whimsical novel, *To Laugh and Grow Rich*, published in Paris by Brentano's. It was something of a success, but when the English publisher Grant Richards brought out a new edition, it was unexpectedly banned by the circulating libraries – a move which seriously affected revenues. In this 'abominable and arbitrary act', as Kahane called it in his *Memoirs of a Bootlegger*, he nevertheless scented 'commercial advantages' – i.e. the allure of forbidden literature. The tone of rhetorical outrage, combined with a sharp sense of money-making possibilities, was to be passed on intact from father to son.

Kahane placed an advertisement in the London press, stating that he was willing to publish any novel refused by a publisher on the grounds that it was obscene. Beleaguered books, usually with titillatingly ambiguous titles, were thus rescued from England's puritanical, joy-denying gloom and set free in Paris. A few would go through seven or eight editions; most would never be heard of again. An example was *To Beg I Am Ashamed* by Sheila Cousins, one of the last originals to appear under the Obelisk imprint. An 'old and respected firm', according to Kahane, had scheduled it for release, but withdrew the book after it had been attacked 'by a couple of popular dailies temporarily short of head-line subjects'. Kahane picked it up . . . and made money.

Making money was not his only aim, however. Kahane dreamed of being taken seriously as a publisher. He was aware that for this to happen, his name would have to be linked with at least one major twentieth-century writer. Sylvia Beach had published *Ulysses* and nothing else, but her place in the publishing hall of fame was secure. Robert McCalmon had issued Hemingway's first book. Harriet Weaver's Egoist Press had put out work by Eliot, Pound, Joyce, Wyndham Lewis and others. In London, Edward Garnett, an editor much admired by Kahane, had made his name by publishing D. H. Lawrence, the ideal type of author for Kahane: a literary genius who wrote about sex.

He was unlikely to emulate those reputations with saucy titles such as his own *The Gay Intrigue*, or Norah James's *Sleeveless Errand*, a portrait of debauched bohemians in London. Eventually, though, Kahane captured his pet genius, in the phallic shape of Henry Miller.

Tropic of Cancer arrived on Kahane's desk in 1932. He took two years to publish it, but *Cancer* was followed by *Black Spring*, and then *Tropic of Capricorn*. Meanwhile, Obelisk published works by Lawrence Durrell (*The Black Book*), Anaïs Nin (*Winter of Artifice*), James Joyce (*Haveth Childers Everywhere* – a portion of *Finnegans Wake* – and *Pomes Pennyeach*). The press was also responsible for *Boy* by James Hanley, *The Well of Loneliness* by Radclyffe Hall, *The Young and Evil* by Charles Henri Ford and Parker Tyler, and *My Life and Loves* by Frank Harris; all banned in England and America for being sexually aberrant (Hanley was accused of promoting pederasty, Hall and the Ford–Tyler duo of portraying homosexual acts); most of them noteworthy for their literary daring.

For all his success in establishing a literary list of high quality, Kahane left little behind him when he died, on the day the Second World War broke out, except 'a collection of bar debts'. His son Maurice then started a publishing firm of his own, but, wishing to free himself from the dubious image many people had of his father – he had already taken his French mother's name – he began by specializing in illustrated art books. But expensive and lavish volumes such as these which Girodias published – he had a particular interest in Norman architecture – did not sell, and he soon found he had taken over the family business.

When the War ended, his publishing activity brought him a distinction never accorded his father: it landed him in court.*
Even as the Cartel d'Action Sociale et Morale was moving in on him for publishing the French translation of *Tropic of Capricorn*, Girodias was reviving the Obelisk Press and reprinting Miller in the original, in most cases printing the true names of author and novel on the cover, but where necessary '*Jane Eyre* by Charlotte Brontë' instead. Next he put together an edition of the *Memoirs of Fanny Hill*, which sold handsomely to American GIs and English smugglers, and he persuaded Miller to make over the rights to *Sexus,* the first part of the projected trilogy. He was a businessman and he had discovered his market. All he needed now was a continuous supply of goods to cater to it.

There were to be several more reverses as his activities caught the attention of the vice squad, the Brigade Mondaine, or 'worldly brigade' (an appellation which caused much amusement in English-speaking circles). First, *Sexus* was almost immediately banned, aborting a likely money-maker. Then he lost his prestigious art publishing imprint, Les Editions du Chêne, in a financial takeover by Hachette. With

*Not for the first time: in 1946, Girodias published a pamphlet by Yves Faye which denounced the official protection given to black-marketeers. Author and publisher were sued by the government, but the case was settled in the publisher's favour.

Chêne went the rights to the other Miller titles, the art books, and much else, including the French edition of Kazantzakis's *Zorba the Greek*. It was at the nadir of this 'near complete bumhood' that the idea dawned on him to create a list of French erotic classics in English translation.

The intellectual ballast was supplied by two of his new friends, Trocchi and Wainhouse. Early catalogue copy for Olympia, written by the former, starts off with some familiar bromides: it was the intention of the publishers to 'place before the general public complete and integral texts' of 'banned masters'; readers must have the right to read what they choose, writers to write, publishers to publish, etc. Yet there was more to it than that – or at least Trocchi could make it seem that there was. From his conversations with Wainhouse in the Tournon and elsewhere ('He understood my situation better than anyone'), Trocchi had imbibed some high-minded ideas and purposes about personal liberation in a constraining social context. He had already floated them into his *Merlin* editorials; now, with a new vehicle to hand, and increasingly grand ideas to steer through, he helped launch Olympia with a lofty vigour, quoting Bertrand Russell and Milton in opposition to censorship, and offering his own view that 'there is no virtue in ignorance'.

> We are dealing here with a subject of vital importance. It is a shorter step than commonly supposed between the rigid suppression of eroticism in literature and the creation of a totalitarian nightmare in which tribal unreason erects its black crematoriums for the living dead.

Freud, Sade, the Holocaust; taken together, they make a potent brew, and Trocchi was writing at the moment of discovering all three. There is more than a touch of humbug about his 'subject of vital importance' and his 'tribal unreason', but this was, even so, the finer spirit of the Olympia Press. Girodias could say that he owed his success 'essentially to the survival of an archaic and semi-religious form of mental oppression: censorship', and then lean back in self-congratulation at the thought of having once again thumbed his nose in the face of the bourgeoisie. But Trocchi was capable of fitting the nose to a head containing ideas:

The proprietors of the *Olympia Press* have the firm conviction that Lord Russell, the eminent British philosopher, is not alone in his contempt for the current laws of censorship in English-speaking countries. While such authors as Chaucer, Boccaccio, Shakespeare, and Congreve are available at least in the metropolis because they are 'classics', each modern work, if it treats of sexual matters – and what serious writer can omit a consideration of them? – is subject at once to the indecent whims and narrow moral codes of the County magistrate. A number of years ago some optimists felt confident that with the final vindication of James Joyce's *Ulysses* an important principle of freedom had been established. Unfortunately, this was not so. No sooner had the enemies of free thought lost on that ground – well-lost, perhaps, since few people had the patience to read *Ulysses* – than they burrowed like the good rabbits they are through each and every book that led man in plain language to look inward at his own sexual nature. The principle established by the legal vindication of *Ulysses* turns out to be a dangerous one. Any book which is courageous and not obscure seems automatically to be branded as obscene without the justification of being of literary value. Mrs Grundy has nothing to fear from the obscure; having given way on that ground she now redoubles her effort in the field of the more outspoken. The book burners are still with us . . . .

Now for the first time in history, the works of Sade and Miller, with full unexpurgated texts, in masterly and exciting translations, are offered at reasonable prices and in handsome book format. We have the courage of our convictions, hoping that in this way many people – the average man as well as the scholar – will be given the opportunity of reading and testing for themselves the greatness of men hitherto condemned to silence by ambiguous laws that have caused our heads to be buried like the ostrich's at the approach of imaginary danger.

There were contradictions involved in being given the key to this moral underworld. Wainhouse, for example, was excited at the thought of being in the engine-room of a 'clandestine' publisher, which was willing to publish his versions of 'dangerous books', to take whatever blame there was, and to give Wainhouse something of a living, as well. But, in the view of the translator himself, there was a drawback. It was picked up by the first reviewer of the Casavini versions of the Marquis de Sade:

> This 'monster author' is about to appear in paperbacks. Sade's writings, rigorously and for sound reason suppressed . . . have served as fuel to the bonfires common sense has lit for 150 years. This summer, on the quays, in the kiosks, tourists will find moderately priced English versions of *Justine* and *La Philosophie dans le boudoir*. . . . The prospect is troubling: Sade a popular novelist! Is it really a service this dauntless young publisher is rendering, who with his scorn for censorship . . . issues pocket editions of Sade? Sade suddenly becomes available! No, I'll not feign to be out of sympathy with the arguments of those who . . . maintain that it would be better for the one totally condemned writer to remain out of sight.

Recognize the fustian tone – 'rigorously and for sound reason'; 'I'll not feign to be out of sympathy', etc.? The reviewer was none other than Austryn Wainhouse, aka Pieralessandro Casavini ('the pseudonym of an American political thinker living in exile in Paris', he told his readers, not failing to remind them that the translations 'have been mistaken for 18th-century performances'). The review appeared in *Merlin*.

The idea of jostling for attention behind Wainhouse's joke was serious enough: he believed in retaining the power of the taboo. Wainhouse – for all his pomposity, finally more serious than Trocchi – understood the paradox of the underground publisher: that to make available to the light that which had been kept from sight in dark prisons is to invite paleness, insipidity, transparency. The force of seditiousness would soon, by this route, be dissipated in cheap imitations.

*

The second batch of Olympia titles was just as classical in tone as the first. It included a translation by Trocchi of Apollinaire's *Onze mille verges*, which he rendered as *The Debauched Hospodar*, and read from, as a work-in-progress, to clusters of friends in cafés. There were also two more by Wainhouse: Sade's *Justine, ou les Malheurs de la vertu* (*Justine, or Good Conduct Well Chastized*), and a short work by the nineteenth-century author Alfred de Musset, *Gamiani, ou Deux nuits d'excès* (*Passion's Evil*). They duly went on sale in the *bouquins* along the quais, and, discreetly, in the English Bookshop (the Librairie Mistral, however, was less than eager to stock them).

Translators had to adopt pseudonyms to avoid the attentions of the Brigade Mondaine. For Sade, Wainhouse retained Casavini, but for the Musset (as for the Bataille), he styled himself 'Audiart'. Trocchi became 'Oscar Mole'. By the end of 1953, Collection Merlin had also issued its first two titles – Beckett's *Watt*, and Logue's book of poems, *Wand and Quadrant* – which, although distinct from Girodias's own list, nevertheless fell into the Olympia embrace.

Occasionally, a stream of high-minded justification would spurt from Girodias's mouth. He claimed to wish to publish 'anything that shocks because it comes before its time, anything that is liable to be banned by the censors because they cannot accept its honesty'. He could be awkward, pointing out that French institutions, tainted by association with the Nazis, were morally bankrupt, and therefore disqualified from imposing moral constraints on the citizenry, whose right to 'liberty' was sacrosanct. How, he was asking, are we to be expected to accept at its own valuation a justice system which allowed French Jews to be shipped to concentration camps, when it tells us what we can and cannot publish and read? When the representatives of a police force that connived with the Nazis visit our editorial offices and seize copies of our books, is it not moral cowardice to give them a free hand to prosecute us on charges of obscenity, and to hope to get off lightly? Isn't it our duty to fight this 'rigid suppression'?

Girodias frequently said or wrote such things, and on the last point was as good as his word. Up till now, all his books were worth fighting for.

He had plans, though, to expand and to start publishing a different sort of book: 'modern fiction', written to order for the most part, by commissioned authors. He took the idea from Gallimard's *Série noire*, the crime series. Girodias would have such a series, too. Instead of French, they would be in English, and instead of crime, they would have sex.

Outlining his plans to Trocchi and company, Girodias had reasoned that the profits from the new series would help to keep both the magazine and Collection Merlin in existence. Even more to the point, they could keep the impoverished authors in existence, too. What Girodias was ordering was pornography – by the yard. In the books he was commissioning, there had to be a sexual encounter of some sort at least every five or six pages; and no jokes. The commission would pay well: approximately a pound per page, which amounted to about £200 or $600 for a book . . . something like six months' subsistence for a hungry writer in 1953–54.

Wishing for the time being to keep the Olympia list for a more discerning readership, Girodias planned to catalogue the new stuff under a different imprint. This series was called the Atlantic Library – it was aimed mainly at Americans, after all – but the publisher of classics, furtively stepping downmarket, massaged his publicity to make it appear that the works he was now bringing into public view had been mouldering for years in obscurity because of repressive legislation.

Once again, the catalogue copy was written by Trocchi. For the most part, it said, the books on the list have been suppressed, or else have passed through the hands of other publishers, their true worth escaping unrecognized. In fact, of ten Atlantic titles, no fewer than four were written, under pseudonyms, by Trocchi himself. The list contained one genuine classic, John Cleland's *Memoirs of a Woman of Pleasure*, but

148

that had already been published by Obelisk anyway (as *Memoirs of Fanny Hill*).

These 'texts', the catalogue reassured any member of Girodias's potential clientele who might be harbouring guilty feelings about sending off for dirty books, have been selected 'from the many manuscripts submitted' by 'approved literary authorities, French and English-speaking' – none other than Girodias and Trocchi. At times, he makes the Atlantic Library sound like a prototype *Joy of Sex*:

> The Atlantic Library is planned to describe aesthetically these areas of human experience usually referred to as 'intimate' or 'private'. Within a creative framework these dark passions are courageously revealed, the key-note being directness, sparing the reader very little as they exactly record the contacts between men and women in this modern age. It is the main-spring of this delicate machinery of human relationships that go to make up our society that these authors touch.

'Two con men,' says Richard Seaver of Girodias and Trocchi; 'it was the perfect match.'

The first Atlantic title was printed in January 1954 – *Three Passionate Lovers* by René Roques – the last in June. Other lists were to follow: Ophelia, Ophir, Othello, Odyssey, and the most famous, The Traveller's Companion. Of the writers associated with *Merlin* – aside from Wainhouse, Seaver and Patrick Bowles, who confined themselves to translations – Logue, Baird Bryant, Denny Bryant, Philip Oxman, John Stephenson and John Coleman all wrote novels for one or other of Girodias's lists, which took their place among titles such as *I'm for Hire*, *Lash*, *The English Governess*, *There's a Whip in My Valise*, and so on. But of this unholy church, in Girodias's phrase, Trocchi was 'the erratic pope' – or, rather, the priestess, since to most of his efforts he attached a woman's name, 'Frances Lengel'. Girodias fell for her instantly: 'a literary lady of little virtue', he styled her.

Trocchi later claimed that the dirty books – db's, as they were known to one and all – were written mainly to earn money to keep *Merlin* going. There is some truth in this. Despite Girodias's offers of help, the magazine was engaged in a constant struggle to stay in existence. Seaver had to undertake teaching work, leaving Paris at a moment when, had he stayed, he might have gained Beckett's vote to translate *Molloy* into English. Trocchi was hatching all sorts of schemes, few of them feasible, and Jane Lougee went back to try and raise money at home in Maine.

But contributing to an endlessly leaking *Merlin* survival fund was not the sole motivation for Trocchi writing the db's. He relished the opportunity which the erotic writing gave him to raise two fingers to the bow-legged of the Establishment, 'to bang at the doors of Grundy, as it were'. This was the age of revolt, and Trocchi, removed by several stages though he was from the great *hommes révoltés* of the period, was none the less engaged in stoking his own rebellion. In time, it would lead to a wholesale repudiation of the society which had produced him. Trocchi surely derived his pseudonym, Frances Lengel, from its initials: an FL is the common name for a condom, or 'French letter', in his native Glasgow. The outrageously pornographic 'texts' he wrote for Girodias were his very own French letters back to his rigidly puritanical homeland.

*

'Trocchi's sex life was a shambles,' says Richard Seaver. 'It was a troubled sexuality, because there was a Don Juanish quality about it.' Though still in love with Jane, he was seldom shy of showing off his talent for seduction. When it came to writing, his talents were again the envy of his friends. He seemed to have the ability to type out his pages, one after the other, without the need for correction.

But he could not ally this gift to the long periods of solitary concentration required for serious creative work. He had an aversion to sitting down alone in a silent room with a blank sheet of paper. Wainhouse, Logue and Seaver were all doing more writing than he was. The novel he had begun on leaving

Glasgow University, *Young Adam*, was still not finished. By commissioning him to write erotic books, however, Girodias provided Trocchi with a métier: now he could be Don Juan at the typewriter as well as away from it.

The first 'Frances Lengel' book was *Helen and Desire*. Trocchi wrote it in little over a week in the early winter, and it was published by the Atlantic Library in January 1954. It tells the story of an Australian girl who runs away to sea with one of her father's farm-workers, eventually being kidnapped by Arabs and 'groomed for love'. Trocchi adopted the technique of Sartre's *La Nausée*, presenting the reader with the first-person narrative of Helen Smith (or Seferis) as a manuscript 'found on some stray Arab' in Mascara, Algeria (Sartre's Roquentin had also travelled in North Africa). This quickfire attempt falls well short of the standards set by the best erotic writing, ancient and modern – too many tremulous breasts, soft and shadowy clefts, moans of pleasure and shattering climaxes; but there are some literary touches, and, here and there, it is possible to detect the influence on the author of the intellectual fashions of the Left Bank:

> The uncertainty of my existence is exasperating. I affirm that existence, nakedly and purely, through my sex.... Sentiments are death. I have shed them all. I want no part of them, want them to be no part of me. Apart from the mind which, for the last time, is taking the trouble to record the events which I shall allow to die as soon as the record is complete, I am only my sex . . .

Trocchi could not have written 'I affirm [my] existence . . . through my sex' had not Genet already said, 'I decided to be what homosexuality made of me.' Helen's 'Sentiments are death. I have shed them all' echoes the show of feelinglessness fatally displayed by Camus's Meursault (who also came to grief in Algeria): 'Mother died today; or maybe yesterday.' This passage also displays for the first time in print a connection – which had troubled Seaver, and which recurs in Trocchi's writing from now on – between sex and death. The

151

friction between them, a sick love of Eros and Thanatos, would provide the spark of his creativity.

Girodias, though, was delighted with the performance of his first lady of lust, and *Helen and Desire* was reprinted within eight months of publication (and many times since, under at least two different titles, another pseudonym – 'Jean Blanche' – and finally under the author's own name in the late 1960s). It was followed by a sequel, *The Carnal Days of Helen Seferis*; then by *School for Sin*, *White Thighs* and *Thongs*, each of them written in less than a fortnight.

*

The books were selling well and the signs for Girodias's continued commercial success were auspicious – which, to a man lately reduced to 'bumhood', was important. Wainhouse went on with translations (three volumes of *The 120 Days of Sodom* were in preparation, after which Wainhouse would continue to work on the five-volume *Story of Juliette*), and Frances Lengel at her lucubrations. But if the business was to flourish, then new books were needed, and new authors to write them.

They would start with a title. For example, *Lust*. Next, someone – either Trocchi, or else Girodias himself – would type up a blurb for the catalogue, which would then be sent to all the addresses on the ever-expanding mailing-list. For *Lust*, the blurb went like this:

> The 'I' in this astounding tale of intrigue and adventure is not [the author] himself. He was given the manuscript by the author's present wife, and, recognizing the wealth of factual detail as a true and uninhibited account of a man's rise to power and fame amongst the decadent and corrupt East European principalities, prepared it for the general public. Here, in an atmosphere of passionate desires and curious liaisons, we have laid bare the naked scramble of beautiful women and powerful men, for position and honour.

So far, so good. The next step was finding someone to write the book. In this case, Girodias lighted on the unlikely but poor (and therefore willing) figure of Christopher Logue, 'pale, ill-fed, ill-garbed', according to the publisher. But: *Lust* by Logue? No, that wouldn't do at all. In order to encourage him in the arduous task that lay ahead, Girodias bestowed on the English poet the splendid *nom de plume*, Count Palmiro Vicarion. Trocchi supplied him with a biography:

> Count Vicarion, born to a heritage of princes but dispossessed by the revolutionary forces of Bela Kun, left Hungary in 1921. . . . During the last war he returned to his own country, first as an agent for the Allies and afterwards as an administrator. At fifty-five he remains an important figure in East-West relations.

Fortified by this surprising history, Logue went off and wrote *Lust*, delivering it in batches of ten or twenty pages at a time, receiving payment from Girodias in instalments. 'He would take your pages from you when you brought them to him in his little office', says Logue, 'and gingerly inspect them for dirty bits. Then he would go into his pocket and draw out this big wad of money which was held together by a clip, and he would peel off what he owed you. . . . He had a certain seedy charm.'

Count Vicarion's *Lust* is a game try, somewhat bedevilled by lyricism and the erotic cliché ('riding her flanks, I took us both into bliss'). The Count was more adept at verse, and his proper contribution to the Olympia list came in the form of two collections, one of limericks, the other of 'bawdy ballads'.

Following the basic principles of diversification in business, Girodias set about the creation of yet another list. This one went under the wittier title (supplied by Wainhouse) of 'The Traveller's Companion'. The books were pocket-sized, with olive-green paper covers, a green border on the title-page, and distinctive black lettering for the name of the book and the author. Once again, they were intended mainly to be bought by Americans, and the design reflected it: it was a matter of exchanging greenbacks for greenbacks.

The need for new authors became even more pressing. John Stephenson, *Merlin*'s business manager ('Not that there was much business to take care of'), was encouraged by Trocchi to try his hand. He wrote a few sample chapters, alighting after due consideration on the choice title *Rape*, and showed them to Girodias, who was still working from the trestle table in the rue Jacob. They were welcomed. Stephenson was immediately commissioned to complete *Rape*, and told by Girodias to 'write as many of these as you like'. Stephenson then went in search of a *nom de plume*. 'It had to sound memorable, and a little bit menacing.' He came up with 'Marcus van Heller', under which name he wrote twelve books, all at high speed.

Yet another *Merlin* associate, John Coleman (author of *The Enormous Bed* by 'Henry Jones' and *The Itch* by 'Stephen Hammer'), recalls getting together at cafés with Girodias and Muffie Wainhouse, wife of Austryn, who began working for Olympia once Girodias could afford to move out of the rue Jacob and into an office of his own. Through the length of the afternoon they would sit, conjuring up titles, blurbs and illustrious pseudonyms, then decide who should be commissioned to write the book. In this way, the Traveller's Companion series came to include *Until She Screams* by Faustino Perez, *Tender Was My Flesh* by Winifred Drake, *The Whip Angels* by XXX, *Darling* by Harriet Daimler, and *Flesh and Bone* by Henry Crannach – all but the first of them, incidentally, written by women.*

*

Girodias's customers seemed to associate the erotic with the exotic, hence Count Palmiro Vicarion's roots in the Hungarian aristocracy, Helen Seferis *née* Smith's adventures in Arabia, and so on. Furthermore, the publisher had many regular clients in the East, particularly India; so, in a somewhat wobbly geographical attempt to match the product to the marketplace, Ataullah Mardaan and Wu Wu Meng were born

*Faustino Perez was Mason Hoffenberg, later to co-author, with Terry Southern, *Candy*; the others, in order, were Denny Bryant, Diane Bataille, Iris Owens and Marilyn Meeske.

(authors of *Kama Houri* and *Houses of Joy*, respectively). One of Girodias's most valuable discoveries was the American artist Norman Rubington. As well as contributing books composed mainly of pictures – notably *Fuzz Against Junk*, which relates 'The Saga of the Narcotics Brigade' in ninety-six pages of collage – Rubington wrote several novels under the name of Akbar del Piombo, including *Who Pushed Paula?*, *Skirts*, and one actually called *The Traveller's Companion*.

Rubington was a large, heavy-drinking, sexually successful man (among his affairs was one lasting several years with the owner of the English Bookshop, Gaïte Frogé) whose Olympian exploits might have borne some relation, at least in spirit, to his day-to-day life. That seems unlikely in the case of another prolific supplier of fiction to the Traveller's Companion series. This was a small Englishman with a trim moustache who appeared in Girodias's office in rue Jacob one day without an appointment. Girodias described him as 'très *proper*, très *dapper*', in appearance exactly the type of English prude he was seeking (a) to scandalize, or (b) to make a subscriber to the Olympia list.

The man's name was Robert Desmond and he worked in a bank in Antwerp, where he lived with his 'plain-looking Belgian wife'. He had already written several novels and wondered if Olympia might wish to publish them. Girodias took the stuff reluctantly, but as soon as he read it he knew it was tailor-made for Traveller's Companion. At their next meeting, he asked Robert Desmond what name he would like his books to appear under. Something with the snap of 'Greta X', perhaps? Or the seductive sibilance of 'Carmencita de las Lunas'? Why, the man replied, puzzled, Robert Desmond, of course. And so, *An Adult's Story*, *The Libertine*, *Heaven, Hell and the Whore*, and five other pornographic novels were published under the bank clerk's real name.

Yet another author was 'Angela Pearson', who wrote *The Whipping Club* ('An account of some of the Activities of a Number of lovely Women who have Men in their power'), *The*

Whipping Post and *Whips Incorporated*. Angela, Girodias confided many years later, was 'a big strapping Englishman teaching in some private school in Athens'. Unlike Robert Desmond, he was 'very anxious' not to let his real name be revealed.

And so it went on. 'It was great fun,' said Girodias. If the Atlantic Library and the Traveller's Companion series brought him notoriety as well as money, he welcomed it. He was wholeheartedly committed to his task, and took a special pleasure in outraging the authoritarian powers of his father's homeland. 'The Anglo-Saxon world was being attacked, invaded, infiltrated, outflanked, and conquered by this erotic armada,' he wrote. 'The Dickensian schoolmasters of England were convulsed with helpless rage, the judges' hair was standing on end beneath their wigs . . .'

Dealers and private customers would cross the Channel from England to Paris just to stock up on Olympia titles, stuffing as many books into their pockets and suitcases as they dared, risking the ignominy of being unmasked and arrested as pornographers at British customs.

Girodias's pioneering mission spawned mercenary initiatives, much to his annoyance. The Olympia titles began to fetch high black-market prices, pirate editions of some of them appeared, and there was even a circulating library operated by a Soho bookseller, from which the customer could borrow *The Chariot of Flesh* or *The 120 Days of Sodom*, leaving behind a fee and a large deposit, the latter to be reclaimed upon return of the book. There must have been many a frustrated customer who, on hearing that a new consignment of the olive-green paperbacks had arrived in London, skulked down to Soho and paid his money, only to find that he had been lent *Molloy*. Or, perhaps worse, that he had entrusted his deposit to the bookseller for the privilege of procuring page after page of euphuistic description of encounters between French transvestites and homosexuals in *Our Lady of the Flowers*.

While this illicit enterprise infuriated Girodias, it could be considered a case of the biter bit. Girodias was carefully informal about paperwork when it came to commissioning the novels. 'The authors being anonymous, I never had contracts for the books I published,' he explained, 'except the ones I considered legit or defensible.' Even those contracts, however, consisted of little more than a page of written agreement, which could seem very flimsy indeed if it came to be tested by law.

Sometimes the authors found their own way of bending the rules. This was so in the case of *Business as Usual* by 'Solomon Peters', a novel included in the Ophelia list. No sooner had Girodias had it printed than 'Peters' sold the book to another publisher on rue Seguier, who issued a rival edition. Never to be outdone, Girodias responded by rewriting the first page of the text and issuing the book – yet again – as *Springtime in Paris* by 'Theobald Lovelace'.

With exceptions, commissioned Olympia fiction was created according to a formula consisting of an exotic locale, an unabatingly hot-blooded relationship between the sexes, a hint of misogyny, descending sometimes into sadism, but redeemed always, at the last, with riots of gasping, writhing and moaning, leading, almost unfailingly, to bliss, utter joy, or, in the case of Helen, the bringing of 'the sacred fire into the most Stygian, the most crepuscular part of me'.

A few samples, chosen more or less at random, indicate the kind of activity taking place mainly on the plains of Olympia:

Ann waited in silence. Yakub smiled seeing her suddenly so docile. 'I suppose you have been wondering why I have been avoiding you recently,' he continued in his gentle voice. 'I shall tell you the truth. You repulse me. I have no stomach for women who are forward, immodest and shameless. You do not yet understand what womanhood is, my child.' Taking her hand gently he guided her to the bed. 'Sit down and do not be afraid, men are what women make them. I am not a beast, I am a simple man of my people. To us the most attractive thing about a woman is her modesty and virtue. I am more excited by a trembling virgin or a virtuous woman who succumbs to me through complete submission than by any bitch who points her breasts indiscriminately at

157

any man! . . . Stand up and undo your pyjamas.'

Ann hesitated. They were seated not far from the little house and she was afraid that one of the villagers might pass by. Then slowly she undid the white cord and let the heavy trousers fall to the ground. . . . He got up from the bed and turning the blonde girl round he made her bend over.

'Open your legs.'

She obeyed. Without any further ceremony he quietly inserted his throbbing organ into the pocket of her womb. Ann gasped. It had been weeks now since she had had a man . . . .

Ataullah Mardaan, *Kama Houri*

They grunted in concentration . . . . 'Keep going,' she gasped, 'keep in me, stay in me, roll in me, that's right, don't stop, don't get lazy, think of other things, think of your mother Macdonald, think of New Year's in Glasgow darling, think of all the Americans you've fucked, yes,' she crooned, 'don't think of me, just fuck Macdonald, fuck me faster darling,' she urged him, 'such a lovely little Scots fucker you are, yes my angel,' she panted, 'don't stop Macdonald, don't stop, don't stop,' and he could feel her cunt throbbing surrender . . . Martha was still screaming, 'Don't stop.'

'Enough darling,' said Macdonald, 'the neighbours will think I'm beating you.'

Harriet Daimler, *Woman*

His penis was sticking out like a pike. He was afraid she might run from the room at the sight of its size, but instead she fixed her fascinated gaze on it as if hypnotized.

'Oh papa I'm frightened – it's so much bigger than Cesare's,' she whispered.

Marcus van Heller, *The House of Borgia*

In real life, 'Ataullah Mardaan', according to Girodias, was 'a beautiful Pakistani girl married to a Dutch photographer', both of whose names he claimed to have forgotten. 'Harriet Daimler' was Iris Owens; the Macdonald in her story is likely to be loosely based on Trocchi, with whom she had an affair. 'Marcus van Heller' is, of course, the prolific John

Stephenson, of *Merlin*.

As the tower of books rose ever higher, the prospect of legal action being taken against the publisher increased. Girodias was unrepentant; righteous, even. 'I insist that no little boys were ever corrupted by bad books of mine . . . ; nobody seems to have died of shock, no reader was ever reported killed by a four-letter word.'

*

He was probably correct – in so far as the danger of corrupting the reader is concerned. But what about the pseudonymous author? Writing, it is said, cannot conceal. The libertine, given licence to express his private fantasies, may inadvertently expose a darker side of his nature than he, or she, knew existed. This is surely true in the case of *Thongs*, by 'Carmencita de las Lunas' – yet another disguise for Alexander Trocchi.

Thongs appeared in the Traveller's Companion list in the spring of 1956. It contained a prefatory note which explained that the manuscript had been edited by 'F.L.' (Frances Lengel, of course), who surprisingly revealed that she was in Madrid as far back as 1925. Browsing in dusty bookshops there, she chanced upon the 'personal notebook of Gertrude Gault, alias Carmencita de las Lunas'. The notebook contained the information that Gertrude Gault hailed from Scotland in the early years of the century. She lived in the notorious Gorbals district, where rival gangs fought for supremacy. Gertrude's father was 'the human wolf known to all Glasgow as the Razor King'.

Thongs was Trocchi's fifth db, and by now he was set to have some fun. However, his idea of fun turns out to be rather unpleasant. The first half of the novel is set in the Gorbals, where Gertrude is initiated by her father into a world of beatings and everyday domestic cruelty. This brutal experience is gradually transformed inside her, until she begins to live in the perverse realm in which pain is pleasure. While Gertrude submits willingly to sodomy and many varieties of sadism, she makes her lovers understand that 'my cunt was a shrine to be worshipped but never penetrated'.

She is introduced by her father's mistress (also a masochist) to a house in Glasgow devoted to sado-masochistic delight, and later is elected High Priestess of a secret order of Pain based in Madrid. There we join her among the Holy Pain Fathers, the Pain Cardinals, and everywhere and always lashings of ritualized whipping.

By this time, Gertrude has become Carmencita. Her lover is Miguel. His ultimate duty – which she begs him to perform manfully – is to crucify her. He does not shirk from the task, and, after being 'whipped mercilessly with fine rods', she dies on the cross, with a metal plate on a silver chain tied round her belly, on which are inscribed the words 'Carmencita de las Lunas *por amor*'. The last line of the book is: 'Miguel, my love, be my executioner.'

An erotic lark, or an unwelcome report from the murk of a troubled sexuality? The evidence favours the latter, as *Thongs* starts to expose an unwholesome liking on the part of the author for violence laced with sex:

> My father would mark her, a small cross cut with a razor on the soft inner surface of her left thigh; his cattle. . . . Everyone knew about the mark. Fourteen women in the Gorbals had been cut already. Normally, my father kept the woman for about two months afterwards. Then they were free to go. The men of the Gorbals fought each other to marry a marked woman.

There is yet another way of gauging corruption, which Girodias appears to have overlooked. Since leaving Glasgow, Trocchi had been toiling on his 'real' novel, *Young Adam*. That he treated it very seriously indeed is proved by an entry he made in his diary on February 9, 1954:

> I sat down to rewrite *YA*, did five pages of the revision; what Gid nor anyone else will understand is that *YA* is merely a 'neutraler', neither good nor bad, against which society comes: thus one sees

society's categories break against neutral existence, crush it perhaps, but with society coming off worst (for its exposed absolutes) through criticism.

Trocchi showed *Young Adam* to 'Gid' (Girodias's nickname), who gave him some good news and some bad news about it. The good news was that he was willing to publish the book in the Atlantic Library; the bad news was that, before that could happen, Trocchi would be required to insert some 'dirty bits' into the text. With an extravagant public display of conscionable reluctance, the author complied.

That really is corruption.

II

Girodias continued to live in the shadow of his father. As a publisher of randy titles he had outstripped him (Kahane's *Sleeveless Errand* could never compete with Olympia's *Ordeal of the Rod*, for instance), but he was still in search of the intellectual repute which his father eventually achieved by publishing Miller, Joyce, Durrell and others. Olympia had Beckett, but Beckett was really a Collection Merlin author, and anyway the public was in no hurry to buy his books. *Helen and Desire* reprinted within a few months of publication; *Watt* took five years.

Girodias continued to depend for a degree of respectability on classic authors – Restif de la Bretonne was added to the list in 1955, with *Pleasures and Follies of a Good-natured Libertine*, translated by Casavini – and with bestsellers originally published by his father. Miller had stood by Girodias, in spite of disagreements over money and contracts (or the absence of money and contracts). In the spring of 1954, the opportunity arose to try his hand with another who had served Kahane and Obelisk well: the Irish journalist, traveller, playboy and all-round knave, Frank Harris.

Harris had had his autobiography, *My Life and Loves*, printed privately in the 1920s – an arduous, exhausting and scarcely profitable business. In 1931, he managed to sell the rights to Kahane, and the four volumes of round-the-world erotic adventures, interspersed with lofty observations on everything, had been good sellers ever since. (Harris died the same year.) Girodias had kept the books in print when reviving Obelisk after the War, but since losing the press in the Hachette takeover of 1950, he had forfeited the right to publish Harris, otherwise he would certainly have introduced the Irishman's fanciful peregrinations on to one of the Olympia lists. Nowadays, it was Hachette that was entitled to enjoy the profits of what had been originally an audacious Kahane enterprise.

Girodias constantly fulminated over the treachery of his enemies. But one day, perhaps at the height of a tantrum, he recalled that his father's contract with Harris made mention of a fifth volume of memoirs, which had never been produced. From time to time, rumours passed through publishers' offices that a manuscript existed. If it did, Madame Nellie Harris, the widow, would surely be willing to sell it; assuming that to be the case, who better to entrust it to than the son of her late husband's fearless patron?

So at any rate Girodias reasoned, as he set off one day by train for Nice, where he had heard Mme Harris lived, hoping first to track her down and then to persuade her to part with the concluding volume of *My Life and Loves* for a very reasonable sum.

His journey seemed to be in vain, however, for he could not even locate Nellie Harris, never mind discover if she possessed the manuscript. Back in Paris, though, he received a letter written in a trembling hand, which said that Mme Harris had been informed of his search; the missive directed him to the office of one 'Maître Adolph', who represented the widow's affairs in Paris. Maître Adolph lived in the seventeenth arrondissement,

in a crepuscular apartment in the frugal fashion typical of the French bourgeoisie of old. I crashed into several chairs on the way

162

15. Maurice Girodias

16. Jacket illustration for an early Obelisk Press edition of *Tropic of Cancer*, drawn by the young Girodias

17. From the first production of *En Attendant Godot* at the Théâtre de Babylone in 1953, showing (from left) Pierre Latour as Estragon, Jean Martin as Lucky, Lucien Raimbourg as Vladimir, and Roger Blin as Pozzo

TROPIC OF CANCER

by
HENRY MILLER

NOT TO BE IMPORTED INTO GREAT BRITAIN OR U.S.A

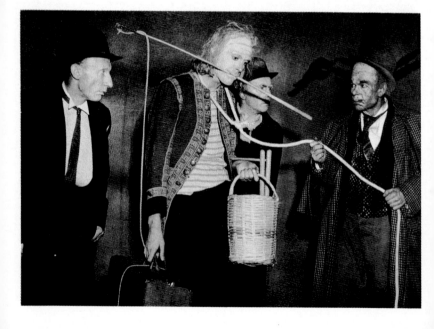

18. Robert Pinget, Samuel Beckett and Claude Simon, outside the
rue Bernard Palissy office of Les Editions de Minuit, mid-1950s

19. Chester Himes with Jean Giono, in the offices of Gallimard, 1958

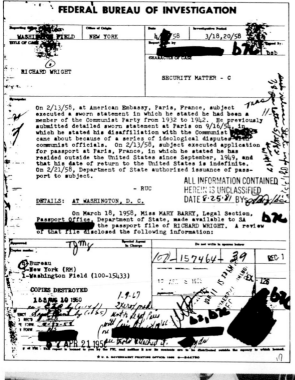

FEDERAL BUREAU OF INVESTIGATION

Reporting Office	Office of Origin	Date	Investigative Period
WASHINGTON FIELD	NEW YORK	4/ /58	3/18,20/58

TITLE OF CASE

RICHARD WRIGHT

CHARACTER OF CASE

SECURITY MATTER - C

On 2/13/58, at American Embassy, Paris, France, subject executed a sworn statement in which he stated he had been a member of the Communist Party from 1932 to 1942. He previously submitted detailed sworn statement at Paris on 9/16/54, in which he stated his disaffiliation with the Communist came about because of a series of ideological disputes with communist officials. On 2/13/58, subject executed application for passport at Paris, France, in which he stated he has resided outside the United States since September, 1949, and that his date of return to the United States is indefinite. On 2/21/58, Department of State authorized issuance of passport to subject.

- RUC

ALL INFORMATION CONTAINED
HEREIN IS UNCLASSIFIED
DATE 8·25·81 BY

DETAILS: AT WASHINGTON, D. C.

On March 18, 1958, Miss MARY BARRY, Legal Section, Passport Office, Department of State, made available to SA
the passport file of RICHARD WRIGHT. A review of that file disclosed the following information:

Approved ____

Copies made:
4-Bureau
3-New York (RM)
1-Washington Field (100-15433)

102- 157464- 39   REC 1
                       EX-126

COPIES DESTROYED

188 AUG 10 1960   1-9-67

57 APR 21 1958

Weight-height-age table for girls of school age

Height, inches	average weight for height in pounds	12	13	14	17 Lolita
50	53	62			
51	61	65			
52	64	67			
53	68	69	71		
54	71	71	73		
55	75	75	77	78	
56	78	79	81	83	
57	94	82	84	88	
58	89	86	88	93	
59	95	(90)	92	96	104
60	101	95	97	101	109
61	108	100	101	103	115
62	114	105	106	109	117
63	118	110	110	112	119

average gain in height

	12	13	14	17
short	54	57	59	61
med.	58	60	62	64
tall	62	64	66	67

average height
av. annual gain in pounds

22. Index cards containing preparatory jottings for *Lolita*

ready for instant service without danger of accidental discharge.

A lightweight arm, compact in design, smooth and flat, powerful and accurate.

This model is particularly well adapted for use in the home and car, as well as on the person [!?]. A significant point in its construction is the solid breech.

Rearsight   frontsight   smokeless powder

magazine spring

magazine with cartridge

8 cm. | push the magazine well home into the butt. press home until you hear or feel the magazine catch engage.

To force a spring catch in the rear of the trigger on the left of the pistol, press it — and withdraw the magazine.

23. Nabokov
in Paris, 1959

24. Dominique Aury,
secretive author of
The Story of O

25. Jean Paulhan,
editor of the *Nouvelle
Revue Française*
and *O*'s sponsor

26. Allen Ginsberg (foreground) with Patrick Shelley, in the Beat Hotel, 1958

27. Ginsberg (right) with Peter Orlovsky, 1958

28. Maurice Girodias and William Burroughs at the time of the publication of *Naked Lunch*, 1959

29. Richard Gibson on his wedding day in Paris. William Gardner Smith is in the background

to his office, as there was strictly no light, electric or otherwise in the hall; then he prudently guided me to a chair and went to sit behind his desk. Gradually my eyes became used to the deep night, and I began to perceive his frail contours.

Girodias heard what he had hoped to hear; yes, indeed, there was a fifth volume of Harris memoirs; yes, it was in Maître Adolph's possession – here, in fact, in the drawer of the very desk at which he sat.

Maître Adolph declined Girodias's invitation to produce the manuscript. Not just yet. Mme Harris was aware of his interest, and Maître Adolph hoped that she might be persuaded to part with the rights. There was no saying; but he assured Girodias that he would use all his influence. 'Up to now,' he said, 'she has refused even to envisage letting it be published.' Too scandalous, was Girodias's gleeful first thought. 'But', Maître Adolph continued, 'she is now a very old lady. We would require a rather substantial advance from you, you must realize that.'

His logic was that Olympia, being a small, independent house, would need to pay more than would be expected from a larger publisher (such as his deadly enemy, Hachette), simply in order to make Mme Harris's investment secure. He invited Girodias to make a 'realistic' offer. The sum of 400,000 francs was mentioned (Beckett, remember, was paid 50,000 francs as an advance for *Watt*). The old man was not impressed, but he promised to put it to Mme Harris, and the meeting ended.

When they came together again, Girodias was told, as expected, that his offer had been rejected. Indeed, Maître Adolph relayed the news that another publishing house, having been invited to bid for the rights, had offered 600,000. Girodias enquired as to who this other house might be. It was Hachette, of course! Far from being pleased with the auction he appeared to be setting in train, Maître Adolph expressed a sense of being retrospectively insulted by Girodias's approaches:

'So, I regret to say that the book will go to them. . . . Unless of course you can make a better offer. Because if such an illustrious publishing house as Hachette offers 50 per cent more than you, what should I conclude? Firstly, no doubt, that you were trying to take advantage of Mme Harris's good will . . .'

Infected with auction fever, Girodias cavalierly offered one million francs (about $2,000). He still had not seen the manuscript, and he had no idea where he was likely to find such a large sum of money; but by now the most important thing seemed to be to prevent Hachette getting their hands on it. Maître Adolph indicated his satisfaction with this renewed offer, and at a third interview in the dark room, told Girodias that the widow had accepted it and that the missing volume of Frank Harris memoirs was his – on condition that an added 5 per cent commission be paid to Adolph himself for having 'so aptly defended your cause to Mme Harris'. He opened a drawer,

and fished out a slim package which he handed to me: 'That is the manuscript,' he asserted.

Stifling the beginning of a hysterical laugh, I took the so-called manuscript and sprang out of the room and into the healthy youthful street, peopled with vigorous cats and dogs. The manuscript was made up of a few sheafs of typed pages, yellowed by time.

In his hands he held about a hundred pages of assorted journalism, bound together with a blue ribbon, which Harris may or may not have intended to use eventually as the foundation for a book. In their actual state, they bore little resemblance to one. They were mostly lacking in the erotic content which principally interested Girodias, who reckoned that maybe fifty pages of the stuff might be publishable. As he walked away from Maître Adolph's cobwebbed, gloomy office, he had to resist an urge to throw the whole lot into the bin.

Instead of doing that, he crossed the river and went to the rue du Sabot, where he found Trocchi, to whom he gave the miserable sheaf, suggesting to him that he do whatever he could with it. Within two weeks, a finger of Harris had been augmented by two fingers of Trocchi, and *My Life and Loves: Fifth Volume* by Frank Harris was at the Imprimerie Richard, being prepared for publication in the Atlantic Library. It appeared in June 1954.

For the Frenchman, it was the thrill of receiving another manuscript 'tingling with sex and fun', and the vindication of his investment. 'I felt that Frank Harris himself would have been proud of it,' he enthused. 'Even the odd 20 per cent of real Harris derived from Maître Adolph's time-stained papers appeared rejuvenated and revitalized in that new context.'*

For the Scotsman, it was the latest role in the drama of playing at being Alexander Trocchi: editor, novelist, translator, poet, publisher, pornographer, *faussaire*; he had been James Fidler, Oscar Mole, Frances Lengel, and now Frank Harris.

Trocchi was less inclined to celebrate his role in the forgery than Girodias was – he called it a send-up, a 'piss-take' – but it was one of the best literary confidence tricks of the time, and one of the best-kept secrets. The 'Fifth Volume' went through successive editions in the years that followed its original publication, but few people suspected it of being a fake. When the popular book *Pornography and the Law* appeared towards the end of the decade, quotations in the section dealing with Frank Harris were taken mainly from the fifth volume, and from that part written by Trocchi.

It is tricky work to separate the hands of the two authors of this unusual collaboration, but the fiercer sex scenes bear the

---

*A definitive edition of Harris's work was published by Grove Press, New York, in 1963: *My Life and Loves, Complete and unexpurgated; five volumes in one*, edited by John Gallagher. Comparison of the Trocchi and the apparently authentic Harris versions suggests that Harris's contribution to Trocchi's apocrypha was more than the '20 per cent' alleged by Girodias. In the introduction, Gallagher writes: 'The fifth volume, as it was published in Paris in 1958 [*sic*], is apparently not authentic, the chapters and portions of chapters having been rearranged and including materials of doubtful origin. The fifth volume, as it appears here, has been checked against Harris's final typescript which is in the possession of the Humanities Research Center of the University of Texas.' It is likely that the 'fifth volume' purchased by Girodias, and that edited by Gallagher, are separate entities, even if identical copies.

stamp of Trocchi, as well as some of the philosophizing. Here we can almost hear him being egged on by his publisher:

> Censorship is dangerous; in the hands of a vicious spirit it can be used to crush the greatest truth. The greatest spirits have always known that truth is its own best defence and that in the end it will always prevail against error. No one denies that bad and vicious books exist. But let us never forget that their existence is the guarantee of the existence of good books . . . .

This was virtually identical to the argument used by Girodias to justify his own enterprise whenever its morality was called into question: the toleration of mountains of trash is the price we must pay for unearthing the occasional treasure.

III

> Well, here at least is the cage, and here is
> this young woman in the cage. All we have
> to do now is listen to her.
> She says: 'You shouldn't be surprised . . .'
>
> Jean Paulhan, 'Happiness in Slavery'

The handwritten manuscript of *Histoire d'O*, in its original French, arrived on Girodias's desk early in 1954, by way of Jean-Jacques Pauvert, lately enjoying the approval of the Left Bank intelligentsia for his French edition of the works of the Marquis de Sade. The two 'clandestine' publishers were by then sharing offices in a building in rue de Nesle, a tiny street in St-Germain near the Seine. Pauvert had received the book from Jean Paulhan, editor of the *Nouvelle Revue Française* and a leading figure in France's literary establishment. Paulhan explained that he had first hoped to have the book published by Gallimard, with which house he was officially connected, but after much indecision, Gallimard reckoned it constituted too great a risk. Paulhan therefore steered *Histoire d'O* in the direction of the less august, more defiant firm of Pauvert.

166

Jean Paulhan indicated that, should Pauvert accept the manuscript for publication, then he, Paulhan, would be willing to add something by way of an introduction or afterword. Such an essay by the *éminence grise* of the *NRF* could make a considerable difference to the book being taken seriously as a work of literature, and not merely of pornography. Paulhan felt that *Histoire d'O* was an important work – so important that it would be considered 'dangerous' – but that, from beginning to end, it was managed 'like some brilliant feat'. It explored, with a literary sensibility unique in erotic writing, the submissive element in female sexuality, and, no less crucial to an understanding of the sexual nature involved, the dialectic whereby 'the slave . . . is destined to become the master'. The story of O, Paulhan noted in the introductory essay which he did write for the published edition, was likely to strike the reader as 'more of a letter' than a secret diary. In other words, there was nothing shameful about it; it was written to be shared.

Pauvert decided to risk legal action and take the book on; and, having read it overnight, Girodias – his *frère d'armes* – agreed to publish an English version. He employed two members of the *Merlin* crowd, Baird and Denny Bryant, to do a quick translation, and brought out *The Story of O* under the Olympia Press imprint in the summer of 1954, simultaneously with the French edition. The title-page of the novel bore a pseudonym: Pauline Réage. This was necessary, Paulhan explained to the publishers, for he had heard that the author was a respectable and highly respected person of letters; scandal, and probably prosecution, would follow his or her exposure. He himself suspected that 'Pauline Réage' was a woman, but he could not say for certain, for he claimed he did not know.

The Story of O can be read at one level as a thoroughly nasty tale of sexual brutality. Many people have read and do read it this way. Erotica? this reader says; why not? But when it comes to the likes of this, no thank you . . .

'O, I'm going to put a gag in your mouth, for I'd like to whip you until you bleed. Will you allow me to?'

'I am yours,' said O. She was standing in the centre of the room, and her upraised arms, which a pair of Roissy bracelets on her wrists held aloft by means of a chain attached to a ring in the ceiling where there had once been a chandelier, made her breasts jut forward. . . . He let go of her and struck . . . .

The beating, with a riding crop, is administered by O's master and current lover, Sir Stephen, to whom her former lover, René – who predates her life as a slave – has 'given' her. That night, René finds O alone in her Paris flat:

René stared for a very long time at that slender body upon which purple welts ran like ropes across shoulders, back, buttocks, belly and breasts, two welts sometimes intersecting. Here and there a drop of blood oozed through the skin. 'Ah, I love you,' he murmured . . . .

The welts on O's body took almost a month to go away . . . .

The novel is set in Paris in the present day, the early 1950s. O is a thoroughly modern woman, who works as a fashion photographer. She is described as having short hair, with a boyish appearance. She has her own flat, a liking, as her job would suggest, for good clothes, and she takes her holidays on the Côte d'Azur.

The story opens with O being driven in a car, together with René, to the château at Roissy, a destination of which she is unaware until they arrive. Once there, she is taken out of René's possession – with his full consent, of course – and out of her own. She is bathed by two female courtiers, then, stage by stage, dressed in a special revealing costume, bound in leather bracelets, blindfolded, and led into a room for inspection by a group of men (which includes René), all of whom use her in different ways. In the succeeding weeks, during which she remains a captive at the château, she is flogged with a variety of whips, including a riding crop, a leather whip consisting of 'six lashes knotted at the end', and a third whip of thin stiff cords which have been soaked in water, 'which marked almost upon contact' – all described in careful detail by Pauline Réage. First of all by René, and later by Sir Stephen, O is offered to other men, for fellatio, sodomy, and prolonged beatings. *The Story of O* does not merely glorify prostitution; it sanctifies it:

> All the mouths that sounded her mouth, all the hands that grasped her breasts and belly, all the sexes that had been sunk into her and which had so abundantly demonstrated her prostitution, had simultaneously demonstrated that she was worthy of prostitution and had in some sort hallowed her.

The book also depicts, in an approving manner, voyeurism, coercion and the apprenticing of a fifteen-year-old girl into the same scheme as O, who is by now branded with hot irons and permanently shackled with elaborate chains attached to her labia. It is basically the tale of a woman's enslavement, her endurance of, and then her profound pleasure in, her pain and her prostitution, ending with her death.

Or perhaps her death – for these are two endings to *The Story of O*. One of them has O in a forest, costumed as an owl, surrounded by admiring onlookers, being possessed in the open air by Sir Stephen and another man, 'now the one, now the other' ('la possedèrent, tour à tour'). But an eerie postscript states: 'In a final chapter, which has been suppressed, O returned to Roissy, where Sir Stephen abandoned her.' It further states:

> There is another ending to the story of O. Seeing herself about to be left by Sir Stephen, she preferred to die. To which he gave his consent.*

*The first part of the postscript is unaccountably missing from the established second Olympia edition of the novel, which was translated (anonymously) by Wainhouse and published in 1957 (originally as *The Wisdom of the Lash*), supplanting the earlier translation by the Bryants. The 'suppressed' chapter was published in French as *Retour à Roissy* in 1969, and two years later in English as *Return to the Château*. In 1965, Grove Press published yet another translation of *Histoire d'O*, by 'Sabine d'Estrée'.

It might seem by now that the description of *The Story of O* as 'a thoroughly nasty tale' is fully deserved. Yet the book has retained a classic status in the library of erotica, in whose vaults most other works rapidly wither. Nothing else is quite as extreme as this, in depicting the affiance between sex and submission, leading to marriage in death. O's will is to lose her will, to drown it in that of her sexual master, a mission to which she applies herself with an ultimate seriousness of purpose. *O* is undeniably a pornographic work – its subject, after all, is prostitution – and yet it has a compelling quality lacking in the majority of pornographic books, a quality in this case not deriving solely from its extreme depiction of sadomasochistic sex. Once begun, it seems imperative to continue, to see how deep O, liberated from her own will, must sink before she can be rescued. And who, or what, will rescue her? It is as if the book contained an account of a treacherous journey – an ordeal we might imagine for ourselves but dare not undertake.

Many writers have treated *O* to high praise. Susan Sontag based a famous essay, 'The Pornographic Imagination', on a study of it. Graham Greene called it 'A pornographic book . . . without a trace of obscenity'. J. G. Ballard referred to it as 'a deeply moral homily'. The 'deeply moral' line is quite a common one in consideration of books branded obscene (the same argument has been used in defence of works as different in character as *The Rainbow* and *Last Exit to Brooklyn*). Jean Paulhan extended this defence beyond the usual rhetorical shorthand in the introduction he wrote for the book's original publication, 'Happiness in Slavery' ('Du Bonheur dans l'esclavage'). Paulhan called *O* a 'dangerous book', but he meant dangerous only in the sense that Pauline Réage breached defences erected to protect the civilized man and woman – and hence the society they compose – from themselves. This is the justification for calling *O* a 'pure' work, for it charts, with clear vision, a passage of pure will. 'If there is any one word that comes to my mind when I think of *The*

Story of O, 'Paulhan wrote, 'It is *decency* [*décence*]. . . . In *O*, there also blows some indefinable, always pure and violent spirit, endless and unadulterated. It is a decisive spirit which nothing disturbs, whether it be moans or horrors, ecstasy or nausea.'

The Marquis de Sade hovers above the passageways of the château at Roissy, where 'doors succeeded doors' and much emphasis is placed on locks and keys, and on costumes: masked men dressed in long purple robes and tights which cover everything except the penis; beautiful chambermaids, past survivors of the voyage on which O is about to embark, dressed in long light skirts, and tight bodices with lace frills. There is also something about the atmosphere of the story which recalls nineteenth-century Gothic fiction, a genre which itself has connections with morbid desire. It excavates a world of terror which is known but not spoken of, and which, once explored, is found to be less terrifying than had been feared, and to contain the answers to certain mysteries, which end by advancing self-knowledge. The true heroine of the book is not O herself but her sexual impulse. The adventure of the story derives from their encounters, one with the other, and it is a very Gothic adventure: she, cool and civilized, the model of decorum; her sex, wild and threatening, but full of promise. There is an element of the fairy tale about the story: the beautiful heroine spirited off to the castle in the forest . . . our fears for her well-being . . . the improbable creatures she encounters there ('the man was masked in a black hood completed by a section of gauze hiding his eyes'), and her ultimate flight to safety. Like a fairy tale, *The Story of O* has a dreamlike surface unreality, which invites us to probe for the true reality underneath which will be disclosed at the moment of the heroine's deliverance. But in this resolutely modern, post-Freudian fairy tale, the happy ending is death.

In an autobiographical essay, 'A Girl in Love', one of only two public revelations made by 'Pauline Réage', she explained that the book began life as a sort of bedtime story for a lover: 'One day a girl in love said to the man she loved: "I could also

171

write the kind of stories you like . . .".' The girl was writing 'the way you speak in the dark to the person you love, when you've held back the words of love too long and they flow at last'. For the author of these dangerous pages, the act of showing them to her lover was a risk commensurate with the risks undertaken by O and René, a full exposure of the nerves of desire. What if her lover had rejected her fantasy in disgust? It was the kind of act dependent on the trust which is itself dependent on love. That is what Greene and the others mean when they refer to the book's lack of obscenity; it deals with the supplication of a devotional spirit, and its subject, finally, is not pain or prostitution but love. Transposed into different terms, but with no shift of emphasis or idiom, *The Story of O* might have been the memoir of a nun:

> She became captivated . . . far down within her heart's and body's secret recesses feeling tied by bonds either subtler, more invisible than the finest hair . . . she was no longer free? Ah! Thank God, no, she was no longer free. But she was buoyant, a cloud-dwelling goddess, a swift-swimming fish of the deeps, but deep-dwelling, forever doomed to happiness.

*

How do we know that the writer of *The Story of O* was a woman, and not a man conjuring up a fantasy of a woman enslaved and in pain? 'Woman you may be . . .,' wrote Paulhan in his integral essay. 'But what kind of woman, and who are you?' He affirmed his total ignorance of the identity of the author – 'I don't even know who you are' – but he made a game attempt to establish the gender:

> Upon the same day that René abandons her to further torments, O keeps her wits about her sufficiently to be able to observe that her lover's slippers have got scuffed and frayed, that a new pair must be bought for him . . . a man would never have fancied such a thing.

There is something in the meticulous attention given in the text to clothes generally – their cut, fabrics, the suitability of

172

accessories, and so on – that supports this suggestion. It gained confirmation in 1969, when Jean-Jacques Pauvert published the 'suppressed' chapter referred to in the postscript, a further, brief instalment of O's adventures, entitled *Return to the Château: Story of O, Part II (Retour à Roissy)*. It was prefaced by 'A Girl in Love', the essay which describes the love-affair which was the occasion for the original novel. Unless some elaborate trick was being played, the author of this autobiographical piece of writing was definitely a woman.

An even better source exists than that essay. In 1975, a book appeared in Paris called *O m'a dit* (later translated into English as *Confessions of O*), which consisted of a long interview between Réage and the French writer Régine Deforges. This established the author of the book once and for all as a woman, though it still did not reveal her name.

A description was given of Pauline Réage:

> She is there; seated; silent. How am I going to bring myself to talk to her about eroticism, sadism, about *The Story of O*? A navy-blue suit, flat heels, no make-up . . . .

In her own account of herself, she confessed to being attached to uniform, conformity, secret societies, and clandestineness in general – correctness, in short. Yet Pauline Réage denied that O's life was a reflection of her own, except possibly as 'the deformed and inverted image'. She admitted to sado-masochistic imaginings – 'my head has been full of them for a long time' – but not to the actual experience. Although she revealed that her fantasies, 'the wildest love . . . the most frightful surrender . . . childish images of whips and chains', were 'beneficent and protected me mysteriously', she claimed to have had at no time the desire to translate them into reality. At only one point did Pauline Réage admit to a deep bond between her own desires and those of her heroine. She liked dangerous situations, she said, particularly of the physical sort. Régine Deforges moved from there to the love-affair which had originally generated the book: what would have been her reaction to demands similar to those made of O? 'What would have happened if, at each stage, more had been demanded of you? Till the next step would have been death itself, as in the case of O?' The lady in the navy-blue suit and flat heels replied, 'Isn't that the supreme temptation?'

＊

The love-affair between Pauline Réage and the man for whom she wrote her bedtime story was an illicit one. Their physical love apart, they could share little, except in the imaginary territory which unfolds in books. 'Books were their only complete freedom,' she wrote in 'A Girl in Love',

> their common country. Together they dwelt in the books they loved as others in their family home; in books they had their compatriots and their brothers; poets had written for them, the letters of lovers from times past came down to them through the obscurity of ancient languages, of modes and mores long since come and gone.

For this author, a book is worthy of the name only if it discloses a secret; the adventure of writing a book (and reading it aloud) is that the secret it contains is discovered at the moment of its being set down, or told:

> Books are full of summonses. Of these, some are constantly heard, others once only. But the fact that there is no end to them, that they outlast forests, even stones, is convincing proof: all our secrets lie there.

Who was this demure woman in a strict suit and sensible shoes, who mixes a quasi-mystical tone with the trappings of Sadean ordeal and the playthings of literary modernism – as well as having alternative endings, *The Story of O* has two beginnings – who wrote one of the most scandalous 'secret' books of the century?

The question was asked the moment *The Story of O* was published. There was a rumour that Paulhan himself had written it (Paulhan: Pauline). He denied this flatly. He had stated in his introduction that he had no idea of the author's true identity – 'I don't even know who you are'.

He was not the author, but he did know who she was. A year after the book was published, the vice squad, the Brigade Mondaine, had a hearing to decide whether or not to take legal action against the book, and its author. Paulhan was called on to make a deposition, in which he denied being Pauline Réage, but revealed that he was well acquainted with the person who was:

> About three years ago, Mme Pauline Réage paid me a visit in my office at the *Nouvelle Revue Française*, a literary monthly of which I am the editor, and submitted to me a thick manuscript entitled *The Story of O*. . . . I had the impression that I had in my hands a work that was very important both in its content and its style, a work that derived much more from the mystical than from the erotic and that might well be for our time what *Letters to a Portuguese Nun* or *Les Liaisons dangereuses* were for theirs. And that is precisely what I told Mme Réage when she came back to see me after I had read the manuscript. . . .
>
> Since Mme Réage came from an academic background, which she was afraid of shocking or offending, she has till now refused to reveal her real name. This was her first novel.

Paulhan added: 'I do see her fairly regularly'; nevertheless, he declined to divulge the identity of the author to the vice squad.

The two publishers, Pauvert and Girodias, felt constrained by a similar vow of silence. Both told the police that although they knew who the author was, they could not be persuaded to tell. Girodias mischievously tried to complicate things at first by claiming that he did not know who wrote the book, only that he knew who Pauvert believed wrote it, and that Pauvert was wrong. And so it went on, and, probably in part owing to their discretion, the author of *The Story of O* escaped prosecution.

Ever since, the identity of Pauline Réage has been protected as a kind of masonic secret, apparently discussed not even among those who are, or claim to be, party to it. 'Yes, I know who wrote *The Story of O*,' says Eric Kahane, Girodias's brother, 'but I'll never tell you – so how do you know I'm not lying when I say I know?' Richard Seaver, a later publisher of *The Story of O* and its sequel in America, is someone likely to have the answer, but he also says: 'I'll never say who it is – therefore you'll never know if I'm lying when I say I know who it is.' As for Pauline Réage herself, she wrote in 'A Girl in Love': 'I promised not to divulge the real name of Pauline Réage, counting on the courtesy and integrity of those who are privy to it to keep the secret as long as I feel bound to keep the promise.'

But there is nothing to prevent those not privy to the secret from trying to unlock it. The chief suspect for a long time, Paulhan, can be discounted. Other prominent names have been mentioned, as Eric Kahane says, 'This person, that person. For a time they were almost convinced that Mme de Gaulle wrote it! It's like a medal, to be suspected of writing *The Story of O*.' Even George Plimpton tried to stake a claim.

The name most frequently mentioned in Paris in connection with the book, after that of Paulhan himself, was that of Dominique Aury, a translator from English (her translations include one of James Hogg's *Confessions of a Justified Sinner*) and the Secrétaire of the *Nouvelle Revue Française*. She had a working relationship with Paulhan, dating from just after the War, when the two edited an anthology of Resistance texts.

The preliminary evidence is suggestive: she comes from 'an academic background', having served on the juries for several literary prizes, and being a member of the Conseil Supérieure des Lettres. Mme Aury has never published a novel under her own name, which would have made *O* her 'first novel', as Paulhan said that it was Réage's first novel. But there is better proof than this: literary proof. Of the two quotations given above, both purporting to be taken from 'A Girl in Love' – beginning 'Books were their only freedom', and then 'Books are full of summonses' – only the first was in fact written by Pauline Réage. The other is taken from a book called *Literary Landfalls* (*Lectures pour tous*) by Dominique Aury. In addition

176

to an identical tone (clear enough even in the English versions), both passages place books at the centre of the speaker's life; both attribute to books the power of holding secrets (that essential O word), both place books beyond the ravages of time: books prevail 'through the obscurity of ancient languages, of modes and mores long since come and gone', says Réage; books 'outlast forests, even stones', says Aury. Really their authors are one and the same.

Literary evidence ought to be sufficient to prove who wrote *The Story of O* ('all our secrets lie there', whispered Aury – meaning in words), but in case material proof is needed, here it is: during one of Pauvert's bankruptcies, a certain author – who wishes not to be named – had the right to see the account of who was owed what, being a creditor himself. Dominique Aury – whose name had never appeared on any book published by Pauvert – was owed 'une somme fabuleuse'.

Another secret in the world of O was that Paulhan had been the regular companion of Dominique Aury since the War.*

IV

> What did she know about Sir Stephen? That he belonged to the Campbell clan and was thus a descendant of the earls of Argyll. That their sombre plaid, with its blue-black and green colours, was the most beautiful of all Scotland, and the most infamous. . . . That he owned a castle somewhere in the northwest corner of Scotland. . . .
> 'I'll take you there next year,' Sir Stephen had said one day.
>
> Pauline Réage, *Return to the Château*

Trocchi, with his gift for floating freely into other postures and personalities, was convinced that the secret world

*While this book was at the printer, Dominique Aury, breaking a forty-year silence, admitted that she was indeed the author of *The Story of O* (*New Yorker*, August 1, 1994).

enclosed by *The Story of O* could be breached and occupied by him. 'A masterpiece', he wrote to Jane Lougee in August 1954, 'which I am going to send you at the beginning of the week. For this, I feel, is what love – if it is to be taken on the level of passion – must become, if it is not to die.'

Jane was by this time back in the United States. Her relationship with Trocchi was in terminal decline and she was planning to marry another man. But Trocchi continued to impose on her, to try to prise her from the embrace of her husband-to-be, into the pair of Roissy bracelets he was holding ready for her.

His courting techniques were bizarre. The letters to Jane show him drifting out in distress to the end of his tether, at one moment adopting the pose of the heartbroken lover, at another parading the endowments of a Don Juan, at yet another attempting to refurnish the hollow spaces of one of his ersatz identities – the Marquis de Sade – with items lately stolen from Pauline Réage. At all points, he is seen moving away from ideas of the social norm, from the very idea of society itself. Like the Marquis, his aim was to break out of the prison in himself; to annihilate, as he put it, '1954 years plus of civilization'.

He urged Jane to read *The Story of O* carefully:

> for I can be your Sir Stephen, or I can be what I am now, in love with you darling, but with the sins of history chaining me to the rock. . . . Am I to guide us through a cauterizing passion as first René and then Sir Stephen did, or are we going to make the best of being civilized . . . and find love when we can? . . . Our problem? It is history's and we can't escape that except by destroying it in ourselves as Sir Stephen did in relation to himself and to O – and you will know all about that when I send you the book.

Jane did as she was asked and read the novel. Did she see in Sir Stephen – who, in one of the touches of Gothic parody which flavour *The Story of O*, is actually a castle-owning Scotsman – the image of her own 'Scottish fellow'? Doubtful.

Or then again, perhaps only too vividly. In either case, her reading did not prevent her from doing as she planned. In a few months' time, she was married.

Trocchi had no choice, if he was to rescue his own floundering ego, but to try and retrieve her. 'Will your husband read your letters? Does it matter? . . . In spite of my truancy, I did and do love you. And I am now lonely. I don't suppose that matters very much. I trust you. And yet to write those words' – see him clubbing himself on the side of the head, out of shame at his own self-abasement – 'to another man's wife.'

A growing sense of derangement spreads over his messages to the woman who had funded his literary dream and put up with his 'truancy', but who was now definitely lost to him. Four months after his exhortations to Jane to read *The Story of O*, promising a cauterizing passion, he was still hankering, dependently, talking in tongues:

I have changed since I came to Montparnasse.
I was dying in St Germain.
It was as though I had seen God.
Jesus Christ was a man called Alexopolis, a New York Greek who came to build furniture. I don't know what would have happened if your letter had arrived while I was still in St Germain. . . .
J'existe.
I am very happy now. Terribly happy.

The reference to the carpenter 'Alexopolis . . . who came to build furniture' is not some lunatic vision of himself, Alex, as a Christ-figure. He was a real person, as a subsequent sentence explains: 'What did I do for Alexopolis? I took his best girl away from him, a beautiful little Indo-Chinese girl called Liane who is now all my very own . . .' And, in case Jane isn't getting the message, he adds, 'I'm fast becoming the bull of Montparnasse.'

Only a few weeks had to elapse before he was writing,

Liane came to see me on Sunday. I found her almost uninteresting. . . . And, as Janet (JF) came to visit me only a couple of hours before, I was not even remotely interested. And so you see you are

179

not the only little girl who can't stay away from me. . . . Does this hurt you?

Not half as much as it was hurting him. The search continued for a means to destroy 'the sins of history' – or perhaps he meant just his own sins – in himself. And eventually he found it, this grail. It was not sado-masochism, after all. 'I tried what Johnnie Welsh takes,' he wrote to Jane in a letter dated 'Dawn, 8 December, 1954'; 'It's wonderful.'

To find a clue to what he is talking about, we may look back to the Frank Harris pastiche, written earlier the same year:

> It was in Shanghai that I first learned that various poisons and aliments are supposed to increase desire or intensify sensation. . . . I was taken by a Chinese I had met shortly after my arrival in Burma to one of the famous 'opium dens' for which China is famous . . . [but] I achieved neither the desired physical effect nor that intense state of clear vision attained by Coleridge on the eve of which he wrote *Kubla Khan*.

In this instance, the pen is definitely Trocchi's and not Harris's own; the reference to Coleridge and *Kubla Khan* – one of his favourite poems – would be enough by itself to pin it down. But what clinches it are the drugs. The thing that 'Johnnie Welsh takes' could have been opium, but was more likely heroin, the substance Trocchi was to use to write the next in his series of improvisations on the theme of himself. (His mention of it in the fifth volume of *My Life and Loves* is a rare sighting of an Olympia writer putting his real life into the usually fantastic fiction.)

Girodias had noticed Trocchi's new departure:

> Alex had separated from Jane Lougee and was living in relative luxury with a charming young Chinese girl who spoke English as fluently as she did French, and who had a very pleasant apartment furnished basically with cushions and carpets. Under this oriental influence, Alex gave himself up to opium and exotic garments.

180

Trocchi was a fluid being, moving from one persona to another in order to evade the flaws in his own make-up. They were deep 'sins', not of history in the grand sense, but of his own history, possibly of adolescent trauma caused by his mother's early death. Future writings suggest an incestuous attraction to the red-haired woman whose untimely departure from the boy in Glasgow might have been an act that could only be avenged by Don Juan, or by the 'bull of Montparnasse', or by Frances Lengel, or any other of his aliases who liked nothing more than to ring the doorbells of well-ordered family life and regulated society, and run away.

In a letter written to Jane at the end of August 1954, Trocchi refers to a new book he was writing. He calls it 'Cain'; it was to be 'a practical experiment in living'. The book took five years to complete, whereupon it was published as *Cain's Book*, a novel of sorts, an autobiographical *tour de force*, which switches between a childhood in Glasgow spent under the warm wing of a beautiful mother prematurely aged by poverty and hard work, and a contemporary existence as a heroin addict in New York. It would be the high point of the Scottish pimpernel's new career.

*

With Jane gone, *Merlin* foundered. Trocchi veered all over the place: Pamplona (with Iris Owens), Mallorca, Athens; he had plans to borrow money from Sinbad Vail and make for the Far East. The magazine owed money to Girodias, who refused to pay for the new issue to be printed before the outstanding debt was settled. It was worth the publisher's while to dig his heels in: *Merlin* owed him over 300,000 francs, about £270 or $800. ('Even money-lenders were consulted at one point,' according to Jane.) The extent of the disaster is made clear in a letter Trocchi wrote to Jane concerning the current issue – as it was to turn out, the penultimate one – for Summer–Autumn 1954. It was typically plump, containing Beckett's story 'The End', Ionesco's play *The New Tenant*, together with an article on the playwright by Daniel Mauroc; there was also a story by Italo Svevo, and the usual helping of poems and reviews. By the end of August, Trocchi told Jane, 'it had sold perhaps ten copies in all'.

There was to be one final issue of the magazine, almost exactly a year later. The publisher is given not as Jane Lougee of Limerick, Maine, as before, but as the Olympia Press, 8 rue de Nesle, Paris. The editorial referred back to *Merlin*'s founding moment, as if conscious of the impending demise. 'We have felt it important to print *reportages*, *chronicles*, *documents* and *notes* that record aspects of the present temper.' It was put together by Wainhouse, who included a piece by himself on *The Story of O* – he deplored the book's sudden popularity, of course: 'Clandestine books belong underground,' he protested, though when Girodias wanted to have the Bryants' translation of the book revised, it was Wainhouse who took the job – as well as poems by Pablo Neruda and pieces by Logue and Richard Gibson. But without Trocchi, the steering power behind the magazine was gone. Without Jane Lougee, the determination was gone, and the money, too.

FIVE

Two Concise Histories:
Lolita and *The Ginger Man*

Girodias's dream of being a heroic warrior in the battle of the books came true in 1955, when he was given the manuscript of *Lolita* by Vladimir Nabokov. It was the novel which caused Olympia to be regarded internationally as a publisher of serious works and not just dirty books. It brought him unexpected wealth – 'the *Lolita* miracle', he tagged it in a letter to Beckett – but it also signalled the end of the party.

Author and publisher fell out over almost every detail pertaining to the book's publication, and even over the facts of their own meeting. Their quarrel, amplified by interjections from certain others, is due for reconstruction.

The Ginger Man by J. P. Donleavy, which forced its way through Girodias's letterbox at roughly the same time as the manuscript of *Lolita*, was to be a more unwelcome intrusion, though that was not how it seemed at the time.

I

Nabokov: The first little throb of *Lolita* went through me late in 1939 or early in 1940, in Paris, when I was laid up with a severe attack of intercostal neuralgia.

Girodias: One day in the early summer of 1955, I received a call from a literary agent, a Russian lady by the name of Doussia Ergaz.

Nabokov: On April 26, 1955, a fatidic date, she said she had found a possible publisher. On May 13, she named that person.

Girodias: I asked Mme Ergaz to send me the manuscript, which promptly turned up complete with a curriculum vita [*sic*] in which I read:

Born 1899, St Petersburg, Russia. Old Russian nobility. Father eminent statesman of the Liberal group, elected member of the first Duma. Paternal grandfather State Minister of Justice under Czar Alexander II. Maternal great grandfather President of Academy of Medicine.

Family escaped from Communist Russia in 1919. England, Germany, France.

Acquired considerable fame in émigré circles as novelist and poet. . . .

Nabokov: For some reason, which presumably I am too naïve to grasp, he starts by citing an old *curriculum vitae* of mine which, he says, was sent to him by my agent together with the typescript of *Lolita*. Such a procedure would have been absurd.

Girodias: There was a certain disarming naïveté in the writer's insistence on such points as 'father eminent statesman' . . .

Nabokov: My files show that only much later, namely on February 8, 1957, *he asked* me to send him 'all the biographical material' available. With the sneer of a hoodlum following an innocent passer-by, Mr Girodias now makes fun of such facts as my father's having been 'an eminent statesman' . . .

Girodias: . . . which I found not to be devoid of charm. But I quickly succumbed to the much more compelling attraction of the book itself.

Dear Mr Girodias,
   I am delighted you are doing *Lolita*. Please rush the proofs and I shall rush them back.

Doussia Ergaz: Girodias finds the book not only admirable from the literary point of view, but thinks that it might lead to change in social attitudes toward the kind of love described in *Lolita*, provided of course that it has this authenticity, this burning and irrepressible ardour.

Nabokov: It was a pious although obviously ridiculous thought but high-minded platitudes are often mouthed by enthusiastic businessmen and nobody bothers to disenchant them.

Eric Kahane (translator of *Lolita* into French): He brought it to Gid and Gid thought it was a great book, which it was; but later Nabokov acted as if it had been stolen from his safe.

Nabokov did some rewriting at Girodias's request.

New York Times Book Review, April 8, 1960

Nabokov: I wish to correct this absurd misstatement. The only alternatives Girodias very diffidently suggested concerned a few trivial French phrases in the English text.

Letter to *NYTBR*, April 22, 1960

Girodias: I bowed to all the terms imposed on me, paid an advance much larger than I could afford at the time, and did not even insist on reserving for my firm a share of the eventual film rights.

Nabokov: No publisher has a right to share motion picture profits with the author.

Memorandum of Agreement . . . made this sixth day of June, nineteen hundred and fifty-five between Mr Vladimir Nabokov, Cornell University, Ithaca, NY, and Olympia Press, 8, rue de Nesle, Paris. . . .

In the event of the Publishers going bankrupt or failing to make accountings and payments as herein specified, then in either event the present agreement becomes automatically null and void and the rights herein granted revert to the Author. . . .

Nabokov: That beautiful, eloquent, almost sapphically modulated . . . 'Revert to the Author', is of great importance for understanding what Mr Girodias calls 'our enigmatic conflict'.

Girodias: I had hardly received the proofs back when Nabokov sent me a cable saying: 'When is *Lolita* appearing. Worried. Please answer my letters . . .' – an entreaty which has been repeated so often in so many cables sent by so many authors to so many publishers.

Nabokov: 'I had hardly received the proofs back' (he received them in July 1955) . . . 'when Nabokov sent me a cable' (August 29, i.e. after a month of Girodiasic silence) 'saying: "When is Lolita appearing. Worried. Please answer my letters" – an entreaty which has been repeated so often in so many cables sent by so many authors to so many (i.e. wise, calm, benevolent) publishers. . . .' The would-be wit and delightful flippancy of this remark should not fool anybody.

Dear Mr Girodias,

I hope you have already started a publicity campaign. When sending out review copies, are you including the following publications: 1. The Partisan Review; 2. The New Yorker; 3. The New York Times Book Review; 4. Saturday Review of Literature; 5. The New York Herald Tribune. That's all I can think of.

Girodias: *Lolita* appeared in September 1955, but was not noticed or reviewed anywhere, and sold very poorly.

Brian Boyd (biographer of Nabokov): In October he received the two pale olive-green paperback volumes of *Lolita* in the Olympia Traveller's Companion series.

Copyright 1955 by Vladimir Nabokov *and* The Olympia Press
First edition of *Lolita*

Dear Mr Girodias,

There is something else I would like to mention: I have received no statements of accounts from you on either of the two dates on which they were due. I would appreciate receiving one now.

Girodias: Those were his last nice words to me.

Graham Greene: I would nominate *Lolita* by Vladimir Nabokov.
Sunday Times, Christmas Books, 1955

John Gordon (*Sunday Express* columnist): The filthiest book I have ever read. Sheer unrestrained pornography. . . . Its central character is a pervert with a passion for debauching what he calls 'nymphets'. These, he explains, are girls aged from 11 to 14. . . . The entire book is devoted to an exhaustive account of his pursuits and successes.

Graham Greene: I have undertaken to write a biography, as yet unauthorized, *The Private Life of John Gordon*, and I should be grateful to any of your readers for any unpublished letters or anecdotes they can supply.

Letter to the New Statesman

Towards the end of 1956 the French government agreed, in response to strong pressure from the British, to invoke its obscenity laws against *Lolita*.

The Times

Lolita was banned, unbanned, banned again, and Girodias embarked on the long process of 'lolitagation'.

Times Literary Supplement

Dear Mr Girodias,
  A *succès de scandale* would distress me.

Girodias: When I decided to fight the *Lolita* ban, my first thought was to ask for Nabokov's help. I was very surprised to receive a very adamant refusal.

Dear Mr Girodias,
  My moral defence of the book is the book itself.

Dear Mr Girodias,
  You are advised that certain copies of this book have been before this office for examination and that they have been released.

Signed, Irving Fishman, Deputy Collector
for the Restricted Merchandise Division,
February 8, 1957

Girodias: In lay language, that meant that . . . *Lolita* could now be published in America with practically no danger.

Dear Mr Girodias,

I suggest that we amend our agreement. Would you like me to send you a new contract or would you like me to send you a draft of such a contract?

Girodias: Only one book earned me a lot of money and that book was *Lolita*.

Nabokov: Mr Girodias declared he had sold only eight copies in America in three months . . . he was sending me the difference, a cheque for fifty cents.

Girodias: In the United States all the big publishers who had turned down Nabokov's manuscript a few years before were biting their nails in chagrin. . . . One publisher spontaneously offered a 20 per cent royalty to get the book.

Nabokov: Mr Girodias does not say who was to get most of that 20 per cent.

Dear Mr Nabokov,

I am prepared to accept this proposal if my share is assured at 12$^{1}/_{2}$ per cent. Would you accept 7$^{1}/_{2}$ per cent as your share?

Doussia Ergaz: *Outrée ces pretensions!*

Dear Mr Nabokov,

Being a rather backward example of that rather backward species, the American publisher, it was only recently that I began to hear about a book called *Lolita*. . . . I am wondering if the book is available for publication.

Sincerely, Walter J. Minton,
President, G. P. Putnam's Sons

Dear Mr Minton,
   Mr Girodias, the owner of Olympia, is a rather difficult person.

> Sincerely, V. Nabokov

Brian Boyd: Doubleday too was ready to sign for the novel. . . . Girodias could have expected a 2.5 per cent royalty for himself. Instead, he insisted he should have a royalty of 10 per cent, leaving the author a mere 5 per cent.

Dear Mr Girodias,
   In view of your failure to submit your statement and to pay me as required by paragraph 9 of our Agreement, I regret to inform you that I am now invoking paragraph 8 of said Agreement and am exercising my right to declare the Agreement null and void.

Dear Mr Minton,
   If this does not do it, I shall admit to defeat.

> Sincerely, V. Nabokov

Nabokov has agreed contract.

> Cable from Walter Minton to Girodias,
> February 11, 1958

Copyright by Vladimir Nabokov, 1955

> Second edition of *Lolita*

Girodias: *Lolita* – that book being the only one that was actually bought from me by a New York publisher instead of being, like all the others, merely stolen.

> Letter to Samuel Beckett

Walter Minton: Actually it is [Vera Nabokov], I think, who is at the bottom of most of the troubles between you and her husband. She is a lovely lady of a very actively suspicious turn of mind.

Letter to Girodias

Girodias: Vera, *l'anti-nymphette!*

Dmitri Nabokov: Minton learned about *Lolita* from 'one-time Latin quarter showgirl' Rosemary Ridgewell. Her finder's fee was 'the equivalent of 10 per cent of the publisher's share of the subsidiary rights for two years'.

Girodias: Rosemary forced Minton to admit that he had never read *Lolita*.

Girodias: I received the visit of a lawyer, Mr Godemert . . . 'I have come to ask you if you could suggest some method to attack you on Mr Nabokov's behalf'.

Nabokov: The elusiveness, the evasiveness, the procrastination, the dodges, the duplicity, the utter irresponsibility.

Girodias: Nabokov, meanwhile, had instructed his much-harassed agent, Doussia Ergaz, to suspend all payment to me of my share of certain foreign royalties due me.

Brian Boyd: Nabokov was quite shocked when a little girl of eight or nine came to his door for candy on Halloween, dressed up by her parents as Lolita.

Brian Boyd: The Texas town of Lolita debated changing its name to Jackson.

The French Ministry immediately banned the novel as pornographic, after a complaint from the British Embassy that tourists were buying the book and taking it to Britain.

The Times, 1958

There is a waiting list in the public library at Tunbridge Wells, town of retired gentlefolk, for *Lolita*, the novel the French Council of State on Wednesday banned as obscene.

Daily Express, 1958

Brian Boyd: Twenty-six-year-old Dmitri Nabokov had let a self-styled publicity agent persuade him to stage a fake casting contest for the part of Lolita. . . . For two days his Milan apartment was invaded by 'decidedly postpubescent aspiring nymphets, some with provincial mothers in tow'. When his father saw a magazine photograph of the 'finalists' surrounding Dmitri on his over-sized, satin-covered bed, he cabled his son at once to stop the 'Lolita publicity' immediately.

Brian Boyd: The process of vulgarization would ultimately lead to such horrors as the life-size Lolita doll with 'French and Greek' apertures.

Groucho Marx: I've put off reading *Lolita* for six years, until she's eighteen.

Brian Boyd: As a *Lolita* movie looked more and more possible, he warned Minton that he 'would veto the use of a real child. Let them find a dwarfess.'

Girodias: I decided to open a futuristic, multi-levelled nightclub in Paris. For five years I certainly had a lot of fun with that new toy, but it lost me much more money than it ever made . . . and as a side effect forced the Olympia Press into bankruptcy as well.

Nabokov: I wrote to Mme Ergaz that I did not wish to make the acquaintance of Mr Girodias when I came to Paris for the launching of the French translation of *Lolita*.

Girodias: I was very perplexed when I received [my invitation]. I did not want to embarrass my friends at Gallimard; and I did not want to look like a coward, being quite as able as anyone else to digest a punch on the nose in case of necessity.

Vera Nabokov: Somebody had brought Girodias and his brother, the translator Kahane, to introduce them to me. Nabokov was either not in the vicinity, or walked away as they approached. I exchanged two or three words with Kahane (not with Girodias), and then left them.

Girodias: I slowly progressed toward the author through a sea of bodies.

Nabokov: A splendid image, that sea.

Girodias: We exchanged a few not unfriendly sentences.

Nabokov: Let me repeat, I have never met Mr Girodias.

Girodias: He had very obviously recognized me.

Nabokov: Very obviously, I could not have recognized somebody I had never seen in my life.

Vera Nabokov: Girodias was *not* introduced to Nabokov.

Brian Boyd: That evening, as they drove away from the party, Doussia Ergaz asked Nabokov how had he found Girodias. He replied, with a surprised look . . . that he had not seen the man.

Girodias: There is a photograph in which I am seen talking with Nabokov; Eric is in the middle. The picture is blurred, rather bad; it's a smallish print . . . that picture will save me piles of argument.

Brian Boyd: The Nabokovs' response to Ergaz's question was to pool their reactions to the man both now knew to be Girodias and decide they 'did not like him a bit'.

Nabokov: I began to curse my association with Olympia as early as 1955.

August 3, 1957
Dear Mr Girodias,
  I shall always be grateful to you for having published *Lolita*.

Girodias: Were it not for my firm, *Lolita* would still be a dusty manuscript in a nostalgic cupboard.

Nabokov: Had not Graham Greene and John Gordon clashed in London in such providential fashion, *Lolita* – especially its second volume which repelled so-called 'amateurs' – might have ended in the common grave of Traveller's Favourites or whatever Olympia's little green books were called.

Girodias: When it became known that his firm proposed to publish the controversial book, Mr Nigel Nicolson MP had to explain, both in the House of Commons and to his Tory electors in Bournemouth, why he felt justified in publishing *Lolita*. Apparently his explanations were not convincing and . . . Mr Nicolson's constituents have now disavowed him and he will have to abandon his seat.

Lolita is the main issue. Suez has been replaced.

British MP, 1960

Girodias: We may therefore lament young Lolita's sorry fate but we must also ask: was she corrupted by a book or by our civilization?

194

Dear Mr Nabokov,
   Our interests are identical.

Dear Mr Girodias,
   I wrote *Lolita*.

II

> People don't realize how dangerous writers
> are. Writers don't know it themselves.
> They are brilliant at law, naturals. . .
>
> J. P. Donleavy

The latent virus which was to destroy Girodias entered the body of Olympia Press in September 1954. It was transferred in a moment of rapture, as the publisher laid open and embraced a certain Sebastian Dangerfield – or 'S.D.', as the original manuscript of *The Ginger Man* was entitled. Its submission had been preceded by a letter from the author to the publisher: 'The obscenity is very much a part of this novel, and its removal would detract from it' – words which, Girodias claimed later, were clearly intended to whet his appetite.

When the parcel of written-over and pasted-together pages arrived, however, it was Girodias's other appetite – for avant-gardism – that was aroused. This was the lesser of the two, but authentic nevertheless. It is difficult to understand how *The Ginger Man* could ever have been thought obscene. There is ribaldry, a touch of scatology, a foul incident with some botched plumbing, another in which a man exposes himself on a train; but nothing to compare with the excesses of Lengel, Vicarion or van Heller. Donleavy's novel is often lyrical and often funny. The ardour of Humbert Humbert might well have been thought likely to deprave and corrupt – 'I gave her to hold in her awkward fist the sceptre of my passion' – but not, surely, the refracted thoughts of Sebastian Dangerfield. *The Ginger Man* switches between straightforward third-person narration and the disconnections of interior monologue, sometimes without signalling. Even in the minds of publishers who had rejected the work as unsaleable, there must have been little doubt that *The Ginger Man* was serious, a Joycean picaresque. There could be no mistaking the quality of the writing. There certainly could be no mistaking it for a work of pornography.

And yet, *The Ginger Man*, which Donleavy went on revising obsessively, was turned down by one American publisher after another. 'Sheer rejection,' Donleavy called it. It led to his quitting his native country for good.

Donleavy was an American who had studied in Dublin and now lived in London. Convinced of his literary destiny, he had pledged never to distract himself with a job. He spent a lot of his time, though, drinking in London pubs with the likes of Brendan Behan, and it was from him that Donleavy first heard about the Olympia Press. Behan recommended Girodias's firm as publishers for books that had proved unpublishable. Donleavy had read Beckett, and he knew that Beckett, like Joyce, had been published in Paris: Joyce (in small amounts) by Kahane, and Beckett by Kahane's son. So when Girodias accepted his novel, Donleavy was pleased to think that his name would sit next to Beckett's on the Collection Merlin list, and perhaps in spirit beside Joyce's.

This was late in 1954, before Girodias had created the Traveller's Companion series, at a time when it could be seriously argued that the good outweighed the bad in Olympia production. Nabokov's retrospective sneer at 'the common grave of Traveller's Favourites or whatever Olympia's little green books were called' lacks his characteristic accuracy, for in its first edition *Lolita* was not published in the Traveller's Companion series but under the plain imprint of the Olympia Press, which at the time included Apollinaire, Bataille, Beckett, Genet, Miller, Restif de la Bretonne and Sade. It was only in their first or second reprints that Nabokov, Beckett, Genet and all the rest were drafted into the Traveller's Companion series.

This may seem a fine point to some, but not to J. P. Donleavy, for whom it became a structural beam of prolonged legal argument.

There was no contract for *The Ginger Man*. Nabokov was unusual among Olympia authors in having a proper written agreement with the publisher, as Girodias preferred to rely on informal methods. His fullest explanation of this came in his autobiography, published in Paris in 1990:

> Donleavy would have wished to have had a classic contract, but . . . since the beginning of Olympia, I had dealt directly with people who had the same reservations as I did about contracts, and who preferred to protect their anonymity in view of our irregular legal situation. Drawing up a contract seemed to me useful only in special situations, such as that of the fifth volume of Frank Harris memoirs. For the rest, I managed with simple pieces of paper, and, more often, with verbal agreements. To those who were surprised by this, I explained pompously that contracts, like virgins, called irresistibly to be violated. The more clauses you strung together, the more room for dispute you created; the agreements became constraints, from which it became a matter of urgency to free oneself. . . . The charm of my enterprise lay in its unsophisticatedness; when working with friends, a handshake would suffice. I was persuaded that if Donleavy were to come to Paris, the question of a contract could be cleared up.

On this last point, he was to be proved right – at first – and then seriously wrong.

In the fullness of time, Donleavy did come to Paris. Girodias threw a party in his apartment overlooking Notre Dame, during which Donleavy drank a generous quantity of his host's 'vins les plus fins'. At the end of the night, he eyed his new publisher and said: 'I've seen you before. Are you Girodias's brother?'

These were, to quote Girodias in a different context, 'his

last nice words to me'.

*

The Ginger Man was accepted by Girodias for publication, in principle, on December 30, 1954. He had a few reservations concerning the pacing and control of the narrative, and he expressed these to the expectant author, whose communications from publishers, until then, had been limited to variations on the phrase 'No thanks'.

Girodias felt that the book failed to engage the reader until about page 100.

> It is hard to explain just why, especially hard when one rereads this opening hundred pages after having gone through the entire book, for then the vagueness disappears, and what seemed inaccessible at first reading is vivid upon second. Nevertheless, several readers have, independently, reached the same conclusion. . . .
> It is not a question of deleting episodes, but of weeding out what blurs them, of sharpening and lightening.

Girodias also felt that 'the deliberate modesty' of the title, 'S.D.' or 'Sebastian Dangerfield', rather than 'giving the book a name, suggests that it lacks one'.

This sounds like good, cogent, constructive criticism, and the young author welcomed it. 'Dear Mr Girodias,' he wrote back to Paris a month and a half later, 'I've finished a revision which includes last one hundred pages from which I've cut thirty-seven. And am now working on first hundred and middle.'

Girodias stood by his usual practice of offering a fixed fee, based upon print-runs (eventually settled at 250,000 francs – about $700 or £200 – for a first printing of 5,000 copies) and on April 15, 1955, set out the terms and conditions in a letter to the author, with his cavalier assertion: 'It is quite unnecessary to have a separate contract.' The clauses in Girodias's letter of terms numbered only four; it was the fourth clause which was to keep these two, author and publisher, at first so

198

appreciative of one another, in court for more than twenty years: 'Every transaction relative to . . . reprints by other publishers . . . should be approved by both parties.'

Donleavy responded to the contract letter with a few questions, but was in general agreement with the terms imposed on him. He had spent years writing his book. He was utterly, unshakeably, convinced of its worth and originality. After barren months of searching, he had lighted on a publisher who was willing to act as party to his self-belief. Nothing in the world, apart from the welfare of his wife and child, was more important to him than to see his creation in print, with his name on the cover.

In the spring of the year, though, shortly after extending the open palm across the Channel to clasp that of Girodias, Donleavy was visited by a premonition. 'Someone somewhere had betrayed me. The foundations of the little house in Fulham shook, and the words "goddamnit" trembling the windowpanes, could be heard reverberating far away up and down the street.' Was it superstition? Was it clairvoyance? No, most probably it was Girodias's way of conveying the advance, which required of Donleavy that he make his way to a dirty-book shop in Soho, ask there for a 'Mr Cliff', and accept his money, which he reckoned to be enough to maintain himself and his family for a year, in the form of a bundle of grubby five-pound notes. The voice told the author that all was not right with his book at Olympia Press.

When, in the middle of 1955, he received the first green-backed copies of the novel, number 7 in the newly created Traveller's Companion series, the earthly foundation for this eerie premonition was made vividly clear. Donleavy had heard the word 'Olympia' linked to the word 'pornography'; he had watched Girodias dispensing with a proper contract; he had ventured into Soho to collect his reward. All this had roused his suspicion. And when he saw, in an advertisement at the back of *The Ginger Man*, who his travelling companions were to be – not *Watt* and *Lolita* and *The Thief's Journal*, but *Rape*,

School for Sin and *Tender Was My Flesh* – he was 'literally infuriated'. His book was 'ruined'. He told Girodias that the novel appearing in this series 'could not get it reviews anywhere', and that, above all, he was opposed to it being presented as a pornographic work.

It was then that Donleavy made for Paris, arriving, unannounced, at the rue de Nesle office one autumn morning.

> As I declared my identity, there was no question but that there was considerable nervous surprise at my sudden unexpected morning presence. Girodias was slowly up out of his seat and from behind his desk offering an apologetically limp hand, with what I am also sure was a fleeting trace of fear.
>
> 'Ah, you are in Paris.'
> 'Yes.'
> 'Ah. I trust your trip was comfortable.'
> 'Yes.'
> 'Ah, please sit down.'

Displaying a polite geniality, generated by a 'clear relief that he was not about to be punched or shot', Girodias proceeded to extend to his new author his professional hospitality. Donleavy was introduced to Muffie Wainhouse, wife of Austryn, who was involved with Olympia. He was taken to good restaurants, and had a small party arranged in his honour.

It was at this party, Donleavy says, that he put it to Girodias that he wished to find an English publisher for his book, and that Girodias thought this 'a good idea'. It was at this party, Girodias claimed, that he thought no such thing a good idea, that no such idea was put to him, in fact, but that his American author with an Irish temperament got well and truly drunk on his 'vins les plus fins', mistook him for his brother, jumped on his back on his way out of the party, and left the next morning without so much as an *au revoir*.

Somehow or other, at a moment impossible to ascertain since the principals' memories disagree, the situation had slipped into the control of the devils of acrimony and revenge. One of Donleavy's queries on receiving the letter in lieu of contract had to do with foreign rights. Girodias liked to control the rights to the books he took such risks in publishing, but Donleavy claimed that they had come to a spoken arrangement at the party, 'whereby I would have all the revenue from the English edition, and that I would then give him 50 per cent of an American edition. He agreed to this verbally. I got nothing in writing.'

Girodias refuted the claim outright, and dared Donleavy to press ahead with an English edition of the novel – he had found a publisher, Neville Spearman – on pain of legal action. He expected Donleavy to back down under this threat. No one had yet dared to act behind his back – even Nabokov would not do so – except pirates operating from no fixed address. When he heard that an English edition of *The Ginger Man* was to be published in late 1956, Girodias wrote to Donleavy: 'If this project is not abandoned immediately, I shall have to take legal action to prevent publication and to obtain adequate damages.' He had no recollection of having made a verbal transfer of English rights to Donleavy at the party. His position was that, having published the book, he owned those rights, 'at least as long as my edition is in print'. This struck him as reasonable, and in accordance with their agreement. How could Donleavy think that he would depart from the letter of the 'contract' over a glass of wine? Why on earth would he?

When the English edition of *The Ginger Man* came out in December – lacking, however, chapter ten, the 'rudest' section (one would hardly reach for a stronger word) – Girodias thought he saw what Donleavy was up to: this was a separate, 'expurgated' edition, to which their agreement would not apply, and by which the treacherous ingrate believed he could circumvent the contract. He wrote to the publisher, Neville Spearman: 'Will you please make known the name and address of your legal counsel so that he can be contacted by mine?'

There began a twenty-year-long battle in the courts over

the right to publish *The Ginger Man*.*

*

The case became a malevolent symbol of all the disagreements with authors, the squabbles over contracts or the lack of them, the unpaid royalties and the claims over rights, the dealings with policemen and lawyers, that Girodias had in the course of his career. When defeated, says the publisher's brother, he took it very badly. So he would find a new strategy, lead with the other fist, hit back, and try to win the next round. The contest for *The Ginger Man* became all-consuming – until, at last, one party swallowed up the other.

Sometime in the mid-1970s, Girodias was declared bankrupt (not for the first time) and the Olympia Press was put up for sale at auction in Paris. Girodias himself attended the auction. Bidding through a nominee, he confidently expected to be able to buy back the firm for a token sum, whereupon he would recommence his commercial activities.

To his surprise, however, he found himself up against a tenacious counter-bidder, an American woman who insistently upped his every bid. Up and up it went, for almost half an hour, until, finally, Girodias was forced to yield, and left the auction in a temper.

Seeking out the identity of his adversary, he discovered she was called Mary Wilson Price, which meant nothing to him. Only later did he find out that she had been bidding under her maiden name. Her husband was J. P. Donleavy.

The litigation continued for a short period after Donleavy assumed control of the Olympia Press, so that he was, at one stage, suing himself.

---

*Typically, Girodias had at the same time spotted a business opportunity which was too good to pass up. By putting into circulation an expurgated edition of *The Ginger Man*, Spearman had unwittingly created a demand for Olympia's unexpurgated one. Girodias had 500 copies of the novel bound in hard covers, cut exactly like the English one, but with the words 'Paris Edition' underneath the title, and shipped to England. However, British Customs intercepted them.

INTERLUDE

Points of departure

The community of little magazines, perennially reflective of the potency of emerging literary life, was disintegrating. A sure sign that a magazine is on the way down is when its editors take a stand to protest its continuing vitality. This happened with *Merlin* in the summer of 1955, shortly after the appearance of issue number six, when Trocchi wrote to the *TLS* to correct the impression given in an earlier article on the Paris scene that, after a gap of almost a year, *Merlin* was starting up afresh under new direction. Not so, said Trocchi; he was still the editor, 'and the future of the magazine seems assured'. *Merlin* never came out again.

The *Paris Review* continued to appear: well-heeled and well-edited, too. The 'Art of Fiction' series of interviews now included Ralph Ellison, Simenon, William Faulkner and Isak Dinesen; it introduced to the genre a depth it had never had before. But 'the Editors', as Plimpton referred to himself and his genial club, were returning home one by one, and from now on the magazine would be edited from New York. Plimpton himself stayed in Paris longer than most of the team, but in 1956 he went too, leaving the review under the Paris stewardship of 'managing editor' Robert Silvers (later to become the founding editor of the *New York Review of Books*).

The contents list reflected the shift: *Paris Review* 11, Winter 1955, contains fiction by the unknown Jack Kerouac

('French-Canadian by birth and a resident of Mexico'), an interview with Nelson Algren, poetry by American poets who had never set foot in Paris. The Summer 1956 issue had an interview with arch-New Yorker Dorothy Parker; its only connection with Paris was a five-page extract from Genet's *Thief's Journal* - without an obscene word, of course - which had been published as an unexpurgated book by Collection Merlin two years earlier.

The cover continued to sport colourful illustrations of this or that *coin de rue*, but that was about all. *Paris Review* 11 was the last to bear the stately rue Garancière address and to boast affiliation with La Table Ronde.

The game was up for *Points*. Sinbad Vail never did take to his task with enthusiasm, only with a sense of obligation, as he ceaselessly reminded his subscribers. By issue 20, the last, the readership had shrunk so much that Vail probably felt he knew every member of it personally. He kept up his air of weary languor to the end, giving as the reason for the delay in arrival of issue 20 in 1955 (*Points* 19 had come out a year before) a lack of decent submissions. Perhaps the money was running out, too:

> It has come to the point where I'm including some of my own work, not that it's better or worse than others, but it's . . . cheaper as I don't have to pay myself.

SIX

Black on Black

> . . . black men have been oppressed for centuries
> – oppressed for so long that their oppression has
> become . . . a kind of culture.
>
> Richard Wright

I

Modernism, the self-conscious preoccupation with the mechanism of the literary construct, was the prospectus for the aesthetes; but for Richard Wright and others cast from a political mould, without modernist guile, the new agenda was simply 'modern man', or 'the modern world'. After the eight-year silence which had followed his removal from the United States, Wright was in a period of great production. Between 1953 and 1958, he published seven books: three novels, three works of travel reportage, and a collection of essays and journalism. None of them caught the attention of the American public. His career, dragged down by the wreckage of *The Outsider*, remained in depression. But the writer himself continued till the end of his life to be full of new ideas and fresh ambition.

Like Sartre, a mentor, Wright was always alert to the political signal coming from below, gauging it, engaging with it, never afraid of finding his own shape altered in the heat of inner debate. Although he did not possess Sartre's faculty of reasoning, likewise his encyclopaedic learning, Wright could yet be dubbed 'Sartre noir' on account of his responsiveness to the moment of political change. He now had little in common politically with Sartre, who moved further to the left with each year while Wright edged the other way – in 1952, Sartre had halted performances of his own play, *Les Mains sales*, in Vienna, because the production was thought to be uncomplimentary to the USSR; it was pressure to shape his work to the will of the party that had led to Wright renouncing Communism a decade earlier – but still he resembled his old friend in his willingness to stand before the new wave, to be touched and changed by it. The greater part of Wright's attention after 1953 was concentrated on global politics as they affected the people gathering together under the banner of 'colour'. The new politics of liberation in Africa and Asia were undoing the imperial dominance of the West, and at the same time altering the division of power which presently existed in the world between capitalism and Communism. Possessed of a political insight which enabled him to grasp the workings of this power, Wright aspired, through his books, his words, to tip the scales – even if only by a feather's weight – in favour of a future which would include his kind.

But, while his political insight was bright and swift, his literary technique was slow-footed and pedestrian, and when it came to expressing his new ideas, it let him down. Wright was a social realist, always had been, always would be. He painted best in broad strokes. The modernist productions of the Olympia Press, which he saw on the shelves of Gaïte Frogé's English Bookshop in rue de Seine, had little attraction for him. In contemplating a book or an author or a movement, Wright's mind would automatically pose the question: 'Left or right?' The bit in the middle – the part that Beckett, Nabokov, even Donleavy explored, not to mention the productions of local genius such as Ionesco or Adamov – held no interest. The closest Wright ever came to literary experimentation was in the stylistically inventive *Lawd Today!*, which pasted collages of newspaper headlines and advertising fliers on to a continuous racy dialogue among four post office workers in Chicago. It was written in the 1930s but not published until after his death.

In the mid-1950s, the 'modern', to Wright, was Africa. The continent's black voices rose in pitch, and Wright imagined he heard the sound of breaking glass in imperial mansions. Returning to Paris from a visit to the land of his ancestors, Wright announced to the company of young admirers at the Café de Tournon: 'It's no longer left or right. It's black or white!'

*

Wright had just come back from the Gold Coast, and he was about to make a book out of his journey. The small West African country (soon to be renamed Ghana) was still a British colony, but it had the first black prime minister in history, Kwame Nkrumah, who had set his sights on making the Gold Coast an independent republic. Wright foresaw that the rest of Africa would follow.

He had met Nkrumah through his friend, the West Indian historian George Padmore, and Nkrumah, mindful of Wright's prestige in America and Europe, invited him to be a guest in his nascent country. Wright informed his agent of his plans: it would be a book not only about the Gold Coast but about the African phenomenon in general. His agent Paul Reynolds replied with enthusiasm which, however, barely disguised his concern about Wright's literary future:

> I am particularly keen because I think this will stimulate you. . . .
> I think your search for material, your going for a purpose, namely
> to find out, will be of great value to you.

In Reynolds's view, Wright had to nourish his roots if he was to develop as a writer. The failure to project himself artistically, coupled with his remoteness from America, could only result in a draining of vitality.

Wright was not in disagreement with the point about roots. But he had no intention of returning to America to reconnect with them. He wished to trace different and, he hoped, deeper roots. The African project had had a long gestation. To his journal six years earlier, he had pledged to write 'the only book about Africa that will be written in my time' (maybe he meant the only 'good' book). And he gave his text a splendidly heraldic title: *Black Power*.

But Wright was lost in Africa, where he had hoped to find himself. His mind was of a different cast from that of the Africans he met, and of a different century. Even the colour of his skin, he discovered, could not be said to be the same as theirs: in Africa, shades of brown tended to be locally specific, whereas the Afro-American experience had melded them. He tried hard to identify with the people, but the people hardly recognized the point of his identification. He was the Outsider here.

Wright may have had pioneering insights into the political future of African peoples, but his ideas about progress are frozen in their era, and some sound startling now, coming from one who considered himself a liberal thinker. In a letter addressed directly to Nkrumah and postscripted to *Black Power*, Wright referred to 'our people' – the people of the Gold Coast – who 'must be made to walk, forced draft, into the twentieth century. The direction of their lives, the duties they must perform to overcome the stagnancy of tribalism, the sacrifices that must be made – all of this must be placed under firm social discipline!'

It's possible that this exclamatory call grew out of his own sensation of having lost his grip on reality in Africa. As he admitted in his book, everything from the religion ('juju' and ancestor worship) to the nudity he witnessed in the villages, either appalled him or left him wondering how to reconcile this ancient 'stagnancy' with the progressive demands of modern society to which he believed the new African nations must aspire. Seeing men holding hands and dancing together in a club, he immediately blamed 'the vices of the English public-school system. . . . Just as the African had taken inordinately to alcohol, had he taken to this too? . . . I leaned toward my host and whispered: "Look here. What's going on?"'

That 'Look here' is pertinently phrased, and speaks volumes. Wright was not an African: he was an American, with at least as many ties to modern Europe as to his ancestral homeland. His host assured him that he had not landed in a scene from James Baldwin's latest novel, but that the men's physical intimacy was an aspect of traditional tribal dancing, a part of the culture. Wright's response was to want to see the culture changed. The 'progressive' thinker on Third World issues was to find, over the coming years, that Third World thinkers themselves considered his ideas reactionary.

*

Wright chose to write about the Gold Coast, rather than any other African country, for several reasons: first, because of its early struggle to gain independence; then because it was British and thus permitted him reflections on the slave trade (he began his journey to Africa in Liverpool); and, of course, because of his personal connection with Nkrumah.

But there was another reason: the Gold Coast was not French. Had the first African state to cry out for self-rule been a part of the French empire, Wright would have left it alone. There was a war going on at that very moment involving a French Third World 'property', Vietnam. And when the French got out of that frying pan, it was only to land in the fire of Algeria. Wright then had an African colonial revolution taking place on his doorstep, posing the 'black or white' question in terms of the immediate vicinity. But far from answering the question apropos of Algeria, Wright never even asked it.

His silence was prudent. Once the Algerian rebels declared their goal as not just social equality on a footing with the white French settlers, but the creation of an independent nation, the French government became intolerant of criticism, at home, of its efforts to put down the rebellion by force. Expatriates, in particular, were expected not to meddle in the political affairs of the host country. They might be deported for attempting to do so. Responding in the pages of the *New Yorker* to the independence demands not just of Algeria but also of Morocco and Tunisia, Janet Flanner referred to 'Bloodshed, terrorism, and a state of small, awful civil war that involves the terrorist natives and the better part of the French Army.' With one eye trained constantly on the American Embassy, Wright did not permit himself even as objective a comment as that about the French-African situation. He avoided mentioning it altogether.

When he did turn his face away from Africa, it was to the East – not towards Indochina but Indonesia. The Bandung Conference of Third World Peoples took place in Jakarta in the spring of 1955, comprising twenty-nine nations, representing over a billion people. It was a show of hands from 'the oppressed peoples' of the world, inspiring confidence in Wright in the potential power of the emerging Third World.

The book which Wright wrote about this event, and about his journey to Indonesia, *The Color Curtain*, was beleaguered from the start, and at all stages reflected its author's vertigo as he lurched between dogma and confusion. First of all, the advance he received for the book was embarrassingly small: $500. Then Harper's, who had commissioned it and had published all his other books, rejected the manuscript. In need of subsidiary funding in order to make the trip to Indonesia at all, Wright had turned to the Congress for Cultural Freedom (CCF), the Paris-based anti-Communist organization which was later exposed as being sponsored by the CIA (incriminating rumours were circulating even at the time). Excerpts from Wright's book were published in the CCF-sponsored magazines *Preuves* and *Encounter*. After the book appeared, Wright was embarrassed when an important journalist in Jakarta who had acted as his host, and on whom Wright had depended for information, wrote an article for *Encounter* claiming that Wright had traduced the views of 'the majority of people with whom [he] came into contact', imputing 'racial' views to them.

Still, Wright insisted on the basic veracity of his report, defending himself against those who criticized or rejected it by claiming that he was 'saying things that Europeans do not want to hear'. Suspicions and conspiracy theories fogged his thoughts now, to the extent that when a Dutch publisher bought the translation rights to *Black Power* and *The Color Curtain*, Wright was taken by surprise: should not Holland, which had taken part in the exploitation of Africa, wish to suppress his books? He seemed to expect to find the publishers and translators in league with the government. He was similarly surprised when the books were bought for publication in England and France.

When his hastily written book about Bandung was about to appear at the beginning of 1956, Wright asked Donald Friede, his editor at his new publisher, World, not to send proofs to Baldwin or Ralph Ellison, such people, he said, not being 'independent enough to give their honest reaction to a book like *The Color Curtain*'. In fact, both Baldwin and Ellison, despite having little in common with each other, were more 'independent' in their views than he was – if what's meant is that they adhered to no particular political system, dogma, or party line. But Wright was now so sensitive to political criticism, or simply difference, that whoever did not share his point of view was automatically placed on the other side of the line.

In this former Communist's mind, Communism now represented the world's primary political evil, and he believed that the West had the duty and the right to intervene in the affairs of Third World countries if, by doing so, it could save them from the Communist threat. Holding up the European nation-state as the model of progressive society, Wright stated that it was in the interests of African 'backward' (his word) societies to aspire to emulate it. He appealed to the West to pledge aid – 'sans narrow, selfish, political motive' – in order to raise the Third World up from its state of poverty. It was in the West's interests to do so, for poverty made the Third World vulnerable to the threat of expansionism from China and the Soviet Union; prosperity would link it to the West.

In the middle of 1956, Wright made this unorthodox and, even for the times, unfashionable statement on the topic:

> In the minds of hundreds of millions of Asians and Africans the traditions of their lives have been psychologically condemned beyond recall. Millions live uneasily with beliefs of which they have been made ashamed. I say 'Bravo!' for that clumsy and cruel deed. Not to the motives, mind you, which were all too often ignoble and base. But I do say 'Bravo!' to the consequences of Western plundering, a plundering that created the conditions for the possible rise of rational societies for the greater majority of mankind.

Black Power, in Wright's lexicon, did not mean what at first it might have seemed to.

*

In the summer of 1956, in Paris, there was a kind of Bandung of his own to attend to: the first Conference of Negro-African Writers and Artists (Congrès des Ecrivains et Artistes Noirs), which was to take place over four days at the Sorbonne. It was organized by the African writers clustered round the Paris-based journal *Présence Africaine*: Léopold Senghor, Léon Damas, Alione Diop, Aimé Césaire and others.

During the early part of his residence in the city, Wright had been closer to the francophone African writers than he was now. He had regarded them as the black literary avant-garde, and saw in his association with the group the *entrée* into Africa he was seeking. For their part, they welcomed him as the world's most famous black writer, hoping that, by embracing him, a little of his bright renown might fall on them. He had been involved with the magazine from its inception, attending the first board meeting at the Brasserie Lipp in October 1946, and contributing a short story to the première issue. Lately, he had found himself in disagreement with the hard-left views of Césaire, and the hard Catholic views of Senghor. Nevertheless, when the delegations for the Conference were

212

discussed by the committee of *Présence Africaine*, Wright's name emerged naturally to head the American one.

Présence Africaine was open to all, stated Diop in the first editorial of the magazine, 'white, yellow and black', who were willing to 'help to define the creativity of the African and to speed his integration into the modern world'. *Présence Africaine* was established as a forum for debating the problems confronting the new African, unable to turn back wholly in the direction of tribalism, equally unwilling to adopt Western civilization wholesale, unsure of his place in the contemporary world, and of how he was regarded by the West. 'We people from overseas countries possess immense moral resources', wrote Diop, 'which constitute the substance to be fertilized by Europe. We cannot do without one another.'

A similar will to synthesis had led to the conception, over a decade earlier, of the movement known as *Négritude*, the exponents of which, mainly poets, came from various French-speaking countries of Africa and the Antilles. Drawing on the resources of both European avant-gardism and African traditional song, the *Négritude* artists aimed to create an 'African originality', in Senghor's phrase – responsive, so to speak, both to the village and the metropolis. A writer like Senghor, who insisted that his poetry should properly be chanted to a musical background, might be said to have been seeking a rhythm in language which would reflect the movement of the African walking through the modern city with ancient melodies in his head.

Opening the Conference of Negro-African Writers on September 19, Diop referred to the gathering as a second Bandung. The people congregated in the Amphithéâtre Descartes, he said, had in common their subjugation to Europe, or at least to the European vision of the world. He regretted the tendency towards assimilation in the colonized African countries, and deplored the opinions of those who wished for an assimilation so complete that the African would be indistinguishable – in dress, in manners, in taste, in culture

– from his conqueror; black wishing to whitewash itself.

When these words were spoken, Wright was stationed on the platform beside Diop and the other leading members of *Présence Africaine*. Any self-doubt which he experienced would have been compounded by the reading aloud of a telegram to the assembly from W. E. B. DuBois, the venerable father of the modern Afro-American intelligentsia. DuBois had been invited by the organizers to attend the conference, but was unable to do so, the telegram stated, because 'the United States Government will not grant me a passport'. DuBois, who described himself in his message as a 'Socialist', was not merely registering his apologies. As *he* had been refused a passport, therefore 'Any Negro-American who travels abroad today must either not discuss race conditions in the United States or say the sort of thing which our State Department wishes the world to believe.'

So much for good wishes – this effectively accused the American delegation of being a bunch of Uncle Toms.

The communiqué was considered extremely ill-timed by the five-man delegation. But did DuBois have a point? The question of which names should be included in the American team had received a good deal of attention from several bodies and individuals. The handing out of invitations was, finally, the business of the conference organizers, but as the cost of transporting the Americans to Europe fell to the USIA, the cultural arm of the Embassy, the Embassy was not willing to pass up the chance to influence the selection.

Wright also wished to have a say in the matter, and did so. He was worried that the political orientation of Diop, Césaire and the rest would result in a left-leaning delegation from America (in which he, as its leader, would find himself out-flanked). It was apparently Wright's concern that

> the members of the (Executive Committee of the Congress) were liberal thinkers and he thought there was a danger the Communists might exploit the Congress to their own ends. Many members of the Presence Africaine, he said, were in search of an

214

idea they could not obtain and as such would be fertile ground for Communist exploitation.

Whether this glib summary adequately represents the views Wright expressed or not is impossible to say for certain. He stated his reservations not at some café table on the Left Bank, but at the US Embassy. There his testimony was written down – and forwarded in a confidential memo to the State Department in Washington, and thence to the FBI. The memo (dated May 3, 1955, and addressed from 'Amembassy PARIS' to 'DEPARTMENT OF STATE') says that

> Richard Wright, American Negro on the Executive Committee of the Presence Africaine and former Communist Party member, believes that, through careful selection of the American delegation to the Congress, the Leftist tendencies of the Congress can be neutralized. . . . On his own initiative, Mr Wright called at the Embassy to express certain concern over the Leftist tendencies of the Executive Committee.

To counteract the danger of the American delegation mirroring this left-leaning bias,

> Mr Wright wondered if the Embassy could assist him in suggesting possible American negro delegates who are well known for their cultural achievements and who could combat the leftist tendencies of the Congress. Mr Wright, the Department will recall, was himself formerly a member of the Communist Party.

He stressed to the Embassy that while he had until recently been on the Committee of *Présence Africaine*, he had been dropped 'because of his present anti-Communist principles'. Wright also contacted Michael Josselson, who was in charge of the Congress for Cultural Freedom and based in Paris, and asked him to call at the Embassy to discuss ways of influencing the politics of the forthcoming conference. Josselson did so, offering 'his collaboration in combating Communist influences'.

Wright would have been deeply compromised had the contents of this conversation become known to his colleagues at

Présence Africaine, or indeed to his fellow American writers. The *raison d'être* of the event was the affirmation of the liberated anti-colonial spirit among 'oppressed peoples', and the United States, where segregation was still in force in the South, was seen as one of the main oppressors. The intellectual drift of the major speeches at the Conference was captured by Aimé Césaire: 'We find ourselves today in cultural chaos, and it is our role to liberate the forces which can organize from this chaos a new synthesis, a synthesis which will deserve the name of culture. We proclaim the right of our people to speak.'

But not to speak to the people Wright had spoken to.

In Wright's defence, it should be noted that the list of possible candidates for inclusion in the American party which he submitted to the Embassy consisted mainly of friends, and they were hardly government stooges. He put forward the names of Ralph Ellison, Chester Himes, William Gardner Smith and Langston Hughes, all of whom, at one time or another, had been of leftist orientation. Probably he was thinking mainly about marshalling his own moral support, in fear of being outdone by the Africans. But the action of going to the Embassy, 'on his own initiative' if the FBI report is to be believed, tipping off the very people he was apt to accuse of being the enemies of freedom, hurts his reputation for independence and integrity.*

He was even more out of touch than he thought he was. For when he rose to his feet to speak on the last day in the Amphithéâtre Descartes, it was to deliver the speech in which he offered two cheers – 'Bravo!' – to 'the consequences of Western plundering'. Colonialism, he told the assembly, had been in many respects a liberation, since it broke old traditions and destroyed strange gods. Wright interrupted himself at one

*In the end, the delegation contained none of the figures suggested by Wright, nor anyone known for holding radical views. It consisted of Mercer Cook, Jim A. Davis, Horace Mann Bond, James Ivy, William T. Fontaine, and Wright himself.

point in the course of making his speech, to admit to the audience that he had been surprised, during the past three days, to discover that few of the other speakers felt the same way about this as he did.

*

Baldwin was not on anyone's list. He was still considered an *ingénue*, with a less solid literary footing than, say, William Gardner Smith. In any case, although he held opinions about colonialism and such subjects as the place of Christianity in Africa, he vexed himself scarcely at all over the upheavals taking place in the continent. It simply wasn't his Third World.

Baldwin wrote little about Africa, besides passing remarks in essays. He never mentioned Wright's book *Black Power* in print. By the time *he* began to concern himself with 'black power', it meant something different. He was even less able to communicate with the Africans he encountered in Paris than Wright had been with those he met in Africa. When Baldwin looked at an African, it only hardened his own sense of himself as an African American. Baldwin's politics were not left or right; they weren't even black or white; they transcended what he saw as fundamentally artificial social categories; his politics were personal, the politics of identity. In one of the few passages in which he attempted to examine the presence of Africa in the soul of the American Negro (in an obituary notice of Richard Wright, as it happens), he went at it with idiosyncratic acuity: 'when [the black American] faces an African, he is facing the unspeakably dark, guilty, erotic past which the Protestant fathers made him bury – for their peace of mind, and for their power – but which lives in his personality and haunts the universe yet'.

Towards the end of the decade, Baldwin gave an interview to the black American journal *Phylon*, in which he ruminated on his intercourse with Africans in France in extraordinarily candid terms. His dealings with Africans in Paris had led him to the realization that the black man from the ancient village and the black man from the New World were separated by both time and space: a gulf of centuries and the culture of a continent – the continent being Europe. As an American Negro, he was committed to Europe, had absorbed European visions, in a way that the African never could. 'They disgusted me,' he told the editor of *Phylon*, Harold Isaacs. Making specific reference to Senghor, he went on:

> They hated America, were full of racial stories, held their attitudes largely on racial grounds. Politically, they knew very little about it. Whenever I was with an African, we would both be uneasy. . . . The terms of our life were so different, we almost needed a dictionary to talk.

Baldwin did attend the Conference at the Sorbonne, however, in the role of reporter, writing about the event for *Encounter*. His commentary on the speeches of Diop, Senghor, George Lamming, Wright and others is penetrating, frequently droll. At one point, Senghor surprised the American contingent in the hall by proclaiming that Wright's autobiography, *Black Boy*, were it to be analysed, would reveal a heritage of 'African tensions and symbols, even though Wright himself had not been aware of this'. Nods of approval from the culturally correct greeted this insight, while Baldwin remarked, 'In the same way, I supposed that Dickens's *A Tale of Two Cities* would, upon analysis, reveal its debt to Aeschylus. It did not seem very important.'

When Richard Wright got up to speak, Baldwin grasped the opportunity to take one more swipe at his former father-figure. Europe had brought the Enlightenment to Africa, Wright said, and 'what was good for Europe was good for all mankind'. Baldwin found this, in present company, 'a tactless way of phrasing a debatable idea'. Wright then went on to express the view that Europe, having given Africa the methods to make itself 'modern', should now allow the African and Asian countries to develop independently, and 'refuse to be shocked' at whatever political methods were used in the cause of social evolution.

It was nothing short of a call for the toleration of dictatorships. Not long before, in a conversation with Gunnar Myrdal, author of *An American Dilemma*, the pioneering work on race prejudice in the United States, Wright had expressed disappointment at 'how little', not how much, Europe had done in Africa. Once delivered from colonial rule, Wright lamented, 'they'll go back to their traditional religion'. But how, Myrdal asked Wright, should the black Western-educated leaders go about altering the mental habits of their people? 'They'd have to impose dictatorial methods,' Wright answered 'readily'.

That readiness reveals Wright to be as much a proponent of social engineering as ever he was in his Communist Party days. Standing before the audience at the Sorbonne, he predicted that once the new social order was in place, these leaders 'would voluntarily surrender the "personal power"'. This was too much for Baldwin. In his essay, he quipped: 'He did not say what would happen then, but I supposed it would be the second coming.'

II

By complying with the Army intelligence unit in 1954 and answering questions about Communists, and then accepting the reward of a fresh passport, Wright left himself open to the possibility of further interviews, further requests, further compromises. By voluntarily consulting the Embassy over the American delegation to the Sorbonne conference, he had let down his African (and American) colleagues. His speech at the conference had aligned him with people and forces incommensurate with his own interests.

Always sensitive to criticism, Wright was now apt to regard any unfavourable comment as a calculated attempt to sabotage his reputation. Simple requests met with wayward responses. When the British MP and journalist Richard Crossman contacted Wright to ask permission to reprint the essay 'I Tried to Be a Communist', which explained Wright's disillusionment with the Communist Party, in a tenth-anniversary edition of Crossman's anthology, *The God that Failed*, the American refused. According to Wright's closest friend, Ollie Harrington, who had lunch with him the next day, Wright told Crossman 'to tell them – and he emphasized the word "them" – that he would write an essay on racism and the cloak and dagger terrorism which was poisoning the climate around the expatriate Paris community'. He exclaimed: 'They can publish that in their god-damned tenth anniversary issue!'

Who does 'them' refer to? Did Wright believe that Crossman – then the assistant editor of the left-wing *New Statesman*, later the editor – or perhaps his publishers were merely puppets of the CIA? Or MI6? Or some other section of the universal department of oppression? There is no way of telling; in a poisoned climate of 'cloak and dagger terrorism', which was how Wright and Harrington now experienced the atmosphere in Paris, 'them' is just *them* – anyone who is not 'us'.

An entry in the journal Wright kept when he first arrived in Paris illustrates the cast of mind that later caused him to be habitually suspicious of other people's motives. Driving his outsized American car through the narrow Paris streets, Wright was continually disconcerted by the French pedestrians' habit of stepping on to the road at street junctions, confidently expecting that the bullying vehicles would stop. Is it that they actually *want* me to hit them, Wright asked his journal – not grasping the mutually arrogant understanding that exists between drivers and pedestrians in Paris – 'so that they can sue?'

Spy stories were bouncing all over the quarter, and the ever-present agents of the CIA were – well, ever-present. And where they themselves were not visible, their shadows were. Chester Himes thought William Gardner Smith was in the pay of the CIA; Smith suspected Wright was; others raised the same suspicion about Harrington, even though he was a committed socialist and later went to live in East Germany. Wright at times gave the impression that just about everybody was, while harbouring especially strong suspicions about Smith and Richard Gibson.

Whispers about Wright himself, of which he caught something more than a breath, added to the fabric of cloak-and-dagger terrorism that so oppressed him. 'There is a story, a rumour, about you that is going about', the writer Kay Boyle warned him in 1956, 'that you are known to be working with the State Department, or the FBI, I don't know which, and that you give information about other Americans in order to keep your passport and be able to travel.'

How did Wright feel when he received that letter, less than a month after the conclusion of the Sorbonne conference? Kay Boyle was a veteran of the Paris scene of the 1920s, a friend of Stein and Sylvia Beach and many of Wright's literary forebears. The 'rumour' must have been very strong to have reached her in Connecticut, where she was writing from, and impressed her deeply, to cause her to approach Wright so boldly.

Wright would have denied the accusation, probably with conviction. To have recognized in the word 'informer' an anagram of his own name was beyond apprehension. All he had done in 1954 was confirm some names which would have been known to the Army as members, or former members, of the Communist Party anyway. And his voluntary trip to the Embassy this year was simply for the purpose of consulting the people who were putting up money for an American delegation, to discuss how that delegation might best be shaped.

If only the detractors listened to what he had learned, they would see that there were in the black colony – in the Café de Tournon, in fact – people who really were employed by government to discredit their fellow blacks.

*

The Algerian question was now the urgent one. For most French intellectuals it was less a question of 'black or white' than of left or right. Camus, agonizing in the ether above the mundane world of 'choice', surprised many by adopting what was seen as a colonialist position: 'I have been alert to Algerian realities and cannot approve either a policy of surrender that would abandon the Arab people to an even greater poverty, tear the French in Algeria from their century-old roots, and favour, to no one's advantage, the new imperialism now threatening the liberty of France and of the West.' The reference to the Soviet empire in the final clause drew sneers of resigned derision from the Sartreans, who regarded scaremongering of this type as the classic excuse whereby capitalist imperialism consolidated itself, by whatever means necessary. The means amounted to thousands of Algerian civilian deaths. 'Such a position satisfies no one today,' lamented Camus, and he was right.

Among the American black writers who considered themselves politically responsible, Algeria presented an awkward dilemma: namely, keep quiet, or else go home. Baldwin, soon to return to America, made what must be regarded as the most authentic choice – he got fed up, he would say later, sitting around in Paris cafés, 'polishing my fingernails and *talking* about Algeria', while at home in the States the brothers and sisters fighting for civil rights were out on the streets, doing the existential thing, choosing the future through present action. (Also finished with mere talk was Camus's particular *bête noire*, Francis Jeanson, whose devastating review of *The Rebel* in *Les Temps Modernes* in 1952 caused the famous rupture with Sartre. Jeanson ran a 'resistance' cell in Algeria against the French, and whenever he returned to Paris was obliged to go underground.)

To keep silent in the face of mounting horror in Algeria could seem to the politically conscious young writers at the Tournon to be the generator of bad faith. To be against but not to act or speak against – what, then, are beliefs for? In founding the Franco-American Fellowship some years earlier, Wright had been at pains to point out that it was American racism in France, not French racism in France, that the organization had been formed to fight. Black Americans were grateful to have found a refuge in Paris, to discover that they were treated like other foreigners; and although the awareness dawned sooner or later that France had its own pariahs, it was unwise to make a fuss about it, neither about the police brutality against Algerians occasionally witnessed on the street, nor the state brutality of the War.

This evasiveness on the part of American blacks did not go unnoticed. An article in the *Reporter* magazine by Ben Burns, a former editor of the black weekly *Ebony* (Burns himself was white), criticized Wright for 'poisoning European thinking about racial problems in America', while ignoring the treatment of Algerians. Wright – though he properly protested that it was not he who had poisoned Europe's view of the race problem in America, but American racism itself – nevertheless felt the sting of Burns's remarks. He regarded the article as further evidence of a concerted attempt to undermine his reputation and influence. That Burns was someone he had once considered a friend made it worse.

At last, somebody in the black intellectual community decided it was time to register a protest. A letter was sent to *Life* magazine stating an objection to an earlier editorial. The letter was published on October 21, 1957:

> *Life* maintains that there will be political and economic chaos in Algeria when France is finally forced to give up her colonial holdings ('Hopeful Plan for Algeria', *Life*, September 30). The chaos *Life* forgot to mention is right here in France. Any American who thinks that France of her own will, will grant Algeria, if not independence, at least some liberal status where seven million Algerians will not be crushed politically by a million Europeans is mad.

The letter was signed: 'Ollie Harrington, Paris, France'.

*

Harrington was quite well known at home as a political cartoonist. He had begun drawing and publishing his work more

223

than twenty years earlier – his most popular character was a wise-fool figure called 'Bootsie' – and had continued to work for black American papers since arriving in Paris in 1951. He was a big, hearty, popular man (Himes called him 'the accepted leader for all the blacks of the quarter'), but profoundly bitter. His experience of racism had thrust him leftwards politically, and he later said that he left America at the beginning of the 1950s having been tipped off that Army intelligence was about to 'investigate' him. In Paris, he grew close to Wright. Whereas Wright had left his Communist convictions behind, however, Harrington kept faith in his.

But no one who read the letter to *Life* said 'Bravo, Ollie.' In fact, Harrington did not write the letter. As someone who had enjoyed the hospitality of the French for five years, he would have been a fool to do so. No worthwhile attention would have been paid to his gesture, no significant outcome could have resulted from it – only trouble. 'My friends said, Ollie, you're crazy! Why on earth did you write that letter? You could be deported because of that. I said, I didn't write that letter. But I have an idea of who did.'

So who wanted to get Harrington into trouble?

About a year before the publication of the letter in *Life*, Harrington had left Paris for three months to go to Sweden. He agreed to sub-let his studio apartment during that time to Richard Gibson. The apartment was in a building in rue de Seine belonging to Raymond Duncan, brother of Isadora, who let out his rooms at low rents, mainly to artists. While in Sweden, Harrington claims, he received a letter from Gibson, 'in which he told me that if I tried to return to France, I would be picked up by the American military authorities the minute I stepped back on French soil, and deported. This was on account of my well-known Communist sympathies.

'I didn't let that stop me. I drove back to Paris and when I went to my apartment and knocked on the door, Gibson wouldn't let me in. He slammed the door and I couldn't get into my own place. I had things there, including frames, sketchpads, kitchen equipment, bedding, and all the rest. It was a crazy situation. Everybody in the quarter knew about it. I had no place to live.'

Slightly younger than most of the Tournon set, Gibson had come to Paris in 1952, following in the footsteps of William Gardner Smith, a friend from youth. In 1953, Gibson published an article in the magazine *Perspectives* (back-to-back with a reprint of Baldwin's essay 'Everybody's Protest Novel'), in which he complained about the stereotyping of Negro writers. In it, Gibson imagined a young writer sitting in the office of a major American publisher.

> 'Now to get down to business,' says our executive in smooth soothing tones, 'we want you to know that this is a liberal firm – why, we've printed the first works of many now-famous Negro authors.' He names them. 'Just what aspect of the Problem does your novel treat, Mr. X?'
> 'None,' replies X.
> 'You mean you haven't dealt with a race theme?'
> 'That's right.'
> The expression on our executive's face changes . . . .

Gibson pleaded for the black writer to be treated as 'a writer who also happens to be a Negro'. In the course of his argument, he referred to Wright as 'a doubtless sincere but defective thinker', which Wright counted as an outburst in the ongoing treasonous fusillade. As a writer, Gibson was not exactly prolific – partly the result, he might have said, of the kind of stultifying liberal bias depicted in his anecdote – but he had settled into a satisfying job as a journalist at Agence France Presse, where he occupied the desk next to Smith; his first novel was scheduled for publication in 1957.

Gibson takes a different view of his obstinate occupancy of Harrington's apartment. While acknowledging that it happened, he claims that the landlord endorsed his taking over the studio, as Harrington owed a large sum in unpaid rent. 'He did not own any of the furniture and there were no paintings in the one-room flat. [Harrington] had no legal title and

Duncan refused to have him back unless he paid what he owed.' Whether or not this was the case, Harrington was reluctant to go to the police, for fear of arousing the interest of the American Embassy in his difficulties, and so had to look for another place in Paris, while Gibson remained at rue de Seine. There was a violent fist-fight outside the Café de Tournon, in which Gibson got hurt, but he stayed in the apartment.

Next came the letter to *Life*. Harrington was certain he could identify the forger, and this time he decided that he would involve the police. He approached a well-known lawyer, Jacques Mercier, who asked Harrington to supply some proof. The letter was retrieved from the files of *Life*, and then, seeking help from among likely associates, Harrington compiled a dossier of letters and other documents written by Gibson, which enabled the comparison of typefaces and handwriting. Harrington next took the case to the DST, the French secret service, who listened while he suggested that there was more to this act than simple spite. It was a deliberate attempt by an American to discredit another American who held left-wing views. The police appeared to see his point, for at the close of questioning, claims Harrington, they told him: '"Don't mention this to anyone." Because – and I'll never forget the phrase – they said, "We want to see what's in this fish's belly."'

As for Wright, this confirmed what he already suspected: in the belly of the fish lurked a government agent, whose job it was to report on the views and opinions of members of the black community, and, where possible, implicate them in scandal. As a socialist, Harrington presented an easy target. Wright saw 'the Gibson affair', as it came to be known, as evidence for his belief that the black Left Bank colony was infiltrated by informers. He began to see them everywhere. He was apt to be outspoken about it. One day he entered a restaurant, walked up to a friend who was waiting for him, and said: 'Give that sonofabitch over there a drink. He's with the Government and he's been on my ass for months.' His idea of a joke was to ask Harrington over lunch: 'Do you know why the cafés in the quarter are crowded up till the last minute? It's because all those CIA informers can't leave until the one customer who ain't an agent leaves with the lady agent he thinks he picked up.' According to Harrington, Wright would 'laugh uproariously' at this type of story.

Wright undertook to get to the bottom of the Gibson affair, and in the process developed an obsession with the man at the centre of it. He drew up a list of questions he wanted Gibson to answer. Many of them dwelt on the role of William Gardner Smith, whom Wright regarded as Gibson's ally. Indeed, from Wright's questions, it would seem that he regarded Smith as the brains behind the plot – a view not disputed by Gibson himself – with Gibson as the hit-man. (Wright probably felt uneasy about Smith's possible knowledge of his own 'friendly' link with the Embassy.)

'Why were Ollie and I linked as targets of Smith?' Wright asked. 'Ollie as an alleged red and I as an alleged FBI man?' 'Could you have any idea why a girl with whom Smith was sleeping would come to my apartment on three occasions and ask to use my typewriter . . .?' She had her own, Wright pointed out; or she could have used Smith's. All this added up, in Wright's mind, to Smith's involvement in the affair. Wright even drew up a floor-plan of Harrington's apartment, showing how the girl, who was called Pamela, could have sneaked in to compose the incriminating letter to *Life* on Harrington's typewriter. Her repeated request to borrow Wright's machine suggested that a similar plot was being hatched which would besmirch him. He kept notes of his progress in uncovering the workings of the affair:

Gibson first tried what he thought would excite my emotions: a racial approach. . . . Gibson attempts an unsuccessful effort at talking and acting like an executive white man. . . . Gibson repeatedly said: I'm not government. But he did not say that he was not an agent!!!! And he had a most detailed knowledge of it in Germany. . . . Whenever I pushed Gibson hard about something he always found a 'personal' rather than a political reason for the action. Hence he says that [X] fought him because he slept once with [X's] wife.

Wright's detective work was aimed at clearing Harrington's reputation, as well as protecting his own. But, at the same time, he was gathering information which might be used in a novel. For what was to be his last work of fiction, which is unfinished and remains unpublished, Wright drew on incidents and characters from the Paris scene. One of the reasons for 'Island of Hallucination' not being published, according to Wright's daughter Julia, is that 'since it is a "roman à clef", it could provoke a certain amount of libel-prone fantasies about who is meant to be whom'.

Gibson himself admits writing the letter to *Life*, and offers his own explanation for the highly irregular action:

It was Bill Smith who set the whole thing up. There was a lot of sympathy for the Algerian national struggle among the American writers, but the problem was, how could you speak out and still stay in France? People wanted to criticize the War, but they wanted to stay in France, so they were caught in a bind. Bill got this mad scheme, in which the idea was that everybody was going to write letters and they'd sign them in someone else's name. If everybody used someone else's name, then when the French police came to you, you could say, quite rightly, 'That's not my signature. That's a fake.' But the damage, from the point of view of publicity, would have been done.

Well, anyway I did it. But I said to Bill: What about Harrington, does he know? 'Oh, yes, it's all right with Ollie.' Because we'd had this fight over the flat. The letter was published in *Life* and the *Observer* in London. And one morning the police arrived, the DST, and I was taken to their headquarters. They showed me the letter and said: 'Did you write this?' More or less overwhelmed by the fact that they knew, I said, 'Well, yes.' And they said, 'We knew all along', and they pulled out a statement – signed by Bill Smith! He had denounced me.

I was never officially arrested, just detained. Apparently people thought I was going to be deported, though I wasn't. And this caused even more consternation – why wasn't I expelled? People assumed that I had been prosecuted, but I never was. It was quite surprising to them that I wasn't banned from France. This was interpreted as proving that I had high protection in the American Embassy or government or CIA, or something like that.

When Gibson returned home after leaving the offices of the DST, he found a *pneumatique* from his employers, AFP, telling him not to come to work next morning. 'I later discovered it was because of Bill Smith – that he had got up a petition from the people on the desk saying they didn't want to work with a person like me.'

Gibson wrote to Wright after this, denouncing Smith as a 'false brother'; he assured Wright that Wright was far too important a figure for anyone to harm, unless they were prepared to enter into a great deal of intrigue (which is, of course, precisely what Wright suspected Gibson and Smith of doing). He tried to keep up a front of cordiality with Wright, presenting him with a signed copy of his novel, *A Mirror for Magistrates*: 'For Richard Wright, the "father of us all", with many thanks for his understanding. Richard Gibson, Paris, Sept, 1958.'

But the understanding existed only in Gibson's head. Wright never forgave him for compromising Harrington, and never ceased believing that Gibson was in the pay of the government. Two years on, he would receive what he took to be further proof of his suspicions when Gibson sent him an open postcard from Cuba, then the focus of every American fear.

> Greetings from revolutionary Cuba – a really free and democratic and progressive land that has dared to shake off the shackles of American imperialism. Sartre is coming back in October – perhaps you would like to come and see for yourself?

Gibson was at that time known in radical (and therefore government) circles for his involvement in the organization of the Fair Play for Cuba campaign. Such a message to Wright could be interpreted as assuming Wright's complicity in

Gibson's own apparent enthusiasm for the Communist regime in Cuba; and since the postcard was open to anyone to read, that made it easily interceptible, if – as Wright would have believed was the case – someone was keeping an eye on his mail.

What was in the fish's belly? As Harrington declined to press charges, the DST never had the opportunity to find out. There was no proper investigation of the Gibson affair beyond that carried on sporadically by Wright. Gibson's troubles continued after leaving Paris. He came to be regarded by certain other people involved in the Fair Play for Cuba campaign, such as the poet Leroi Jones (later Amiri Baraka), as being a government agent. In 1964, the Paris-based political magazine, *Révolution*, edited by Jacques Vergès, for which Gibson had worked as US Editor, published a denunciation of him, 'following grave accusations by certain comrades in New York, London and Accra, which have been confirmed by investigation'.

*

The Gibson affair caused a fracture in the black *cénacle* in Paris. Even with Gibson gone – he left the city in 1958 – Wright felt vulnerable, and continued to believe that he was being targeted from the other side of the ocean. In the autumn of 1958, a journalist from *Time* arrived in Paris in order to write an article about the black literary colony, motivated mainly by the recent award to Chester Himes of the Grand Prix de Littérature Policière for his novel *La Reine des Pommes* (*A Rage in Harlem*).

Wright declined to be interviewed, believing that the reporter would say only what he had made up his mind in advance to say, no matter what Wright told him. Himes, Harrington and Smith were more co-operative, and each was quoted. However, it must have come as a shock to all of them that the article, 'Amid the Alien Corn', which appeared in *Time* on November 17, should end with a quote from Gibson, expressing precisely the sort of views with which Wright in particular wished to avoid being publicly associated, especially in journals such as *Time*.

> 'All those people are in Europe because of social and political causes, which everybody knows. The bright young white boys, after the end of their Fulbright scholarships, are able to return with reasonably light hearts to the dens of Madison Avenue or to the provincial Ph.D factories. It is still impossible for an American Negro to return to the land of his birth in the same spirit.'

In the prominence given to his enemy, Wright would have seen confirmation of his suspicion that the *Time* journalist had approached the principal topic with the intention of dirtying the reputations of the black writers in the eyes of the public and of the government. He would have been pleased with his decision to remain aloof.

So it was with incredulity that he discovered that he *was* quoted in the article – in fact, the page was laid out around a photograph of him, mouth open and arm outstretched, as if leaning disputatiously towards the photographer.

> Richard (*Native Son*) Wright, the dean of Negro writers abroad, says bluntly: 'I like to live in France because it is a free country. Then there are my daughters. They are receiving an excellent education in France.' What of the dangers of getting out of touch with US life? Snaps Wright: 'The Negro problem has not changed in 300 years.'

Wright had snapped no such thing – at least not to any journalist from *Time*. The person to whom he had said these things – or things roughly similar, for the views attributed to him were roughly his views – was the photographer Gisèle Freund, credited next to the photograph, who had claimed at the time to be taking pictures for her own agency. It seemed that *Time* questioned her about her conversation with Wright, and then quoted the remarks made by the reluctant 'dean' as if he had been speaking to its own reporter. Freund's 'reward', though she may have acted unwittingly, was to have one of her photographs reproduced in *Time*.

231

Wright felt frustrated all the way. He threatened to sue, but withdrew when the cost of such an action was pointed out to him. He demanded a retraction, which *Time* refused to issue. 'Did not see your reporter,' he fumed in a cable to the editor. 'Are you now aping Communist tactics of character assassination?' *Time* remained unmoved.

Wright's mind was a firetrap of loose wires. What might seem to the detached observer to be a relatively minor infringement was likely to blow a fuse. In fact, his whole experience of exile, which had begun shortly after the Liberation and had reflected his personal liberation, had done just that. Paris no longer contained the power to seduce him. International literary success – the strangest thing that could have happened to a boy from Mississippi sharecropping farms, just a couple of generations removed from slavery – had ebbed away, leaving him at the mercy of accursed historical – which is to say racial – determinants.

Wright is not to be judged harshly for his fear and suspicion, for he incorporated them, and the tension that resulted from their breeding, like a gene. He was virtually programmed to feel like a 'hunted being', as he himself put it in his early Paris journal. He formulated the black man's dilemma like this: born and reared to express his sense of the ethical values of his own country (the country which had enslaved him), he then lived in fear of the same expression bringing down an unforeseeable punishment on his head. No matter what you did, or how you did it; no matter where you looked, or who or what you looked at, you were looking at the wrong thing, at the wrong person, in the wrong way. Wright had been among the first black Americans to 'jump free' (when he arrived in Paris, he would not have used the quotation marks) of that mentality, only to find that he had landed in a different corner of the same pit.

Near the end of his life, he delivered a lecture in Paris on the subject of the difficulties confronting the black writer abroad. It expresses his fear of Gibson, his dislike of Baldwin, his groundless contempt for Ralph Ellison, who, having spent two years in Rome, according to Wright, feared that the cultural establishment – his 'white sponsors' – might accuse him of disloyalty and hold his expatriation against him. Towards the close, Wright came out with a statement which is the key to the experience of the second half of his life in France:

> This is the fear with which we Negro artists and intellectuals live. It shapes our work. And he who escapes from the circle that controls his expression, is damned.

III

During the months leading up to the Conference of Negro-African Writers and Artists at the Sorbonne, black students in the Southern states of America, on their way to attend classes at previously all-white universities, had to walk between rows of policemen holding back mobs of jeering white protestors. In February, the *New York Herald-Tribune* reported that Autherine Lucy, the first black student at the University of Alabama, had almost been lynched as she tried to enter the building. The next day, she was temporarily barred from classes, 'as a safety measure'. One day round about the time of the actual conference, Baldwin had read a similar story in the papers, which seemed to him to have deep relevance to the matters discussed at the Sorbonne, even though it had nothing to do with Africa. The front pages showed photographs of a fifteen-year-old girl, Dorothy Counts, being reviled and spat upon by a mob as she made her way to school in Charlotte, North Carolina . . . 'it made me ashamed. Some of us should have been there with her!'

This was *his* Third World: a colonial struggle taking place in towns where his people were subjugated. The speeches at the conference, some invigorating, some vague, had inspired a variety of reactions in him, as the place of the African in the modern world was debated. Now the moment of the African in America had come, and it wasn't happening over here but over there. As he read the story and looked at the pictures, Baldwin knew he was leaving France.

Baldwin had, in fact, just written his first words on the subject of civil rights, in the form of an essay addressing the political foolishness of William Faulkner. In an interview with the *Reporter*, the great novelist had come out with a series of statements about race relations in the South, which ranged from the silly to the deranged. For example, he said that things were getting better in the South, as witnessed by the fact that 'only six Negroes were killed by whites in Mississippi last year, according to the police figures'. He also gave his opinion that eventually 'the Negro race will vanish by intermarriage'. The low point in what was probably a drunken ramble came when he proclaimed that 'if it came to fighting I'd fight for Mississippi against the United States even if it meant going out into the street and shooting Negroes'.

Faulkner's disavowal of the views attributed to him in a subsequent issue of the magazine (he himself called them 'foolish and dangerous'; but the interviewer stuck to his story) came too late to prevent Baldwin, still in France, from issuing a pithy rejoinder in the pages of *Partisan Review*. It proves him to be a man increasingly engaged, in charge of an increasingly supple pen. He dealt with Faulkner's alleged remarks reasonably and efficiently, brushing aside, for example, the consolatory statistic of 'only six Negroes' killed by police in Mississippi. Retorted Baldwin: 'Faulkner surely knows . . . something about "police figures" in the Deep South.' In the prefacing remarks to his essay, Baldwin displays the literary confidence, and moral humanism, that had already marked him out as the most promising young writer in Paris, and would, within a few years, turn him into the American conflict's recording angel:

> Any real change implies the break-up of the world as one has always known it, the loss of all that gave one an identity, the end of safety. And at such a moment, unable to see and not daring to

234

imagine what the future will now bring forth, one clings to what one knew, or thought one knew; to what one possessed or thought one possessed. Yet, it is only when a man is able, without bitterness or self-pity, to surrender a dream he has long cherished or a privilege he has long possessed that he is set free – he has to set himself free – for higher dreams, for greater privileges. All men have gone through this, go through it, each according to his degree, throughout their lives. It is one of the irreducible facts of life. And remembering this, especially since I am a Negro, affords me my only means of understanding what is happening in the minds of white Southerners today.

This is intelligence motivated and guided by emotion. But the feeling that powered Baldwin's insight, even when, as here, he was writing about a social crisis, was frequently generated by a private crisis. It was not a failure of talent; rather it was its strength. It was by means of this balancing of public mind and individual conscience that Baldwin's prose achieved its authority. 'I am the man, I suffered, I was there': he chose the line from Whitman as the epigraph for *Giovanni's Room*, but it could have been affixed to almost any of his writing – novel or short story, essay or play.

Simply by lopping off its final sentence, the splendid paragraph which opens his reply to Faulkner could be applied directly to a man with a broken heart, trying to lift himself out of a failed love-affair – to Baldwin himself, in fact, even as he wrote these words. His relationship with a young jazz drummer from Harlem, named Arnold, had come to grief, and the distress it caused him was as much behind Baldwin's compulsion to quit Paris, and eventually France, as the duty to witness and participate in the struggle for civil rights. 'It was on that bright afternoon that I knew I was leaving France,' Baldwin wrote in his memoir, *No Name in the Street* (1972), recollecting that he had been hit by images of Dorothy Counts's ordeal on the newsstands as he left the conference; but his memory had played a trick on him, for none of the leading papers ran desegregation stories over that weekend, and anyway he remained in

235

France, trying to heal his broken heart, for another year.

He went from Paris to Corsica, where he stayed, sifting through the wreckage, accompanied at first by Arnold, and then alone, for about nine months. In a sheaf of letters written to his friends Gordon Heath and Leslie Schenk from his tiny village ('no bigger than the Flore', he told Schenk, 'and closed much earlier'), he never once mentioned civil rights or the Third World, just developed the theme of himself and his failings, as he perceived them, as if his stone cottage was a darkroom in which he might achieve self-exposure . . . 'it is only when a man is able, without bitterness or self-pity, to surrender a dream he has long cherished . . . that he is set free'.

He had had trouble getting *Giovanni's Room* published – Knopf, the New York publishers of *Go Tell It on the Mountain,* had turned it down because of its too-torrid subject matter – but another publisher, Dial, finally brought it out while he was still in Corsica. Alone in his cottage, he could flick through the pages and reflect that it, too, was prescient. Although the novel about the transforming power of love, the fear of one individual to accept it, and the tragic consequences that result, was written before the start of the love-affair that had just ended, it had turned out to be about it anyway.

Did he ever contemplate taking *Giovanni's Room* to Girodias, publisher of unpublishable books? Doubtful. And anyway, had he done so, it's unlikely that Girodias would have taken it on. Not that the homosexual detail in itself would have deterred him – more likely he would have complained that there wasn't enough of it. Olympia had already published *The Thief's Journal* and would soon do *Our Lady of the Flowers* and other books with the same theme. But the love-affair at the heart of *Giovanni's Room* would have struck the pornographer as too sensitive, too fragrant, lacking in the necessary sexual athletics.

Returning to Paris from Corsica in the summer of 1957, Baldwin paused briefly in the city before sailing on to New York. It was then that he made his way to the trouble spots in the American South. His 'Paris Years' were over. He had had scarcely any contact with the native writers in the country which had given him, on the whole, hospitable lodging since 1948; less contact than Wright by far, and less contact with the French reading public than Himes, who these days referred to himself, in bitter jest, as a 'French writer'. But Baldwin had become more Parisian than the others in one respect: he was now fully *engagé*.

The ticket that exploded

For the writers who lived in Paris after the Second World War, the example of the generation of the 1920s was unavoidable, if not actually an ideal. Richard Wright had received the baton in person from Gertrude Stein, just weeks before she died, leaving him the most celebrated of expatriate English-speaking writers in the city. 'She has realized acutely the difference between Yesterday and Today,' Wright said in his profile of Stein for *PM* magazine in 1946. With the death of Stein, she was Yesterday, he was Today.

In his very first letter to Stein, from New York, in 1945, he said that he hoped to find Paris 'as so many have said it used to be', adding that all American writers, sooner or later, wanted to visit Paris, the Paris which had been made real to Americans by the writers of the 1920s.

Baldwin came to France to look for Wright, but he rejected Wright as a literary model. In that domain, his mentors were Hemingway – Baldwin's first short story, 'Previous Condition', published in October 1948, a month before his arrival, bears the clear imprint of Hemingway – and, later, Henry James, a symbolic American-in-Paris of a yet earlier generation.

Peggy Guggenheim, a lover of Beckett and friend of many other Twenties writers, bestowed enough money on her son, Sinbad Vail, for him to found a literary magazine, precisely because she wished to keep the 'published-in-Paris' tradition alive, under her auspices. The *Paris Review* group were more self-conscious and candid about the connection with their café-writing forebears than any other. Christopher Logue, opening himself to the breath of Pound, felt that by coming to the place where Pound – and, to an extent, Eliot – had written poetry, he, Logue, might write poetry, too. And did. Trocchi came looking for Joyce's footprints, and by tracing them found Beckett. And so on.

Sometime in the late middle of the 1950s, the ethos changed. It was no longer the past that was the 'thing' – that usage being enough by itself to suggest the change – but the future. For the blacks, it had to do with Africa and civil rights in the American South. For the whites, even where they were not fully aware of it, it had to do with blacks.

SEVEN

Black and White Negroes

I

'We gotta go and never stop going till we
get there.'
'Where we going, man?'
'I don't know, but we gotta go.'

Jack Kerouac, *On the Road*

The Sixties arrived in Paris in 1957. In a dismal November,
Allen Ginsberg checked into a dismal hotel near the Seine, in
a narrow street connecting the Quai des Grands Augustins
with rue St-André-des-arts. Ginsberg had been in Europe for
six months. On the road: Tangier, Barcelona, Florence, Ischia
– where he sought out W. H. Auden, was insulted by the poet
(Auden thought Ginsberg's poems were 'full of the author
feeling sorry for himself'), and delivered a stronger insult in
return ('a bunch of shits', he called Auden and his friends) –
and now Paris.

Like others before him, Ginsberg looked in Paris for a
refuge from the puritanical strictures of his home country. But
he was not tracking the ghosts of Hemingway and Fitzgerald,
already, to his mind, exemplars of an old way of thinking.
Ginsberg wanted the City of Light to be his place of inner
illumination. He possessed a headful of visionary enthusiasm.

240

If there was inspiration in Paris past, it was the Paris of Baudelaire and Rimbaud; he would stir the poet within by walking where they had walked, seeing what they had seen, and smoking what they had smoked. It was also a city famed for its sexual constituency, past and present – city of Genet, of O, of Olympia, *Sexus*, *Nexus* and *Plexus* – among which he hoped to find an address.

His immediate address was the small hotel at 9 rue Gît-le-coeur, named after its proprietor, Madame Rachou. Of the nine categories of hotel in Paris, the Hôtel Rachou was the lowest: hole-in-the-floor lavatories, with newsprint for toilet paper; leaking roofs and dream-disturbing plumbing. The hotel possessed only one bath, the use of which required advanced reservation and exacted a surcharge. Everything was topsy-turvy; even the floors sloped.

On the credit side, each room had a gas ring and a small table, so that guests could eat cheaply 'at home'. Mme Rachou, a tiny woman with a startling blue rinse, ran a small bistro on the ground floor, where you could drink coffee and meet the other residents. In Ginsberg's time, they included a photographer who hadn't spoken to anyone for two years, and an artist who filled his room with straw. The Rachous were tolerant folk. There had once been a Monsieur Rachou, who had shared his wife's old-fashioned reverence for artists and writers, as well as her patience when the rent fell due, but he had recently died.

Ginsberg stayed in the Hôtel Rachou for ten months, together with his lover, Peter Orlovsky, and another aspiring poet, Gregory Corso. With her liking for bohemian types, Mme Rachou could be bafflingly particular about whom to admit to her dingy rooms and whom not to – many a plain-seeming applicant was turned away with a brusque 'complet' – but she apparently favoured this trio, and they all slept together in a sagging bed in a third-floor, front-facing room. One of her best: French windows giving on to the blank wall of the building across the street – spitting distance – and hot

241

water at weekends.

The other group for which Mme Rachou had a tender spot was policemen. Every morning, she entertained a clutch of gendarmes with cups of espresso and helpings of local gossip in her ground-floor bar, occasionally throwing in lunch as well. This gave a fright to Ginsberg and his crew. They were using drugs – heroin as well as marijuana, both of which had become cheap and easy to obtain in Paris – and generally following the route of disorderliness as a poetic creed: Rimbaud's 'dérèglement de tous les sens', updated to include jazz and a homegrown mendicant philosophy of the unwashed.

Ginsberg had arrived in Europe in March 1957, unknown. He had published one book from a small press in California, *Howl and other poems*, had a history of mental illness, and had got into trouble at university. He had been suspended from Columbia for tracing the words 'Fuck the Jews' on a dusty window. As Ginsberg was Jewish himself, this behaviour puzzled some (though not all). He had also become involved with the law in New York over his foolish and half-hearted participation in a series of burglaries masterminded by a Bonnie-and-Clyde team called Vickie Russell and 'Little Jack' Melody. Thanks to his teachers at Columbia, principally the critic Lionel Trilling, he was not sent to prison but was required to undergo psychiatric treatment, after which he was able to resume his studies and his writing.

Within a few months of arriving in Europe, however, and before he checked into the Hôtel Rachou, Ginsberg was famous. Not in Paris, but at home in America. The reason for the sudden success was that his long poem 'Howl' had been prosecuted in San Francisco. Lawrence Ferlinghetti, owner of the City Lights Bookshop (which he modelled on George Whitman's Librairie Mistral in the rue de la Bûcherie) and publisher of *Howl and other poems*, was arrested for selling the book. A trial was ordered, which Ginsberg was not required to attend. Several West Coast writers testified on behalf of the poem's literary merit, and in October a judge ruled that

'Howl' was not obscene.

Then, during the same summer, Jack Kerouac's novel *On the Road* was published to a highly favourable reception. The Beat Generation was on the go . . . it had publicity and an outrageous leader who went to tea with Dame Edith Sitwell and offered her heroin. Or so said *Life* magazine, which ran a story on Ginsberg and the beats, the philosophy of beat, the meaning of beat ('beatitude', or just 'beat-up'?), during the poet's absence in Europe.

*

About a year after taking up residence in the Hôtel Rachou, the three-in-a-bed group of Ginsberg, Orlovsky and Corso reassembled at Ginsberg's alma mater, Columbia University, to give a poetry reading. Poetry, in the late 1950s, was treated with caution and reverence at Columbia, where there was deep respect for tradition. The first evening of Beat poetry was introduced by the critic F. W. Dupee, who began pointedly by saying that the last poet he had introduced from this platform was T. S. Eliot. He admitted that he didn't much care for the poetry he and the 1,500 people in the McMillan Theater were about to hear, but thought it right that this suddenly prominent 'generation' should have its say. Other members of the English department agreed with his opinions about poetry but not about freedom of spoken verse, and stayed away in protest.

The critic Diana Trilling attended the reading. She was the wife of Lionel (absent) and the friend of Auden (also absent), another member of the faculty. Her comments about the appearance and hygiene of the poets are suggestive of the way people thought about this new and menacing force – youth – when it first caught the headlines, the gossip columns, and the talk in the polite salons, including the Trillings':

> For me, it was of some note that the auditorium smelled fresh. The place was already full when we arrived: I took one look at the crowd and was certain that it would smell bad. But I was mistaken. These people may think they're dirty inside and dress up to it.

Nevertheless, they smell all right. The audience was clean and Ginsberg was clean and Corso was clean and Orlovsky was clean. Maybe Ginsberg says he doesn't bathe or shave; Corso, I know, declares that he has never combed his hair; Orlovsky has a line in one of the two poems he read . . . 'If I should shave, I know the bugs would go away.' . . . Kerouac, in crisis, didn't appear, but if he had come he would have been clean and shaven too. . . . And anyway, there's nothing dirty about a checked shirt or a lumberjacket and blue jeans, they're standard uniform in the best nursery schools.

When Ginsberg dedicated a poem to her husband, Mrs Trilling was surprised by how much she liked it – she heard it as a 'passionate love poem'. (Ginsberg had actually intended the dedication ironically.) She was also impressed by the way in which Ginsberg resisted attempts during the question-answer period to make him speak about the 'philosophy' of the Beat Generation, explaining his production instead in terms of inspiration, ecstasy, illumination. She was less taken with Orlovsky, who, the audience was told, had read only two poems because he was still writing his third, and with Corso whom she saw as a small boy carrying on a private battle against powerful grown-ups. But of Ginsberg, she wrote, in one of her ever-spreading, encompassing sentences, with a kind of motherly impatience:

> Ginsberg, with his poems in which there was never quite enough talent or hard work, and with his ambiguous need to tell his teacher exactly what flagrancy he was now exploring with his Gide-talking friends at the West End Café had at any rate the distinction of being more crudely justified in his emotional disturbance than most; he had also the distinction of carrying mental unbalance in the direction of criminality, a territory one preferred to leave uncharted by student or friend.

Without quite intending to, Diana Trilling managed to pin to the floor with one stroke of the pen two of the fakirs of the era in store: the poet-as-psychopath and the poet-as-outlaw. Robert Lowell's *Life Studies*, the first book by a major poet (apart from *Howl* itself) to make its subject matter the mental

244

disturbance of the poet, was published in 1959, the same year as her essay appeared. Other contemplations of the poet's own psychopathology – by Sylvia Plath, John Berryman, Anne Sexton – would follow.

But it was the parallel career – poet-as-outlaw – that was taken by the Beats, Ginsberg's stay in the mental ward notwithstanding. His poems do not so much explore illness in the hope of healing the poet, as they seek to do to social norms and intellectual conventionality what, he wrote to Ferlinghetti, he had wanted to do to his old university on the night of the poetry reading: 'break its reactionary back'. It was society's requirement of uniform behaviour and its rejection of aliens which was, Ginsberg believed, the cause of his mental crisis. Instead of accepting the doctors' and professors' opinions (this was what Mrs Trilling failed to understand) and trying to 'adjust', he should embrace his maladjustedness in the cause of ultimate self-fulfilment. He wanted the freedom of his visions, the freedom to write poems with titles like 'Under the World There's a Lot of Ass, a Lot of Cunt', containing lines such as 'There's a lot of Shit under the world, flowing beneath cities into rivers,/a lot of urine floating under the world,/a lot of snot', and to write about his mother's vagina and his own anus. He wanted the freedom to undress in front of the camera, or anywhere else, to make love in the street if he felt like it, and not to pretend in interviews that his literary focus was purely intellectual, or even that his literary habits were purely literary: 'As I often do, I had been jacking off while reading,' he told an interviewer, momentarily interrupting an exposition of 'Supreme Reality with a capital S and R'.

With nothing of the hard criminal in him, this was Ginsberg's way of chipping at the stubborn, bland, smothering social fabric. Some of his friends had been more orthodox in their ways of subversion. Corso, a genuine streetboy, had spent three years in prison. Lucien Carr, another member of the circle, though not a writer, had also done time for stabbing and killing a man who made a pass at him (the motive for the

245

crime, and its ramifications, inspired Baldwin's early drafts for *Giovanni's Room*). William Burroughs had shot his wife in the head in 1951 during a game of 'William Tell', though he managed to convince the police that her death was an accident, and escaped punishment. Neal Cassady, the original for Dean Moriarty in *On the Road*, was a larger-than-life, irresponsible sponger, with an appetite for women and cars and petty crime.

The Beats found other ways of being outside the law. Ginsberg, Orlovsky, Burroughs and occasionally Cassady were sexual 'criminals', being homosexual, or bisexual, while Burroughs and several of his less literary (but more authentically 'beat-up') friends were junkies. Kerouac was more interested in drink than in drugs, and in women than in men, but he cut loose from everyday regulation by taking flight with Cassady and writing *On the Road* to the rhythm of the internal-combustion engine.

The Beat Generation raises its head as the suppressed demon in ordinary American life, as the urge for total anarchical freedom, without respect for laws or civilizing norms. The form which they gave to this impulse was not only in verse and prose, but in a lifestyle. Ginsberg and Kerouac did not just write about ways to be free; they *were* free. *Life* magazine had caught them in the act. And American youth realized, much more quickly than its elders, that the pre-eminent characteristics of the Beat Generation were not beards and uncleanliness, as Diana Trilling seemed to think, but rebellion and eroticism, and the beguiling dance between the two.

While the Beat writers were still unknown and largely unpublished, Hollywood provided a prototype. Marlon Brando in *On the Waterfront* is casual in manner and style, unimpressed by authority, if not downright disrespectful of it, conferring some sort of nobility on the rebel which he had previously wanted. Until then, the rebel, in modern myth, had been the feckless hobo or the always ambiguous red. Brando also made it clear – as James Dean did – that sex existed as more than an immobile screen kiss, or as bait used by women to ensnare husbands. Their sexual language was body language, but the Beats transferred the knowledge to the language of poetry and prose. A large amount of Beat Generation sexuality is homosexuality, which remains an unexplored part of its appeal, although a simple explanation would be to say that the clubbing together of boys, unencumbered by domesticating girls, creates an ethos of freedom and the promise of adventure which might lead to misadventure.

They gained their education, of course, not only from Parisian writers, but from writers who could only be published in Paris, mainly Henry Miller and Jean Genet. 'Have Genet's *Journal of a Thief* [sic] in English,' Burroughs wrote from Tangier to Ginsberg in New York in 1955, 'and have read it over many times. I think he is the greatest living writer of prose.'

If Miller is the father of the Beat Generation, Genet is its transvestite mother. An outlaw of the pre-war world, Genet committed himself to his criminality and homosexuality as articles of faith: he pledged to serve them. So Ginsberg tried to keep faith in his visions, and, later, to be as open about his homosexuality in public as about blowing his nose. 'I decided to be what crime made of me,' Genet had said, and Ginsberg and Kerouac might have appropriated and adapted the phrase: 'I decided to be what being *beat* made of me.'

From its outpost in Paris, the movement which had begun in New York as a fraternity of unsuccessful writers began to spread, leaving traces everywhere. No country in the Western world was untouched by the liberal revolution which the Beat Generation had started.

A monument survives on rue Gît-le-coeur, where, for ever after, Mme Rachou's establishment would be known as the Beat Hotel.

*

247

Ginsberg was writing all the time while in Europe and he
reached Paris with a bag full of papers. He could write – and
recite – anywhere, and gratefully took his seat in the local tradition of café-writing.

Nobody would have noticed another American scribbling in
his notebook – Ginsberg did not have his long beard and strag-
gly black hair at the time – except that, being Ginsberg, he
brought something extra to his toil: 'I sat weeping in the Cafe
Select . . .', he wrote to Kerouac in the month of his arrival. 'I
write best when I weep . . . I gotta get up a rhythm to cry.'

The poem he worked on in the Select was 'Kaddish', an
elegy for his mother, and he included some of his lines in the
letter to Kerouac:

> Farewell
> with long black shoe
> Farewell
> smoking corsets & ribs of steel
> Farewell
> communist party and broken stocking . . .
> with your eyes of shock
> with your eyes of lobotomy
> with your eyes of stroke
> with your eyes of divorce
> with your eyes alone . . .

It was not only his own writing that Ginsberg had brought
with him. All the way from Tangier, through Spain and Italy,
he had carried a manuscript by his friend and one-time lover
William Burroughs, who had stayed behind in North Africa.
Burroughs had published scarcely anything, and nothing at all
under his own name. The bundle in Ginsberg's rucksack was
the manuscript of *Naked Lunch*, in which Burroughs seemed to

be making a bid for total unpublishability. He had doubts about his calling anyway, suspecting that he was not really meant to be a writer. 'I am essentially active and will always seek solution in activity,' he wrote to Ginsberg. If his activity was to be in the literary arena, then he wanted to practise a form of writing that had 'the urgency of bullfighting'. In so far as it makes any sense at all to say so, in *Naked Lunch* he succeeded.

Stranded in Tangier during the second half of the 1950s, addicted to heroin, lovesick for Ginsberg, gorging himself on paid-for sex with Spanish boys, Burroughs began to record his impressions of the city in a series of bulletins to the poet. Tangier was then an 'international zone', colonized by eight foreign powers, and technically not a part of Morocco. Eager and admiring but also critically objective, Ginsberg was felt to be the perfect 'receptor' for what Burroughs called his 'routines': short, phantasmagorical prose pieces, usually involving mutations of people and events seen or experienced in Tangier. Over time, a book began to emerge from the impressionistic mass, to which Burroughs gave various titles: 'Interzone', 'Ignorant Armies', etc. (By a curious coincidence, the latter was also an early title for Baldwin's story based on the Lucien Carr case.)

Whenever Burroughs tried to turn his hand to other types of writing – for a magazine, for instance, in the hope of earning some money – he only had to begin typing to find he was writing another routine. In December 1954, he told Kerouac that he had

> sat down seriously to write a best-seller Book of the Month Club job on Tangier. So here is what comes out in the first sentence:
> 'The only native in Interzone who is neither queer nor available is Andrew Keif's chauffeur, which is not an affectation on Keif's part but a useful pretext to break off relations with anyone he doesn't want to see: "You made a pass at Aracknid last night. I can't have you in the house again."'

Vile grotesquerie ensues, and the passage was later refined and used to form the opening of the 'interzone' section of *Naked*

Lunch. (In a PS, Burroughs adds: 'Andrew Keif is Paul Bowles, of course.') Other routines contain characters, such as Spare Ass Annie, who 'had an auxiliary asshole in her forehead'; or Doctor Schafer, the Lobotomy Kid; or the Displaced Fuzz – out-of-work policemen – who find employment in the private sector repossessing artificial kidneys.

Burroughs came from a wealthy family (his grandfather patented the Burroughs Adding Machine), and for years had used his allowance to avoid work and buy boys and drugs, but his delinquent life eventually led to him being cut off by the family. He had taken jobs at everything from barman to vermin exterminator. He was always an extremist. In 1939, in a Van Gogh-like attempt to impress a young man in whom he was sexually interested, he had sliced off the top joint of one of his fingers. He began writing seriously in 1950, when in his late thirties, possibly in an effort to displace one type of occupation – the all-absorbing inaction of the drug addict – by another. A more or less straightforward account of the drug addict's life in New York, *Junkie*, was published in 1953 under the pseudonym William Lee – the name Burroughs later used to represent himself in his own fiction (Lee was his mother's name). The novel was presented as a 'confessions of . . .' type of book by its nervous publishers, who packaged it in one volume with the memoirs of a narcotics agent. A first attempt, it falls on to the page in a style which is fully formed. The original intention was to follow it with *Queer*, a companion piece on the theme of homosexual obsession. But after the completion of *Junkie*, Burroughs's ideas about writing changed. By 1952, he was persuaded of his need for medium-as-message innovation. 'A medium suitable for me does not yet exist, unless I invent it,' he told Ginsberg in May of that year. Three years later, fully committed to his new style, he wrote: 'It's almost like automatic writing produced by a hostile, independent entity who is saying in effect, "I will write what I please" . . . only the most extreme material is available to me.'

The prose style of *Junkie* could have been fitted to any other low-life subject, but the grammar of *Naked Lunch* is custom-built to carry the unforeseen engine which powers it. From his letters to Ginsberg, it is clear that Burroughs was dissatisfied with his previous efforts. 'What I do is only evasion, sidetrack, notes. I am walking around the shores of a lake, afraid to jump in, but pretending to study the flora and fauna.'

He worked methodically on his prose – sometimes writing more than one draft of a letter to Ginsberg, when he thought it would add to his stock of routines – quite aware of the nature of the book emanating from his transmissions. The picture, often given by chroniclers of the Beat Generation, of Burroughs friendless and penniless in Tangier, floating on a raft of junk amid the scattered pages of *Naked Lunch*, is not borne out by his correspondence with Ginsberg. When he wrote to his friend, 'Read in any order. It makes no difference', it was not lack of interest but the affirmation of a surrealist aesthetic of chance: 'The selection chapters [*sic*] form a sort of mosaic, with the cryptic significance of juxtaposition, like objects abandoned in a hotel drawer, a form of still life.' Two years later, he wrote: 'I am beginning to see now where I have been going all along. It's beginning to look like a modern inferno.'

Naked Lunch was a collage of styles – science-fiction, pornography, surrealism, music-hall humour, American tough-guy vernacular – with no obvious narrative progression. Randomness is its design; but from a different point of view, everything looks securely organized, for everything in *Naked Lunch* emanates directly from its basic energy, which is the energy of a convulsion attempting to shake off a sickness.

'A.J.'s annual party' gives the flavour:

She bites away Johnny's lips and nose and sucks out his eye with a pop . . . She tears off great hunks of cheek . . . Now she lunches on his prick . . . Mark walks over to her and she looks up from Johnny's half-eaten genitals, her face covered with blood, eyes phosphorescent . . . Mark puts his foot on her shoulder and kicks

her over on her back . . . He leaps on her, fucking her insanely . . .
they roll from one end of the room to the other, pinwheel end-
over-end and leap high in the air like great hooked fish.

'Let me hang you, Mark . . . Let me hang you . . . Please, Mark,
let me hang you!'

'Sure, baby.' He pulls her brutally to her feet and pins her
hands behind her.

'No, Mark! No! No! No,' she screams, shitting and pissing in
terror as he drags her to the platform.

Passing through Paris in 1957, Kerouac, who, like
Ginsberg, was fully convinced of Burroughs's genius (he provided the title for the novel), had shown part of *Naked Lunch*
to Genet's translator, Bernard Frechtman, in the hope of
securing a recommendation to Girodias. But Frechtman was
not interested, and now, with Kerouac back in the States, it
was left to Ginsberg to act as the agent.

Olympia still seemed the best hope and it so happened that
staying at the Beat Hotel was a young South African called
Sinclair Beiles, who did occasional editorial work for Girodias
and who had also written an orientalist db, *Houses of Joy*,
under the pseudonym Wu Wu Meng ('Behold! Her lovely
form is bathed in moonlight'). Beiles effected the introduc-
tions, and Ginsberg took the manuscript across the Place St-
Michel to Girodias's new office on rue St-Séverin.

When he saw what was being presented to him, however,
Girodias shook his head. The thing was appalling. It was
unreadable. Not only did *Naked Lunch*, to the naked eye, not
make sense but the manuscript was in a dreadful state. Pages
were tattered and ripped, some of them stuck together with
paste; additions were made in this way or else scribbled in the
margins. It was, as Ginsberg admitted later, 'just fragment
after fragment strung together'. Even the rats of Paris had had
a go at it, nibbling away at the margins so that Burroughs's
vaudevillian prose looked in places like poetry. Lover of outrageous books that he was, Girodias couldn't quite believe in
one *this* outrageous. He turned it down.

In appearance, Burroughs was unlike the other Beats. He was about ten years older, for a start, and he dressed with almost parodic sobriety, seldom being seen without a shirt, tie, grey suit and hat. He was bespectacled and rarely smiled in front of the camera. In an early sketch, he provided a self-portrait:

Lee was the last of an archaic line, perhaps a subspecies of *homo non sapiens*, or the first here from another space-time way. In any case he was without context, of no class and no place.

Lee's face, his whole person, seemed at first glance completely anonymous. He looked like an FBI man, like anybody. But the absence of trappings, of anything remotely picturesque or baroque, distinguished and delineated Lee, so that seen twice you would not forget him. Sometimes his face looked blurred, then it would come suddenly into focus, etched sharp and naked by the flash bulb of urgency. An electric distinction poured out of him, impregnated his shabby clothes, his steel-rimmed glasses, his dirty gray felt hat. These objects could be recognized anywhere as belonging to Lee.

Burroughs possessed odd pieces of arcane knowledge: he was interested in South American native cultures, and he had gone on anthropological field trips to Peru and Ecuador, in order to make contact with Indians and study the effects of mind-expanding drugs. The term 'mind-expanding' sounds dated now, but it is where Burroughs links up with the other Beats. His private mission was to stretch the mind so that it finally broke the perimeter of social control, releasing the individual into a free zone.

On January 6, 1958, he wrote to Ginsberg from Tangier, asking him to reserve a room at the Hôtel Rachou. 'Must absolutely get out of here for my health. The place is plague-ridden . . .' He reached Paris a week later, taking up residence beside Ginsberg and the others on the rue Gît-le-coeur.

Burroughs was disappointed at the rejection of his book by Olympia Press. But it wasn't unexpected, and he was opposed to any sort of compromise. He had other purposes in coming to Paris, anyway, namely the desire to see Ginsberg again, and also to go into analysis. By the time he started his course, he was 'half-hooked on paragoric', a tincture of opium freely available in Paris from pharmacies. In April, he sent his manuscript off to Lawrence Ferlinghetti of City Lights Books in San Francisco, Ginsberg's publisher. Again, it was rejected.

II

> Negro speech is vivid largely because it is private. It is a kind of emotional shorthand – or sleight-of-hand – by means of which Negroes express, not only their relationship to each other, but their judgement of the white world. And, as the white world takes over this vocabulary – without the faintest notion of what it really means – the vocabulary is forced to change.

> James Baldwin, *New York Times*,
> March 29, 1959

Ginsberg, Burroughs and Corso made the Beat Hotel famous, but none of that trio was the first writer in this story to have enjoyed the eccentrically tolerant management style of Mme Rachou. In 1956–57, Chester Himes had stayed at the rue Gît-le-coeur for several months, on and off, as he passed in and out of Paris, a new woman in tow, a faithful dog at heel, another car with a faulty starter. If there existed a Burroughsian archive of writers' recurring dreams, it would surely contain an entry under *Himes*: 'car with faulty starter'.

Like the Beats, Himes was on the run from conventional society. In fact, Himes was the example for the Beat Generation. Well, not Himes himself, exactly, but the Negro, the soul brother, the cool cat who soothed his senses with jazz and anaesthetized his nerves with horse and weed. Years before Kerouac, Himes had said 'We gotta go'. He had long since dropped out; he had been on the road all his life. Society had dropped *him*. He derived no consolation from the imagery of the rebel: long hair, casual dress, drugs, cool music; he was, as Baldwin would say, just trying to live.

Himes's stay at the Hôtel Rachou coincided with the lowest point of his term in Paris:

> We ate dogmeat cooked with leeks to kill the odor, and potatoes boiled with beans, and day-old bread and anything we could get for nothing to stem the gnawing pangs of hunger at our bowels, and tried to defy the scorn and contempt which had become our lot.

The disgust in that sentence is not at the beginning – the dogmeat (by which Himes presumably means meat for dogs) – but at the end, and it is self-disgust: 'scorn and contempt' for Himes – even in Paris – were synonymous with fate.

Himes had quit Mme Rachou's establishment by the time Ginsberg arrived, but suppose that he had come back there in 1958 and that they had met in the lobby: on the way in, the bedraggled boy (Ginsberg was over thirty, but he was still a boy), Jewish and self-conscious about it ('Fuck the Jews'), homosexual but not yet comfortable with it, far less proud of it (he had taken 'cures', and often slept with women), stoned on heroin or marijuana, carrying a sheaf of poetic visions under his arm ('under the world there's a lot of come, a lot of saliva dripping into brooks . . .'), and a letter of introduction to Baudelaire in his head; and on the way out, the sharp-suited Negro with soft brown eyes and a trim moustache, carrying a heavy chip on his shoulder, a switchblade in his pocket ('I had to walk the streets, didn't I?'), and a copy of one of his very angry novels in his hand.

What would they have found to talk about, bound together yet separated by a common nationality, and now bound and separated by a common culture? The scorn and contempt of their peers? Hardly, for the words, and the history lying behind the words, would have meant entirely different things to the two men. Ginsberg might have expressed a polite inter-

255

est in Himes's writing, but would have been too busy with Burroughs to read any of it. He would have asked after Jimmy Baldwin, whom he had known vaguely in Greenwich Village. Himes would have read into the enquiry the information that Ginsberg was (as he would have said) a faggot, and it also would have confirmed his suspicion that Baldwin was over-friendly with whites. He would have evaded a question about drugs – anyway, he preferred whisky – and probably would have seen Ginsberg and his friends as just another bunch of middle-class white kids slumming it on his territory, as he had seen them all his life. They would have parted without having established any common ground, these two, one black, elegant, very hard and very cool, the other half-consciously expressing the black man's style, adopting his music and plundering his language.

*

The most articulate explicator of Hip was neither black nor, really, a hipster. Norman Mailer had spent the summer of 1956 in Paris. He never met Himes or Harrington or any of the other soul brothers from the Tournon, but one night, in the Montparnasse apartment of his French translator, Jean Malaquais, he was introduced to Baldwin, who took a liking to this confident, boastful character, whom he remembered later 'striding through the soft Paris nights like a gladiator'. Baldwin in turn introduced Mailer to some of his black jazz-musician friends, and when Mailer returned to the United States, he brought together the best of them and the best of him, and wrote the essay which defines the essentials of Hip. He called it 'The White Negro'.

Mailer was a founder of the radical New York paper the *Village Voice*, and was then its leading commentator. His column was full of talk of hipsterism, psychic outlaws, 'the murderous message of marijuana', the struggle in each human being between God and the Devil, the urgency of jazz, the meaning of its popularity. He was reading the French existen-

256

tialists, and in his adroit, frequently brilliant mind was using ideas skimmed from Sartre to reflect the emergent anti-hero of the New York scene, the hipster, 'whose psychic style derives from the best Negroes to come up from the bottom'.

Mailer's essay opens with a brief disquisition on the effect of the 'psychic havoc of the concentration camps and the atom bomb upon the unconscious mind of almost everyone alive'; he preaches the moral requirement of the individual to make fast his private dissent in the face of the contradictions and 'inexorable agonies . . . of super-states'. Contemplating the perils of this falsification of existence – this 'non-existence' – in his defence of Sade in *Merlin* some years earlier, Austryn Wainhouse had declared, 'there is nothing else to do but live the important, the essential, part of our lives underground'. In Mailer's perception, the feat was already accomplished; the result was the hipster,

> the man who knows that if our collective condition is to live with instant death by atomic war . . . why then the only life-giving answer is to accept the terms of death, to live with death as imme-diate danger, to divorce oneself from society, to exist without roots, to set out on that uncharted journey into the rebellious imperatives of the self.

There was an American who had been living in this state of constant existential rebellion all his life. He lived next door – or, rather, on the other side of the tracks:

> And in this wedding of the white and the black it was the Negro who brought the cultural dowry. Any Negro who wishes to live must live with danger from his first day, and no experience can ever be casual to him, no Negro can saunter down a street with any real certainty that violence will not visit him on his walk. The cameos of security for the average white: mother and home, job and family, are not even a mockery to millions of Negroes; they are impossible. The Negro has the simplest of alternatives: live a life of ever-threatening humility or ever-threatening danger.

The hipster had absorbed 'the existentialist synapses of the

Negro'. He had learned a lesson from his black neighbour in how to live in the margin between totalitarianism and democracy, and could, for practical purposes, 'be considered a white Negro'.

*

> I walked with every muscle aching among the lights of 27th and Welton in the Denver colored section, wishing I were a Negro, feeling that the best the white world had offered was not enough ecstasy for me, not enough life, joy, kicks, darkness, music, not enough night.
>
> Jack Kerouac, *On the Road*

> This is absolute nonsense, of course . . . I would hate to be in Kerouac's shoes if he should ever be mad enough to read this aloud from the stage of Harlem's Apollo Theater.
>
> James Baldwin, 'The Black Boy Looks at the White Boy'

Mailer was right to insist in his essay that the hipster took his key, his beat, from the Negro, and that the two shared a place on the margin of a society which, though free, constantly threatened them. He omitted to stress a crucial distinction, however: the hipster refused to accept conventional society; the Negro was refused by it. Mailer's essay is bursting with insight, but his black man was still an invisible man. He did not pause to consider what the negro Negro thought about all this white Negro stuff. His new-found friend from Paris, Baldwin, whom he began to see regularly back in New York, was about to inform him.

Baldwin, though he had friends who considered themselves beatniks or hipsters (Mailer's distinction was that hipster was a beatnik who reads), was inclined to be contemptuous of their 'we-gotta-go' ways of conceiving freedom. To him, being free could never be a matter of dropping out of school, or giving up your job, and hitching a lift to Denver. The people Baldwin had grown up with in Harlem had little chance of getting *in* to school. And he could hardly ever find a proper job. At the end of the 1940s, Baldwin had had difficulty getting a place to rent in Greenwich Village (supposedly the most liberal section of New York), and not because of a shortage of rooms.

And now the bars and streets were overrun with white kids saying 'man' and 'cool' and digging chicks and smoking reefers and blowing horns and looking for kicks and bringing down squares as a drag – as if these things had just been discovered. Chester Himes may not have been able to give a baroque definition of 'cool', but he knew what it meant. He had learned it 'in the body'. Compare what Mailer wrote about the white hipster's reaction to 'ever-threatening danger' with how Himes responded to the danger he felt surrounded him, even in the free atmosphere of Paris:

> I remained the same, a thinking animal, filled with regrets, experiencing hunger, stirred by anger along with the acceptance of the necessity to live. . . . I had become very violent, dangerous, with a wild skyrocketing temper. Sex and violence held me in a vice.

In 'The Black Boy Looks at the White Boy', a personal essay about Mailer written in 1960, Baldwin looked back on their Paris nights fondly, but he could not help a little weariness creeping in when forced to consider his friend's intellectual romance with the outlaw. Baldwin administered a gentle but effective put-down, which was, however, intended to make a serious point about Hip and the different perspectives of black and white.

'I could not, with the best will in the world,' Baldwin wrote, 'make any sense out of "The White Negro".' In searching for the likely spark of Mailer's essay, he recalled their nights in Paris:

> the Negro jazz musicians, among whom we sometimes found ourselves, who really liked Norman, did not for an instant consider him as being even remotely 'hip' and Norman did not know this and I could not tell him. He never broke through to them . . . and

259

they were far too 'hip', if that is the word I want, even to consider breaking through to him. They thought he was a real sweet ofay cat, but a little frantic.

Baldwin is having fun, but it's hardly surprising that he should have taken up an attitude before 'The White Negro'. What makes hip language a special language, Mailer wrote, 'is that it cannot really be taught'. Which is just what Baldwin was trying to tell him.

*

Ginsberg had moved back to the States early in 1959, leaving Burroughs in residence at the Beat Hotel, together with his new 'number one receptor', Brion Gysin, a café-owner and artist whom he had known in Tangier. Gysin had invented a device which he called a Dream Machine, a cylinder with slits lit from inside, which revolved on a turntable. It produced alpha waves corresponding to thirteen flashes per second, which acted on the optic nerve in such a way as to produce hallucinations. Gysin and Burroughs could sit for hours in the Hôtel Rachou, looking at it and having visions.

Burroughs was moving farther and farther out, believing in Gysin's genius, believing in L. Ron Hubbard and Scientology, believing in his own weird psychic explorations and metamorphoses: 'What is happening now,' he wrote to Ginsberg from rue Gît-le-coeur in the middle of 1959,

> is that I literally turn into someone else, not a human-creature but man-like: He wears some sort of green uniform. The face is full of black-boiling fuzz. . . . I have been seeing him for some time in the mirror. . . . Brion has seen him (or it).

He also told Ginsberg that he had found a new method of writing, which he could not explain 'until you have the necessary training'.

Meanwhile, in the spring of 1959, a few chapters from *Naked Lunch* were published in an American magazine, *Big*

Table, which was immediately declared obscene by the US Post Office, banned, and sent for trial. Burroughs was dismayed, for this made American publication of the novel impossible in the foreseeable future. But news of the scandal reached the offices of Olympia Press, where nothing was more welcome than a banned book.

'Dear Mr Burroughs,' Girodias wrote on June 6, 1959, 'what about letting me have another look at *Naked Lunch*?'

*

Burroughs was given $800 and one of Girodias's rare contracts.* He was asked to have the manuscript ready for the printers in ten days' time. The sections were typed up, with the help of friends, and sent to the printers, once again in random order – 'You can cut into *Naked Lunch* at any intersection' – which Burroughs saw no reason to alter when he received the galleys. It was bound and ready for sale in July 1959, with a cover designed by Burroughs himself. Five thousand copies were printed, followed shortly afterwards by a similar reprint.

The literary table-talk in France at the time was of the *nouveau roman*, and in particular its hardline proponent Alain Robbe-Grillet. Marking out modern French literature like a football pitch, Robbe-Grillet grouped in his own half the team of Natalie Sarraute, Claude Simon, Michel Butor, Francis Ponge, plus a few more, and on the other side – the rest. Be 'new' or be redundant. It was a group with a manifesto, like the surrealists, and the *nouveau romanciers* were described as the heirs of surrealism. Burroughs had probably never heard of the *nouveau roman*, but he used the leftovers of surrealism

*It didn't do him much good. Swindling the author of *Naked Lunch* out of his foreign-language monies was among the few transgressions against authors which Girodias owned up to (letter from Girodias to Patrick J. Kearney; in possession of Mr Kearney). The novel was published as *The Naked Lunch*, the title still used in English editions. For American publication, however, the definite article was dropped; *Naked Lunch* is how the book is referred to in Burroughs's bibliography, and apparently the title preferred by the author.

to more inventive effect than anything by Robbe-Grillet and his colleagues. Nothing was more new in Paris at the end of the 1950s than this American new novel.

Naked Lunch had effectively been completed for some years now, and Burroughs was in the process of advancing the new technique he had advised Ginsberg of – the cut-up method – which he would incorporate into his pseudo-science of addiction. Drugs and sex control the body, but control over the mind is exercised by 'word and image locks' – which cut-ups set free by juggling the alphabet of consciousness.

Having assaulted language in every way open to him in *Naked Lunch*, he was now assaulting it using actual sharp implements. The concept behind the cut-ups came from Gysin, and they would occupy Burroughs for much of the decade to come. In 1961 and 1962, Olympia Press published the first two cut-up novels, *The Soft Machine* and *The Ticket that Exploded*. But on this guerrilla mission to subvert the word, the man who was 'literally' turning into 'someone else' had his most successful campaign with *Naked Lunch*, the last original novel to be published by Girodias during the 1950s.

III

William Burroughs had spent the entire decade trying to break his narcotics addiction: 'the Chinaman' was how he referred to it, writing repeatedly to Ginsberg and Kerouac that he was struggling 'to get this Chinaman off my back'. Occasionally he would succeed for a short while, only to lapse into renewed dependence. He had a lucky escape from prison in 1959 when an incriminating letter sent to Paris by a friend in Morocco fell into the hands of the French police, implicating Burroughs in a deal to smuggle marijuana from Tangier. Burroughs got off with a suspended sentence, owing to the efforts of Girodias's lawyer who played on the French reverence for writers.

In New York, Alexander Trocchi, putting the finishing

touches to a drug novel, *Cain's Book* – begun several years before, in Paris – was in happy partnership with his Chinaman, and included rapturous descriptions of the Chinaman's talents in the book. Trocchi was not the slave of drugs but their apostle, or so he believed. Without mentioning Mailer's essay (though he must have read it), he took up his own 'white Negro' stance, as personified in the narrator of *Cain's Book*, Joe Necchi:

> The identity of the junkie (not only a figure of the underground, but the social leper of the 1950s in New York) was consciously chosen. The resulting experience is by definition that of an alien in a society of conformers, a personal cosmology of inner space.

Trocchi had travelled a long way from St-Germain, from the cultured iconoclast revered by Logue, admired by Beckett, valued by Girodias, loved by Jane Lougee, liked – and a little bit feared – by Plimpton and almost everyone else. Going into orbit in inner space, he turned his back on Literature, attacking it with determined destructiveness in *Cain's Book*, which is both a novel and a critique of The Novel, a work broken into pieces and then fitted together again with precision intelligence. In adopting the identity of the drug addict, Trocchi was testing to see how far out a man could go without falling off the edge. He was setting himself up as a laboratory wherein he could conduct experiments on alienation. 'I reject the entire system,' he wrote to a relative in Britain. 'I am outside your world and am no longer governed by your laws.' The junkie was as outside as the outsider – the white outsider – could get.

There are strong hints of what was to come in his letters to Jane from Paris, after she had left him and *Merlin* to go back to the United States and marriage. Recall what he wrote to her in 1954, after reading *The Story of O*, about 'the sins of history chaining me to the rock', and about 'our problem' being 'history's' – 'we can't escape that except by destroying it in ourselves'.

This was written at about the time that Trocchi first used heroin ('I tried what Johnnie Welsh takes'), and in heroin ('It's wonderful') he found, or thought he found, the means to erase history's sins as they were stamped on his mind and being. He conceived freedom as Sade had conceived it; he strove to obliterate the repressive civilization in himself.

In a section written for *Cain's Book* but not actually included in the novel, Trocchi described how he would typically go about scoring drugs in New York:

> I took the subway up to the Bronx. At that time of night, long after the rush hour, it was grey, bleak, cold, and lonely, especially at a station like 23rd Street. I was the only passenger to get on. But there was no alternative. I had to cop some heroin from our connection, Wolfie. A long journey it seemed in that all but empty carriage. . . . God, I used to hate that journey, even when I remembered to take a book which, for some reason or other, this evening I hadn't. At 42nd Street, a few more people got on. But they were all muffled up, nipped by the cold, and in that garish but still dim light of the old subway carriage their pitiful look contributed to my own low spirits. Who would be out on a night like this if he could help it? And where I was going I had no real wish to be. I never felt relaxed in that chromium-plated nightmare that was Wolfie's pad.

The police raided Wolfie's place while Trocchi was there, but he claimed to be just a visitor and escaped arrest. A trick he used in order to avoid the law in New York was to carry a portable soapbox 'pulpit' on a strap over his shoulder. At the first sign of police while he was on the scent of drugs, Trocchi would get up on his soapbox like a street-corner preacher and deliver a sermon with a good Scottish accent and Calvinist zeal.

On more than one occasion, though, he was arrested and put in prison, and when he finally departed New York for London it was as a fugitive travelling with a false passport. He used the name of Baird Bryant, who was the original translator of *The Story of O*, and was now married to Jane Lougee (her first marriage having ended). Thus Trocchi on the run, under yet another pseudonym, subliminally fulfilled three wishes all at once: he was a genuine outlaw, married in name to Jane, and married symbolically to the author of *The Story of O*, Pauline Réage.

*

Ginsberg called Trocchi 'the most brilliant man I've ever met'. Mailer was in awe of him, as a writer and extreme hipster. Here was someone living at an edge so precipitous that few among the Hip would dare to approach it. 'It is difficult to explain to the underprivileged that play is more serious than work,' Trocchi said, and who would dare to disagree? He set up a 'Methedrine University' for play in his pad on Avenue C in New York, named after the amphetamine he took in order to write.

Ginsberg and Mailer visited it together one night. They found about thirty people engaged in making 'garbage art', some of them sitting around mumbling to themselves, all involved in painting, in intricate detail, little bits of wood picked up from the street. Hours would be spent scrubbing the sticks clean, then the speed freaks would paint them with shiny enamel in bright colours. Every so often, someone would go over to the table and give himself another shot of Methedrine. Ginsberg remembered how Trocchi beamed 'all over his bony face'. As they went out into the street, close to dawn, the neighbourhood was asleep, except for Trocchi's pad, burning with high-intensity light-bulbs in the dark.

He put the finishing touches to *Cain's Book* in August 1959, just as *Naked Lunch* hit the English-language bookstands in Paris. It was published the following year by his old *Merlin* colleague Richard Seaver, now an editor at Grove Press. It is the mastercrime he had always known he was capable of committing. *Cain's Book* is autobiography and fiction at once, a stage-by-stage account of the junkie's odyssey in New York, coupled with flashbacks to his childhood in Glasgow. Here the Paris pornographer meets the Scottish philosopher, fusing in the drug-addicted alien.

To adopt the identity of the junkie was to be avant-garde in one's person, to become the anti-man. Trocchi implied that his was a moral position. Only by the way did he invoke ortho-dox justifications for drug-use, by claiming that he was 'experimenting', like Aldous Huxley seeking to unlock con-cealed compartments of the mind. Trocchi barely counte-nanced the notion that his addiction could debilitate him physically, or erode his talents. On the contrary, he made hero-in sound positively beneficial:

> It's somehow undignified to speak of the past or to think about the future. I don't seriously occupy myself with the question in the 'here-and-now', lying on my bunk and, under the influence of heroin, inviolable. That is one of the virtues of the drug, that it empties such questions of all anguish, transports them to another region, a painless theoretical region, a play region, surprising, fer-tile, and unmoral. One is no longer grotesquely involved in the becoming. One simply is.

Trocchi writes of himself in the novel (as Joe Necchi) stepping between cities, luggage in hand, one suitcase packed with notes and scraps of text. Quotations are given in *Cain's Book* from 'Cain's Book', aphoristic fragments which do not appear in the main body of the novel. The philosopher Trocchi invites his reader to consider the paradox which says: 'This statement is not true.' For the ingenuity of *Cain's Book*, the tease that draws the reader into it again and again, is that it questions its own validity at every turn, refusing its status as a 'novel', yet finally existing freely as a work of art.

It took a long time to fall into place, but in 1959 it finally did so. On the last page, Trocchi writes as if discussing another book entirely:

> as soon as I have finished this last paragraph [I intend] to go into the next room and turn on. Later I shall phone those who have intimated their willingness to publish the document and tell them that it is ready now, or as ready as it will ever be . . . .

266

Trocchi wrote nothing else of note before his death twenty-five years later, and he never came off heroin. The writing in *Cain's Book* is much taken up with that fashionable French topic, the death of the novel. The novel didn't die, after all, but, following *Cain's Book*, Trocchi's part in it did.

IV

On June 23, 1959, at ten in the morning, a black American author sneaked uninvited into a small cinema near the Champs-Elysées to watch the preview of a film made from one of his novels. It involved a black man who can pass for white, who is much liked by the boys and girls in the small town to which he has drifted, and it ends with him savagely murdering two white sisters. The 'invisibility' of the novelist in the Salle du Petit Marbeuf was due to the fact that the screen version of his story, directed by Michel Gast, was one which he disapproved of but was powerless to prevent. In the darkened theatre, as the projector whirred, he had a heart attack and died.

The author was Boris Vian. He was thirty-nine and had long since been exposed as 'Vernon Sullivan', who wrote *J'irai cracher sur vos tombes* in 1946. The first white Negro came from St-Germain-des-Prés.

EIGHT

Waiting for the End, Boys

Il n'y a plus d'après
à St-Germain-des-Prés

Juliette Gréco (G. Béart)

I

Albert Camus survived Vian by six months and twelve days. On January 4, 1960, he was being driven from Lyons to Paris in a Facel-Véga sports car by his publisher, Michel Gallimard, when the vehicle left the road and hit two trees. The clock on the dashboard stopped at the moment of impact, recording Camus's death at 1.54 p.m. Michel Gallimard lived for another six days.

Richard Wright died at the end of the same year, as if, to invoke a romantic fallacy, by appointment (strictly speaking, 1960 was the final year of the decade). He was fifty-two.

These three names could be taken together as a triangulation of time and space in 1950s Paris. Camus was friendly with both Wright and Vian, but close to neither. He has come to seem the very type of the post-war Parisian intellectual: committed, rigorous, diversifying outwards from fiction into theatre and the essay, integrating literature, politics and philosophy, all woven together into a consistent system of belief.

268

Camus's ethical quarrel with the Sartreans left a wound too bloody to be healed in his lifetime. When she heard the news, Simone de Beauvoir's first reaction was: 'I'm not going to start crying. He didn't mean anything to me any more.' Later, however, she got out of bed and walked through the night, mourning the man who had been part of their bright circle in the days when Paris was newly liberated and St-Germain was the centre of the world.

If it were necessary to elect a single figure from among that circle to act as an emblem of the 1950s, the choice would not be Camus, nor Sartre or de Beauvoir, but Boris Vian.

Vian was the opposite of Camus: playful, irreverent, satirical, iconoclastic, a man of likes rather than beliefs. Going into Vian's house, someone said, was like going on holiday. He was in the vanguard of everything he turned his hand to, and he turned his hand to everything. He had studied to be an engineer and enjoyed tinkering with 'inventions' throughout his life (one of his fictional creations was a piano which mixed cocktails according to the tune played on it); in addition to novels, he wrote plays and operas, poems and songs, filmscripts for impossible films, science fiction and pornography; he made collages and drew the cover artwork for his own books; he led a jazz band; he restored old cars, and carried out metamorphoses in their design. Critics have ranked him among the pioneers of the Theatre of the Absurd, on the strength of his early play, *Les Bâtisseurs d'empire* (*The Empire Builders*), which was never performed in his lifetime. Writing of a play that was performed, in 1950, Cocteau elevated Vian above 'the rest of us timid people, limited as we are to confronting the plural with the singular'.

In the column he wrote in the 1940s for *Les Temps Modernes*, 'Chronique du menteur', Vian joked about the magazine's dullness, its bad rates of pay, its awkward design. He made fun of the sombre pronouncements of Meloir de Beauvartre and Pontartre de Merlebeauvy. Merleau-Ponty, the general editor of *Les Temps Modernes*, was less than amused: a piece in which Vian teased the hard-left philosopher for taking up too many pages in the magazine ('He is a capitalist') was rejected, and the 'Chronique' did not appear again. But nothing could stop Vian. One of his musical turns in the St-Germain *caves* was to have the singer Henri Salvador do a blues to a background of readings from *Being and Nothingness*.

Richard Wright hardly knew Vian, but he would have recognized the tall young man with the strong nose as the one who led on trumpet at Club du Tabou ('white boys would . . . tell me the deep meanings buried in solo trumpet'), who had translated one of Wright's stories for *Présence Africaine* in 1946, and in the same year had written a novel under the pretence of being a black boy. Wright might even have noticed that the theme of *J'irai cracher sur vos tombes* bears strong similarities to that of *Native Son*.

The work of Camus, Vian and Wright – an Algerian who was considered French, a Frenchman who pretended to be Afro-American and an Afro-American who dreamed of being just an American – reserves their place in the integrated pantheon of literature, but the nature of their deaths belongs to legend: Vian expiring in the cinema, cursing another's abuse of his book; Camus, who had lived under the shadow of tuberculosis, dying in a sports car; as for Wright . . . he died two deaths.

*

At the beginning of November 1960, two months after his fifty-second birthday, Wright began to experience the symptoms of flu. It was only the latest in a succession of ailments, and it developed into a severe bout, with dizzy spells and the return of a persistent stomach complaint – amoebic dysentery – which had troubled him since his trip to Africa. He rallied sufficiently to deliver his lecture at the American Church in Paris on 'The Position of the Negro Artist and Intellectual' on November 8, but his fever returned, and for the next two weeks he was constantly tired, and frustrated by being unable to work.

During the past year, Wright had changed doctors. His new physician, Dr Victor Schwartzmann, a Russian, was a genial man, and he pleased Wright by making a point of reading his books. On one of his first visits to Dr Schwartzmann, Wright was touched to notice a copy of his recent collection of essays and journalism, *White Man, Listen!*, on the doctor's desk. In the spring of 1960, Wright had accompanied Schwartzmann and his father to Leiden in Holland to attend a medical conference, at the doctor's suggestion. Although he was put off by what he considered the doctor's overbearing friendliness, he tried to rationalize his feelings and separate them from other fears – the 'real' fears – which continued to assail him, resulting from sinister happenings and communications in Paris. His unjustified aversion to the doctor could lead to behaviour which further disturbed him.

For example, on arrival in Leiden, he told Schwartzmann and his father that there was no room for them at the hotel, even though two rooms had been reserved in advance by Margrit de Sablonière, Wright's friend and Dutch translator, and the major correspondent of his final year, who lived in the town. Wright fretted over his behaviour in a letter to Sablonière, putting it down to something subliminal 'between me and the doctor that creates tension'. Yet, he admitted, in a state of bewilderment, 'the doctor and his father are friends of mine and only wish me well'. It was not the first time, he continued, that he had felt an unconscious aversion to people without knowing why.

Wright's friends were familiar with his fears of surveillance and persecution, arising from the knowledge that, at one time or another, the black community at the Café de Tournon, and the meetings of the Franco-American Fellowship, had been infiltrated by spies reporting back to the American Embassy, which in turn recorded the information for use by the CIA and the FBI. Of course, you never knew when, and you couldn't say with certainty who. Therefore, almost everyone was under suspicion.

271

Those closest to Wright had watched his obsession grow over the years of his residence in Paris, developing out of the angry knowledge that the FBI continued to maintain a keen interest in his actions, movements, friendships and beliefs, all because of Communist convictions he had publicly renounced in the *Atlantic Monthly* in 1944, into a state of suspiciousness in which he had difficulty distinguishing between happenstance and plot. The loose dots of conspiracy were embedded in the most trivial incident, just waiting for the practised eye to join them up and say 'Look!' – while others could see nothing at all.

On returning from Holland to France, Wright prepared to travel straight to the town of Nancy. He was due to give a lecture at the university there on April 27, on the subject of 'The psychological reactions of oppressed peoples' (the irony of which he was surely alert to). At the last minute, however, he was notified that the lecture had been cancelled. The official excuse was that the filmmaker Robert Bresson was speaking on the same evening, and consequently Wright would most likely find himself in the embarrassing position of talking to a small audience.

This was a tactless way of breaking an engagement, but Wright was convinced that there was more to it than that. Suspecting that the American government had intervened with the university to stave off unwelcome discussion of problems in Africa by the likes of him, Wright made discreet enquiries through friends at Nancy, with the aim of confirming his suspicions. They came to nothing.

He learned that Chester Himes had written a detective novel (*A Case of Rape*), which contained a character based on him. 'He's got all his information from undercover agents of the American CIA,' Wright told Sablonière, without specifying the basis of this accusation against one of his oldest friends. Himes and Wright had fallen out some three years earlier, leaving Himes with the feeling that Wright was apt to turn against a 'brother' at the slightest provocation.

Some provocations were not so slight. Back in February, he had been astonished to receive a letter from Sartre, attacking him and his work. It turned out to be a forgery. To Sablonière, he wrote: 'I know the direction from which this comes', again without being specific (the letter from 'Sartre' has apparently been lost), though it is not hard to guess what he was getting at. According to Dorothy Padmore, wife of the Africanist George Padmore, 'He . . . declared himself the victim of a plot, evidence of which he had gathered, and which implicated the French security, the American FBI (perhaps CIA) and ex-Trotskyists.'

The real fertilized the illusory, and created paranoia. His fears, that spring, were pervasive, and they included the ultimate fear. On March 30, he wrote to Sablonière:

> You must not worry about my being in danger . . . I am not exact-
> ly unknown here and I have personal friends in de Gaulle's cabi-
> net itself. Of course, I don't want anything to happen to me, but
> if it does, my friends will know exactly where it comes from. . . .
> So far as the Americans are concerned, I am worse than a
> Communist, for my work falls like a shadow across their policy in
> Asia and Africa. That's the problem; they've asked me time and
> again to work for them, but I'd rather die first . . . .

Towards the end of November, still suffering from the effects of dysentery and what he called 'grippe', Wright, on the advice of Schwartzmann, decided to spend some days in hospital. He had been mostly unwell since July of 1959, as he told Sablonière in February 1960. A month later he referred to a 'serious illness', the first he had ever had. By July 1960, his complaints had proliferated to include debilitating fatigue, weight loss, depression, stomach spasms, recurring fever, and 'nervousness'. He had been in the habit of having regular check-ups, usually in the American Hospital, but this time he chose the Eugène Gibez Clinic on rue Vaugirard. Schwartzmann had prescribed a variety of medicines, including the recognized antidote of arsenic, in very small doses, for the stomach problem – 'rat poison' Wright called it in the

273

company of his friends. He was also taking penicillin, emetine, bismuth, sulpha and tranquillizers in order to help him sleep. He had stopped drinking alcohol and was thinking of giving up coffee.

Wright's wife was away in London. His eldest daughter was due to begin studying at Cambridge in the autumn. The house in the country and the fine apartment on rue Monsieur le Prince had both been sold, and Wright was living alone in a small place on rue Régis, close to Sèvres Babylone. Hours before a car arrived to pick him up to deliver him to the clinic, he was visited by the poet Langston Hughes. Hughes found Wright in good spirits, in spite of his ailments. 'As he talked, he seemed and looked very much like the young Dick Wright I had known in Chicago – vigorous, questioning, very much alive.'

Hughes was the last person to see him in his proper surroundings. At about eleven o'clock on the night of the twenty-eighth, lying on his hospital bed and witnessed by no one, Richard Wright had a heart attack and died.

*

> It breaks my heart in two, Lord
> And I just can't forget
> Old F. B. Eye ain't ended yet.
>
> Richard Wright, 'F. B. Eye Blues'

That is the official story of Wright's death. There exists another version of it, which came into being even while his funeral was in train, largely as a consequence of Ollie Harrington receiving a telegram which, in retrospect, appeared highly suspicious.

The alternative version of the death of Richard Wright goes as follows: two days after leaving Hughes at the door of his rue Régis apartment on November 26, Wright was visited in the evening at the Eugène Gibez Clinic by a woman. Her identity is not established, but there are rumours that she was a

274

Hungarian refugee, recognizable from Left Bank cafés but thought to have been deported from France some years before. No one enquired of her purpose as she entered the clinic, though her presence was noted by the telephone operator. Under the pretence of paying Wright a get-well visit, she administered, probably by injection, a fatal dose of a drug – possibly belladonna – capable of inducing cardiac arrest. She left unimpeded.

Wright got up and went to the operator's office – apparently not in obvious distress – and asked for a telegram to be sent to Harrington, who was in Normandy. The message said: 'Ollie, please come immediately.' He then returned to bed. When Harrington received the telegram, he headed straight back to Paris, arriving the next day. Asking at the clinic to be allowed to see his friend, he was told: 'You can't. Monsieur Wright died last night.' It was from the telephone operator that he learned of the woman visitor.

On December 3, following a small, private ceremony at Père Lachaise Cemetery, Wright's remains were cremated. No post-mortem was carried out. The Hungarian woman has not been seen or heard of since. If anyone knows her identity, they have never disclosed it.

*

The more sinister account is stoutly defended by Harrington. 'I *know* Richard Wright was assassinated,' he says. 'I've never met a black person who does *not* believe [he] was done in.' He has some impressive backers. Chester Himes is no longer here to state his own opinion of the circumstances, but his widow, Lesley, says: 'Richard was murdered. I have no doubt about it.' Asked if her husband felt the same way, she replies: 'Oh yes.' By the end of his life, James Baldwin had also come to believe that Wright's death was suspicious, even though he had not seen his old adversary during his final years. Wright's daughter, Julia, gives credence to 'a CIA plot to isolate him, in order to make him more vulnerable. . . . It was sufficient that a man be sick, isolated and poor to drive him to his death.'

Why would anyone want to kill him? His standing as a public spokesman for black people was greatly diminished since
the days of *Native Son* and *Black Boy*; he had little contact
with the new generation of civil rights leaders and activists,
and had not been to America for almost ten years. His work,
which he defiantly claimed fell 'like a shadow' over American
policy in Asia and Africa, was selling in ever-reduced quanti-
ties, and it's hard to see that it would have troubled the top ech-
elons of government as much as he believed. The people at the
American Embassy in Paris who had asked him 'time and again
to work for them', would have been frustrated by a refusal, but
surely not to the extent of ordering his assassination.

Perhaps there was a personal element to the intrigue?
Describing the 'sullen' atmosphere at the Tournon before the
funeral in his memoir, Himes put a name to the danger which
Wright believed was menacing him. 'For a long time Dick had
had an obsession that he was being persecuted by Richard
Gibson, the soul brother who had had a fight with Ollie
Harrington in 1956.' Gibson had left Paris to return to the
United States in 1958, but the persecution continued, in
Wright's eyes, through such strategic assaults as the potentially incriminating postcard from Cuba. And forged letters like
the one purporting to come from Sartre would always bring to
mind the letter signed in Harrington's name and sent to *Life*.
Rumour spread and connected with other rumours, and the
woman alleged to have visited Wright on his deathbed was
even said by some to have been a close friend of Gibson, but
there was no evidence to corroborate the suggestion.

Indeed, attempts to probe deeper into the circumstances
surrounding Wright's death run aground on the plain fact that
there are no facts to investigate. Since Wright's body was cremated, there was no possibility, once the talk started, of looking for traces of poison or anything else which might indicate
foul play. The Hungarian woman – 'quite well known in the
quarter', according to Harrington, who nevertheless cannot

identify her – remains obstinately faceless and nameless. Discussions with many people close to the events have failed to produce one piece of evidence which would upgrade the rumour to something closer to fact.

Rumour takes on a life of its own, however, and adapts itself to fit the conviction. 'He was in perfect health,' says Lesley Himes, 'he wasn't ill' – but he was, quite seriously so, according to his letters to Margrit de Sablonière. Harrington broods over the anomaly of the Eugène Gibez Clinic: why didn't he go to the American Hospital as usual, where he would have been safer? – 'He thought there were people out to get him, but he thought they probably wouldn't try to do it in the American Hospital' – overlooking the fact that it was recommended by Dr Schwartzmann. Schwartzmann himself, who actually became a personal friend of Wright, has become in some accounts 'the strange Russian doctor'. On BBC radio, Julia Wright referred to the passage in the letter to Sablonière as having been written 'a few days before his death', whereas it was actually written eight months earlier. No one has explained why a man who had just realized he was the victim of a poisoner would send his SOS to someone in Normandy, and without giving the hospital operator who took the message any impression that he was in distress.

Perhaps there is something in the travail of Richard Wright which calls out for a final adventure, a dramatic end – the ultimate convergence of his life's experience with his philosophy of opposition. To many of those who surrounded him, protected him, admired his fortitude, an ordinary death seems not to be enough.

When Wright arrived in France, he told William Gardner Smith, the experience of leaving the United States was like the feeling of a corpse slipping off his back. In the intervening years, Paris had been hospitable to him – 'city of refuge', he called it – but gradually the tensions of his early life in Mississippi, for so long repressed, began to reveal themselves, like the lines of ageing forewritten in the face. At the end of his life, the corpse was on his back again. Supernaturally, it seems to have survived him.

'My husband lived with tension all his life,' says Ellen Wright, 'every day, awful tension.' A life of tension, and, most probably, a death from tension, too.

II

By this time, the life – the real life – of the Olympia Press had practically run its course. Its energy was dissipated in legal problems and authors' dejection. For the 'great fun' of making English judges' hair stand on end beneath their wigs, there was a price to pay in France. As the decade wore on, the Brigade Mondaine – the worldly brigade – began to make frequent visits to Olympia's offices. The clean-up at first targeted only books bearing the name of Henry Miller, but it soon spread to embrace almost any title published by Olympia.

The blanket banning led to ludicrous situations. For example, at the same time as Genet was being lauded universally as a great French writer, his *Oeuvres complètes* published by Gallimard and displayed prominently in bookshops throughout Paris, the English translation of *Notre-Dame-des-Fleurs*, published by Olympia in 1957, was banned from sale in the very same shops.

Already familiar with the insides of the police headquarters on rue des Saussaies, Girodias became adept at making the law work to his own advantage. Informed that a book – or twenty books – had been banned by the Minister of the Interior, Girodias would go on the offensive and sue the Ministry; and often the Administrative Tribunal of Paris, or the Conseil d'Etat – the highest court in the land – would find in his favour.

Even when the bans were not overturned, he had a way of sneaking his books past the worldly brigade. When the police issued a writ banning the sale of *Helen and Desire*, *Seeds of the*

Rainbow, Candy and the *Memoirs of Fanny Hill*, Girodias had the covers reprinted with different titles – thus *Desire and Helen, Pearls of the Rainbow, Lollipop* and *Fanny* – and distributed the books all over again. The police, who couldn't read English, didn't know the difference.

By 1960, Olympia had done what it existed to do (even where that was different from what Girodias had set out to do) and the cause of freedom from censorship in literature could now be taken up elsewhere. Girodias could never have built up his celebrated list of classics and modern masters without the intellectual assistance of the *Merlin* writers. And where writers blaze the trail, publishers naturally follow. The literary part of Olympia's list could now be exported to the United States and Britain, where it was republished by Grove Press (founded by Barney Rosset and run together with Seaver) and John Calder. In co-operation, or separately, these two firms brought out the works of Beckett, Burroughs, Bataille, Genet, Miller, Trocchi, the Marquis de Sade and Pauline Réage, among other Olympia 'discoveries'. Rosset and Calder had to fight battles too, including legal battles, and sometimes the credit for placing such 'clandestine' books before the public fell to the American or British publisher, leaving Girodias the reputation of a man who, as Trocchi later put it unkindly (no doubt piqued by further non-payment of royalties), published *Watt* under the impression that it was just another dirty book.

Girodias was proud of publishing the modernists; but he did not attempt to disown the other side of his industry. He embraced it with a type of honesty that can be called noble. In a testimonial worthy of Genet, he wrote, late in life, 'I accepted in principle my unworthiness, my image as a publisher of the scandalous, the clandestine . . .'. He showed a finer awareness than Trocchi did of his true strength when he wrote, in a letter to Beckett in 1986, that he had persuaded a reluctant John Calder to publish *Tropic of Cancer* in Britain after Grove Press's victory in the US Supreme Court in 1964: 'Later, he thanked me many times for having virtually forced him to take

279

that chance, since that is what made him a "real publisher" in the eyes of his peers.' The world of publishing is perennially dominated by a small minority of risk-takers – the avant-garde, in fact – and Girodias occupies a place in the front rank.

After 1960–61 – during which period he published or republished several modern classics, including *Steiner's Tour* by Philip O'Connor, *The Young and Evil* by Charles Henri Ford and Parker Tyler (originally put out by his father), *The Soft Machine* by Burroughs, and a batch of 'collage novels' by Akbar del Piombo (Norman Rubington) – Girodias began to find himself all but immobilized by legal entanglements. He faced accumulated prison sentences totalling six years, numerous fines, and a suspension from publishing activities in France for ninety years. In the mid Sixties, he moved his press to New York, where he developed a new list, depending less on literature and more on its sub-species.

*

The two sides of the story integrate in one of Olympia's last serious publications. Hearing word that Chester Himes was back in Paris at the turn of the year 1960–61, and that he had an unplaced manuscript on his desk, Girodias got in touch and asked to be allowed to read it. After he had done so – overnight, as usual when his instinct was strong – he told Himes that if he put in 'six good sex scenes' he would give him a contract and a thousand dollars advance.

Was Himes put off by the suggestion that he deprave and corrupt his own work? Not much. He needed the money badly, and soon got into the spirit of things: 'I put in so many sex scenes that I had to take two-thirds of them out again.' The novel was *Pinktoes*, and Himes the pornographer gave his sex scenes a *beat* all their own:

> So what happened to the unidentified distinguished-looking white lady and the young dark Negro poet . . .? They left Mamie's to go somewhere and make some poetry, and, oh, brother, they are making it, white and black poetry, that is.

This poetry is not only being made but it is being said, between pants and grunts and groans, that is.

He: Birmingham.
She: Oh, you poor lamb.
He: Ku-Klux-Klan
She: Oh, you poor black man.
He: Lynch mob.
She: Oh, you make me sob.
He: Little Rock.
She: Oh, what an awful shock.
He: Jim Crow.
She: Oh, you suffering Negro.
He: Denied my rights.
She: Oh, take my delights.
He: Segregation.
She: Oh, but integration.
He: They killed my pappy.
She: Oh, let me make you happy.
He: They call me low.
She: Oh, you beautiful Negro.

Finally, the verse ceased as the rhythm increased to a crashing crescendo with a long wailing finale:

He: Oooooooooooooooo!
She: Negroooooooooooooooooo!

By going to Olympia with this novel, Himes was entering the zone of unending erogeneity peopled by such fabled creatures as Greta X, Count Palmiro Vicarion, B. von Soda, Pieralessandro Casavini, Carmencita de las Lunas, and other members of the secret order of Pleasure. There was already, in Paris, a line of aspirants queuing up to confess to being the author of *The Story of O*, the supremely liberated architect of the hidden castle of desire (who, in actual life, her sole interviewer commented, 'looks like a nun'). Himes might have enjoyed this company, but only for the length of time it took for him to drink long and deep from what was on offer, before hightailing it back to the Tournon. One day, while there, he met a woman on the terrace who claimed to have written a bestseller

281

for Olympia Press. She told him it was called *White Thighs*.

She did not give her name. Had Himes asked, might she have replied: 'Frances Lengel, first lady of lust'? The true author of *White Thighs* was, of course, Alexander Trocchi.

*

There is no summing up. The people who came to the Left Bank in the years after the Second World War, and stayed, did not see themselves as living in 'Paris in the Fifties'. The characterization of decades – 'roaring', 'swinging', etc. – is a contrivance. But if one were to isolate a single force guiding the actions and inspiring the inventiveness of the people described here, it would be the claim to freedom – from racism, from sexual restraint, the frenzy of anti-Communism, the monotony of work, freedom from Calvinist ethics, from conventional dress and conventional opinion and inhibiting families, from artificial rhyme and stiff rhythm, from linear narrative and arrangements of words that repress as wickedly as wicked governments, from the tyranny of the living-room and the totalitarianism of the new thing, television. The source of this civilizing energy, in both native French society and amid the anglophone colonies, lies in the liberation of the City of Light from the Nazi darkness.

Notes

3 *'most important writer'* Joseph Barry to Richard Wright, 26 April 1945; Beinecke Rare Book and Manuscript Library (BRBML), Yale University.

3 *'You, of course'* Richard Wright to Gertrude Stein, 23 June 1945; BRBML.

3 *'but for writing'* RW to GS, 27 May 1945; BRBML.

3 *'deep Negro dialect'* RW, journal, 28 January 1945; BRBML. Quoted in Michel Fabre, *The Unfinished Quest of Richard Wright*, New York, 1973.

4 *'I'd say'* Ibid.

4 *'We were generally'* *New York Post*, 17 June 1946.

5 *'the dirtiest'* Congressman Thomas Bilbo, *Proceedings and Debates of the 70th Congress*, Vol. 91, 27 June 1945. Quoted in Fabre, *op. cit.*

5 *Wright's arrival Combat*, 11 May 1946.

6 *'How beautiful'* Douglas Schneider, 'Souvenir de Richard Wright', *France Etats-Unis*, December 1960.

7 *underwear* Janet Flanner, *New Yorker*, 22 May 1946. See also Flanner, *Paris Journal, 1944–65*, edited by William Shawn, New York, 1965.

9 *'an account'* *Les Temps Modernes*, January 1946.

10 *'Too gloomy'* RW to GS, 28 March 1946; BRBML.

13 *carrying a corpse* William Gardner Smith, 'Black Boy in France', *Ebony*, July 1953.

13 *'My home'* interview with Raphael Tardon, *Action*, Paris, 24 October 1946.

13 *'Nigger lover'* RW to Sylvia Beach, 30 May 1947; Sylvia Beach

papers (SB), Princeton University Library.

13 *'thousand little dramas'* RW to GS, 27 May 1945; BRBML.

14 *'Intellectuals don't fit'* Richard Wright, *American Hunger*, New York, 1977.

14 'I Tried to Be a Communist' was published in the *Atlantic Monthly* in August and September 1944; it was reprinted in Richard Crossman's anthology, *The God that Failed*, London, 1949, and later incorporated into *American Hunger*.

14 *'loathsome, filthy'* David Caute, *The Great Fear*, London, 1978.

15 *Shakespeare and Company* Wright was not successful; Beach's book, *Shakespeare and Company*, was eventually published by Harcourt, Brace in 1959.

15 *'If I could'* RW to Sylvia Beach, 3 May 1947; SB.

17 *'I don't know'* RW, journal, 15 August 1947.

18 *de Beauvoir's affection* letters to Jean-Paul Sartre, 31 January 1947, 7 February 1947 etc.; see Simone de Beauvoir, *Letters to Sartre*, translated and edited by Quentin Hoare, London, 1991.

18 *Wright's introduction The Respectful Prostitute*, London, 1948.

19 In 1857, Flaubert had been charged with offending public morals, upon publication of *Madame Bovary* in the *Revue de Paris*, and summoned to appear before the court in Paris.

21 *'French weeklies'* RW to Owen Dodson, 9 April 1946; published in *New Letters*, Winter 1971.

22 The French editor of *Points* was Marcel Bisieux.

23 *'enough manuscripts'* Christopher Logue to author.

23 *'It was'* Points 18, Winter 1953–54.

25 *'A young seventeen-year-old'* Hoetis to author.

25 *Marlon Brando* see James Campbell, *Talking at the Gates: A Life of James Baldwin*, London, 1991.

26 *'violent, anarchic'* Baldwin to William Phillips, April 1949; *Partisan Review* Collection.

28 *'went to pieces'* Fern Marja Eckman, *The Furious Passage of James Baldwin*, New York, 1966.

28 *'explained everything'* Otto Friedrich to author.

28 *'In some deep'* 'Equal in Paris', in *Notes of a Native Son*, Boston, 1955.

29 *'Somehow this turned'* Otto Friedrich, 'Jimmy', in *The Grave of Alice B. Toklas*, New York, 1989.

30 '*So, they said*' Ibid.

31 '*I was in*' Ibid.

31 *Stuck in his typewriter* Hoetis to author.

32 'Zero *was here*' Baldwin to Philips *op. cit.*

34 '*Richard accused*' 'Alas, Poor Richard', in *Nobody Knows My Name*, New York, 1961.

34 'Many Thousands Gone' was first published in *Partisan Review*, Nov.–Dec. 1951, and reprinted in *Notes of a Native Son*.

36 '*It's always the same*' RW to Margrit de Sablonière, 8 April 1960; Schomburg Center for Research in Black Culture (SCRBC), New York Public Library.

36 '*faggot*' Bernard Hassell to author.

38 '*In no country*' *Les Temps Modernes*, January 1950.

39 '*Existentialists hide*' *Samedi-Soir*, 3 May 1947.

40 Jean-Sol Partre is to be found in *L'Ecume des jours* (*Froth on the Daydream*), Paris, 1947.

41 '*dimmed with humiliation*' Elliot Paul, *Springtime in Paris*, London, 1951.

42 '*The hucksters*' *New Yorker*, 25 January 1950; see Flanner, *op. cit.*

43 '*The fear*' Simone de Beauvoir, *La Force des Choses* (*Force of Circumstance*), Paris, 1963.

44 '*Camped outside*' Trocchi, journal, 4 October 1950; Alexander Trocchi papers (AT), Washington University Library, St Louis.

46 '*Faded now*' taken from a fragment of an autobiographical novel, published posthumously in *The Invisible Insurrection of a Million Minds: A Trocchi reader*, edited by Andrew Murray Scott, Edinburgh, 1991.

46 *didn't like him* Baldwin to author.

47 '*Very well*' Christopher Logue, 'Alexander Trocchi and the beginning of *Merlin*', *Edinburgh Review* 70, August 1985.

48 '*Alex didn't mind*' Logue to author.

48 '*The words*' 'A diaristic itinerary', 30 April 1951; AT.

49 '*his ego*' Richard Seaver to author.

49 '*I had hoped*' 'A diaristic itinerary', 4 May 1951.

51 '*Beckett is*' Points 11–12, Winter 1951–52.

51 '*so-called*' Richard Seaver, introduction to a reissue of *Cain's Book* by Alexander Trocchi, New York, 1992.

52 '*out of a complete*' Logue to author; also interview with *Quarto*, London, November 1981.

54 '*Yet it was*' 'Suez' by Patrick Brangwyn.

55 Trocchi to Riddell, 28 April 1952; AT.

57 *Camus* de Beauvoir, *Force of Circumstance*.

59 '*I passed*' Seaver, introduction to *I Can't Go On, I'll Go On: A selection from Samuel Beckett's work*, edited by Richard Seaver, New York, 1976.

60 '*By the look*' Seaver, introduction to *I Can't Go On*; A. Alvarez, *Beckett*, London, 1972.

61 '*We had*' Seaver, introduction to *I Can't Go On*.

62 '*We met*' Ibid.

64 *French* lycées Jane Lougee to author.

65 '*fundamental sounds*' Beckett, letter to Alan Schneider, quoted in 'Waiting for Beckett: A personal chronicle', *Chelsea Review*, New York, September 1958.

65 *Beckett's characters* from 'Paris letter', written for the London magazine *Nimbus*, but not published.

67 '*The words*' Arthur Adamov, *L'Aveu*, Paris, 1946; passage dated '1938'.

68 '*To my astonishment* Ionesco, 'La tragédie du langage', *Spectacles*, Paris, July 1958.

69 *Tzara Roger Blin, Souvenirs et Propos*, edited by L. B. Peskine, Paris, 1986.

69 '*In* Godot' Ibid.; also interview with Mary Benson, *Theater*, New York, Fall 1978.

70 '*as Pozzo is fat*' Jean Martin, 'Creating Godot', in *Beckett in Dublin*, edited by S. E. Wilmer, Dublin, 1992.

72 'Paris Review' By a coincidence, a cast-off title for the *Paris Review* was 'Ms', as in 'manuscript', the plural of which – 'Mss' – had been considered as a title for *Merlin*.

72 '*The literary hopefuls*' 'The *Paris Review* Sketchbook' by George Plimpton and others, in *Paris Review* 79, Spring 1981.

73 '*The news*' Burford to Trocchi, 13 October 1952; AT.

75 '*The two*' '*Paris Review* Sketchbook'.

75 *TLS*, 27 May 1955.

77 '*The* Paris Review *was funded*' Friedrich to author.

78 *working for the CIA* Plimpton to author.

78 '*potential James Joyce*' 13 September 1946, Secker & Warburg papers, Reading University Library.

80 'A check' Austryn Wainhouse to Beckett, 6 November 1953. Also: Trocchi to Beckett, 31 July 1954; Beckett to Trocchi, 3 August 1954 and 27 August 1954; Trocchi to Beckett, 30 August 1954; Samuel Beckett papers, McMaster University Library, Ontario.

81 'first-class man' Wainhouse to Trocchi, 22 July 1953; AT.

83 'To Libertines' La Philosophie dans le boudoir (The Bedroom Philosophers).

84 'Impertinence' Austryn Wainhouse, 'On Translating Sade', Evergreen Review, August 1966.

85 'Where madness defines' 'Of the Clandestinite', Merlin, Vol. 2, No. 2, 1953; a revised version of the same essay appeared in Writers in Revolt, edited by Terry Southern, Richard Seaver and Alexander Trocchi, New York, 1963.

89 Deux Magots/Select Wainhouse, 'On Translating Sade'; Maurice Girodias, Une Journée sur la terre, Paris, 1990.

89 'Of the sort' 'On Translating Sade'.

94 'Tintin' Combat, 16 May 1950. For a full account of the J'irai cracher affair, see Philippe Boggio, Boris Vian, Paris, 1993.

95 'unable to sit still' Boris Vian, Manuel de St-Germain-des-Prés, Paris, 1974.

96 'old Eugénie' Anne-Marie Cazalis, Les Mémoires d'une Anne, Paris, 1976.

97 'In the pinball' Alexander Trocchi, Cain's Book, New York, 1960.

98 'not immaculately' William Gardner Smith, Return to Black America, Englewood Cliffs, NJ, 1970.

98 'kind of silence' 'Paris Review Sketchbook'.

99 Baldwin explained Baldwin to author.

99 'hash-hish' see Campbell, op. cit.

100 'chess partner' 'On Translating Sade'.

100 Plimpton claims Plimpton to author.

100 'black voices' Logue, Guardian, 1 December 1992.

102 'en-ga-jay' Ibid.; Logue to author.

102 'I applied' New York Post, 25 March 1959.

103 'Definitely' Lesley Himes to author.

104 'our horror' 'Alas, Poor Richard'.

104 never acted Ebony, January 1951.

105 'character and destiny' RW to Paul Reynolds, 1 May 1952. Quoted in Fabre, The Unfinished Quest.

106 Paul Reynolds to RW, 6 May 1953; *ibid.*

107 '*all his friends*' Chester Himes, *The Quality of Hurt: The autobiography of Chester Himes*, Vol. I, New York, 1972.

107 '*pinball machine*' 'Alas, Poor Richard'.

107 '*strange perturbation*' Wright, 'I Choose Exile', *c.* 1952; unpublished.

108 '*I'll define*' Ibid.

109 *FAF The Crisis*, June–July 1951.

110 '*How, I asked*' 'Alas, Poor Richard'.

113 *Katzenjammer Kids* Flanner, *op. cit.*

113 '*That stupid*' *The Quality of Hurt.*

114 '*Going into*' RW to Paul Reynolds, 24 May 1952; quoted in Fabre, *The Unfinished Quest.*

114 '*On September 16*' FBI File on Wright, incorporating files from the Army, CIA and other intelligence agencies; released in censored form under the Freedom of Information Act.

116 *Baldwin joked* see Campbell, *op. cit.*

117 *500 American Negroes The Crisis*, June–July 1951.

118 '*The musicians*' Miles Davis with Quincy Troupe, *Miles: The autobiography*, New York, 1989.

118 '*Anyway*' Chester Himes to Carl Van Vechten, 12 May 1953; BRBML.

119 '*Given my disposition*' Chester Himes, *My Life of Absurdity: The autobiography of Chester Himes*, Vol. II, New York, 1976.

120 '*raconteur*' . . . '*spiv*' Gibson and Logue to author.

121 '*This is to me*' Targ to Himes, *c.* June 1954; quoted in a letter from Himes to Van Vechten, 7 July 1954; BRBML.

122 *the largest advance* 'My Man Himes', interview by John A. Williams, *Amistad* 1, 1970.

122 '*One joker*' Chester Himes, *A Rage in Harlem*; first published as *For Love of Imabelle*, New York, 1957; first French publication, *La Reine des pommes*, Paris, 1958.

123 '*Gitanes filtres*' Lesley Himes to author.

123 '*Dick had*' *The Quality of Hurt.*

125 *Wright on Baldwin* 'The Position of the Negro Artist and Intellectual in American Society'; BRBML.

127 '*We hurried*' *The Quality of Hurt.*

128 '*Once, one evening*' 'Alas, Poor Richard'.

128 '*Your obsession*' Schenk to Baldwin, 5 March 1957; Leslie Schenk private papers.

129 '*Now Baldwin*' *The Quality of Hurt*.

129 '*I am rather despairingly*' JB to William Cole, January 1953; Lilly Library (LL), Indiana University. '*At one stage*' Ross to Keen, 9 September 1953; private collection. '*I'd like*' JB to William Cole, 2 April 1954; '*I would like to borrow*' JB to Jennie Bradley, 18 January 1954; Harry Ransom Humanities Research Center (HRHRC), University of Texas at Austin.

130 '*Jimmy Baldwin*' 'William Styron' in George Plimpton, *The Best of Plimpton*, New York, 1991.

131 '*On the evening*' 'Equal in Paris', in *Notes of a Native Son*.

131 '*departure*' JB to William Cole, 13 January 1954; LL.

137 '*Un pornographe*' Maurice Girodias, *Une Journée sur la terre*.

138 '*Our friend*' *New York Herald-Tribune*, 5 November 1949.

139 '*My staff*' 'The view from Mount Olympus', *Playboy*, April 1961.

140 '*the shiny black Citroën*' Seaver, postscript to an excerpt from *Watt* in *The Olympia Reader*, edited by Maurice Girodias, New York, 1965.

141 '*old and respected*' Jack Kahane, *Memoirs of a Bootlegger*, London, 1939. For a general account of Kahane's fortunes, see Hugh Ford, *Published in Paris*, London, 1975.

143 '*bar debts*' Introduction to *The Olympia Reader*; published elsewhere under the title 'Confessions of a Bootlegger's Son'.

149 '*Two con men*' Seaver to author.

149 *Frances Lengel* Introduction to *The Olympia Reader*.

150 '*Grundy*' Trocchi to author.

150 '*Trocchi's sex life*' Seaver to author.

152 '*pale, ill-fed*' Introduction to *The Olympia Reader*.

154 '*Marcus van Heller*' Stephenson to author.

155 '*très proper*' *Une Journée sur la terre*.

155 '*plain-looking*' MG to Patrick Kearney, 4 February 1979; Patrick Kearney private papers.

155 '*big strapping*' Ibid.

156 '*Dickensian*' Introduction to *The Olympia Reader*.

161 The two versions of *Young Adam* differ from one another markedly. Both versions remain in print. In the pornographic version, published by the New York house Masquerade Books, the author is given as 'Anonymous', although Trocchi's name appears on the title-page.

162 *Maître Adolph* Girodias wrote the story of how he obtained

the Frank Harris manuscript more than once. This version is based on the accounts in his autobiography, *Une Journée sur la terre*, and in *The Olympia Reader*.

165 *'tingling'* from the introduction to an undated New York edition of the book, issued under the title, *What Frank Harris Did Not Say*.

165 *'piss-take'* from a 1966 Brandon House edition of the book, published under the name 'Frances Lengel'.

165 *Pornography and the Law: The psychology of erotic realism and 'hard core' pornography*, by Drs Eberhard and Phyllis Kronhausen, New York, 1959.

173 *'my head'* 'A Girl in Love'; *'no time the desire'* *Conversations with O*.

175 *'About three years'* quoted in *Conversations with O*.

175 *Girodias mischievously The Olympia Reader*.

176 *'I'll never tell you'* Kahane to author; Seaver to author.

176 *Plimpton* Plimpton to author.

176 *Lectures pour tous*, Paris, 1958; English edition, *Literary Landfalls*, London, 1960; translated by Denise Folliot.

178 *'A masterpiece'* AT to Lougee, 20 August 1954; Jane Lougee private papers (JL).

178 *'1954 years'* Ibid.

179 *'Will your husband'* Ibid., 8 February 1955; JL.

179 *'I have changed'* Ibid., 8 December 1954; JL.

179 *'Liane'* Ibid., 9 February 1955; JL.

180 *'Alex had'* *Une Journée sur la terre*.

181 *red-haired woman* for a fuller discussion of this topic, see James Campbell, 'Alexander Trocchi', *London Magazine*, April–May 1992.

181 *The magazine owed money* AT to Wainhouse, 2 August 1955; AT.

181 *300,000 francs* AT to Lougee, 19 September 1954; JL.

182 *'ten copies'* AT to Lougee, 29 August 1954; JL.

183 *Lolita* The imaginary exchange between Nabokov, Girodias and others has been sewn together using a variety of materials, including: Vladimir Nabokov: 'On a book entitled *Lolita*' (published as a postscript to most editions of the novel); '*Lolita* and Mr Girodias' (*Evergreen Review*, February 1967); *Selected Letters 1940–77*, edited by Dmitri Nabokov, New York, 1989. Maurice Girodias: 'A Sad, Ungraceful History of

Lolita' (*The Olympia Reader*); 'Publisher's Digression' (published as a preface to the third – 1959 – Olympia edition of *Lolita*); Preface to *The Paris Olympia Press* by Patrick J. Kearney; *Une Journée sur la terre*; 'Letter to Samuel Beckett' (*Frank: An international journal of contemporary writing and art*, Paris, Winter–Spring 1991). Brian Boyd: *Vladimir Nabokov: The American Years*, New York, 1991. *New Statesman*, 24 January 1959; *The Times*, 14 May 1957, 17 November 1958; *TLS*, 14 February 1991; *Time* magazine, 17 January 1958; *Daily Express*, 19 December 1958.

195 Donleavy quote taken from an interview published in the magazine *Passport* 5, Huntingdon 1993.

195 '*The obscenity*' J. P. Donleavy to MG, quoted in *Une Journée sur la terre*.

196 '*Sheer rejection*' interview with *Passport*.

197 '*Donleavy would have*' *Une Journée sur la terre* (translated by JC).

197 '*Girodias's brother*' Ibid.

198 '*It is hard*' MG to Donleavy, 30 December 1954.

198 '*I've finished*' Donleavy to MG, 10 February 1955, quoted in J. P. Donleavy, *The History of The Ginger Man*, London, 1994.

199 '*Someone somewhere*' Ibid.

200 '*literally infuriated*' Donleavy to author.

200 '*As I declared*' Donleavy, *op. cit.*

201 '*all the revenue*' Interview with Donleavy in the *Paris Review* 63, Fall 1975.

201 '*If this project*' MG to Donleavy, 26 October 1956.

201 '*at least as long*' MG to Donleavy, 24 August 1956.

201 Girodias's version of the disagreement over the 'contract' is set out in *Une Journée*; Donleavy's in *The History of The Ginger Man*.

201 '*Will you please*' MG to Neville Spearman, 6 November 1956.

202 *Her husband* Donleavy to author.

203 Trocchi, letter to *TLS*, 10 June 1955.

204 '*It has come*' *Points* 20, May 1955.

205 quotation from Wright's foreword to George Padmore, *Pan-Africanism or Communism?*, London, 1956.

207 '*no longer*' Gibson to author.

207 '*I am*' Reynolds to RW, 6 April 1953; quoted in Fabre, *The*

Unfinished Quest.

210 '*the majority*' Mochtar Lubis, 'Through Coloured Glasses', *Encounter*, March 1956.

211 '*saying things*' RW to Margrit de Sablonière, 17 January 1955; SCRBC.

212 '*In the minds*' Wright's speech was printed in a special issue of *Présence Africaine* devoted to the Sorbonne conference (Numéro Spécial, 8–10, June–November 1956).

217 Baldwin's obituary of RW was incorporated into the essay 'Alas, Poor Richard'.

218 '*They hated*' *Phylon*, Winter 1960.

219 *Wright and Myrdal* taken from a written account of the conversation, recorded by Wright; private collection.

220 '*to tell them*' Oliver W. Harrington, 'The Mysterious Death of Richard Wright', *Daily World*, New York, 17 December 1977; reprinted in *Why I Left America and other essays*, Mississippi, 1993.

220 *Chester Himes thought* Lesley Himes to author.

221 Kay Boyle to RW, 6 October 1956; Kay Boyle papers, Southern Illinois University at Carbondale.

222 '*I have been*' Albert Camus, *Actuelles III*, Paris, 1958; translated and published in *Resistance, Rebellion and Death*, London, 1961.

222 '*polishing*' Baldwin to author.

223 '*poisoning European*' Ben Burns, 'They're not Uncle Tom's Children', *Ebony*, March 1956.

224 '*the accepted*' *My Life of Absurdity*.

224 *tipped off* Harrington, 'Why I Left America', in *Why I Left America*.

224 '*My friends*' Harrington to author.

224 '*I didn't let*' Harrington to author.

225 Gibson's essay 'A No to Nothing' was published in *Perspectives* 2, Winter 1953.

225 '*He did not*' letter from Gibson to Leroy Hodges, 26 June 1977, quoted in Leroy Hodges, *Portrait of an Expatriate*, Connecticut, 1985.

226 '*Give that*' quoted in Addison Gayle, *Richard Wright: Ordeal of a Native Son*, New York, 1980.

227 '*Do you know*' Harrington, 'The Mysterious Death of Richard Wright'.

227 '*Gibson first tried*' quoted in Fabre, *The Unfinished Quest*.

228 The manuscript of 'Island of Hallucination' is sealed at the BRBML.

228 '*roman à clef*' Julia Wright, foreword to Harrington, *op. cit.*

228 '*It was Bill*' Gibson to author.

229 *Gibson wrote to Wright* see Fabre, *The Unfinished Quest*.

229 '*For Richard*' see Fabre, *Richard Wright: Books and Writers*, Mississippi, 1990.

229 '*Greetings*' Gibson to RW, 6 July 1960; BRBML.

230 '*following grave*' *Révolution*, July–August 1964.

233 '*This is*' 'The position of the Negro Artist and Intellectual in Society'; BRBML.

233 *In February New York Herald-Tribune*, 6 February 1956.

233 '*it made me*' Baldwin, *No Name in the Street*, New York, 1972.

000 *drunken ramble* 'A Talk with William Faulkner' by Russell Warren Howe, *Reporter*, 22 March 1956.

234 '*Any real*' Baldwin, 'Faulkner and Desegregation', *Partisan Review*, Winter 1956, reprinted in *Nobody Knows My Name*.

240 '*feeling sorry for himself*' Barry Miles, *Ginsberg: A biography*, New York, 1989.

241 For general information on the Beat Hotel and Ginsberg's residence there, see Miles, *op. cit.*, and Ted Morgan, *Literary Outlaw: The life and times of William S. Burroughs*, New York, 1988.

243 *Life* 30 November 1959.

243 '*For me*' Diana Trilling, 'The Other Night at Columbia', *Partisan Review*, Spring 1959, reprinted in *Claremont Essays*, New York, 1964.

244 *Ginsberg had actually intended* Miles, *op. cit.*

244 '*Ginsberg, with his poems*' Trilling, *op cit.*

245 '*jacking off*' Ginsberg, interview with the *Paris Review*, 37, Spring 1966.

248 *The poem he worked on* Miles, *op. cit.*

249 '*sat down*' Burroughs to Jack Kerouac, 7 December 1954, *The Letters of William Burroughs, 1945–59*, edited by Oliver Harris, London, 1993.

251 '*The selection*' Burroughs, *Letters*, 25 October 1955.

253 '*Lee was*' William Burroughs, *Early Routines*, Santa Barbara, 1982.

254 *half-hooked* Burroughs, *Letters*, 16 February 1958.

254 *rejected Ibid.*, 18 April 1958.

255 *'We ate' My Life of Absurdity*.

256 *'striding through'* 'The Black Boy Looks at the White Boy', in *Nobody Knows My Name*.

257 *'the man' The White Negro*, New York, 1957, reprinted in *Advertisements for Myself*, New York, 1959.

259 *'I remained' My Life of Absurdity*.

260 *'What is happening'* Burroughs, *Letters*, July 1959.

261 *'Dear Mr Burroughs'* Morgan, *op. cit.*

261 *'You can cut'* from the 'Atrophied Preface' to *Naked Lunch*, not included in the Olympia edition.

263 *'The identity'* from the jacket of the first London edition of *Cain's Book*, 1963.

264 *'I took'* published in *The Invisible Insurrection*.

264 *soapbox* see Andrew Murray Scott, *Alexander Trocchi: The Making of the Monster*, Edinburgh, 1991.

265 *'Methedrine University'* see Miles, *op. cit.*

269 *first reaction* de Beauvoir, *Force of Circumstance*.

269 *Cocteau* 'Salut à Boris Vian', *Opéra*, 3 May 1950.

271 *Wright and the doctor* RW to Margrit de Sablonière, 26 April 1960; SCRBC.

272 *'He's got'* RW to M de S, 16 April 1960; SCRBC.

272 *Himes and Wright My Life of Absurdity*.

273 *letter from 'Sartre'* RW to M de S, 28 March 1960; SCRBC.

273 Dorothy Padmore's remarks are quoted in Fabre, *The Unfinished Quest*.

273 *'serious illness'* RW to M de S, 20 February 1960; SCRBC.

274 *Hughes* 'Richard Wright's Last Guest at Home', *Ebony*, 16 February 1961.

275 *telegram* Harrington to author.

275 *'I* know' Harrington to author.

275 *'I've never met'* Harrington, 'Why I Left America', in Harrington, *op. cit.*

275 *'Richard was murdered'* Lesley Himes to author.

275 *Wright's daughter* from a BBC Radio 4 profile of Wright, broadcast on 28 October 1990.

276 *Himes put a name My Life of Absurdity*.

276 *close friend* an article on the subject, by Schofield Coryell, appeared in the English-language *Paris Passion* in January 1986. The allegations concerning Gibson were later retracted.

276 *'quite well known'* Harrington to author.

277 *Discussions with many* I have interviewed the following people on the subject of Wright's death: Michel Fabre, the late Addison Gayle, Richard Gibson, Ollie Harrington, Lesley Himes, John A. Williams.

277 *'He was'* Lesley Himes to author.

277 *'He thought'* Harrington to author.

277 *'strange Russian'* BBC Radio 4, 28 September 1990.

278 *'My husband'* Ellen Wright to author.

279 *'my unworthiness'* Une Journée sur la terre.

280 *'real publisher'* 'Letter to Samuel Beckett'.

280 *Himes and Olympia My Life of Absurdity*; Lesley Himes to author.

282 *White Thighs My Life of Absurdity*.

Index

The letters *e.* and *n.* following page references indicate epigraphs and footnotes.

301

302